Blackmail, Sex and Lies

Based on the True Story of Madeleine Hamilton Smith

Kathryn McMaster

BLACKMAIL, SEX AND LIES

Copyright © 2017 Kathryn McMaster

DEDICATION

For Philip, a wonderful husband and father; a beautiful man

FOREWORD

I first encountered Kathryn via social media - as so many contacts are made these days. I have never met her in the flesh and yet she has influenced my writing and specifically my understanding of the Indie book world more profoundly than anyone else.

Her work through the One Stop Fiction Authors' Resource Group has impacted thousands of writers like me, wising us up to the harsh realities of writing and marketing Indie fiction. She selflessly shares advice and resources amongst her peers, fostering a co-operative mind-set amongst those who might otherwise have seen themselves as in competition. For the first time in my writing career I feel that, far from being a solitary scribbler in a chilly attic, I am, in fact, part of a massive, mutually supportive body of creative talent.

It has been a privilege to play a small part in giving back to Kathryn what she has given so abundantly to me, by reading and offering suggestions on her manuscript. It is no surprise to find her book encompasses both the thoroughgoing, sometimes shocking, empiricism of indisputable historical fact - she is a realist - and the wondrous faculty of the imagination to speculate on what we cannot absolutely know for sure - she is a writer.

Allie Cresswell
https://www.amazon.co.uk/Allie-Cresswell/e/B00J7OIC0K/

ACKNOWLEDGMENTS

Thank you to my editorial team: Ansley Blackstock, Allie Cresswell, Suzanne Merrick-Zewan, Angela Petch, Lilly Brock, Gemma Haworth, Kathryn Marley, and Colin Garrow. A big thanks too, to my cover artist, Adrijus Guscia from **Rocking Book Covers** for designing a fabulous cover. Last, but not least, to my son Kent, from **One Stop Fiction**, working hard as my social media manager in getting this book launched. Without all of your help, this book would not have been possible.

NOTE TO THE READER

All letters found in this book are the original correspondence written between the two main characters, Madeleine Hamilton Smith and Pierre Emile L'Angelier. There were more than 200 letters between them. In this book you will only find just a few of these. If you would like to read the rest, please visit my website: **www.kathrynmcmaster.com**

Opportunity, like a sudden gust,
Hath swell'd my calmer thoughts into a tempest.
Accursed opportunity!
That works our thoughts into desires; desires
To resolutions: those being ripened and quickened
Thou giv'st them birth, and bring'st them forth to action.

Denham

1 ARSENIC, AN OLD FRIEND
EDINBURGH, 1851

Pierre Emile L'Angelier thrashed and writhed in excruciating agony. He clawed at his intestines as spasms pushed hot coals of pain through all twenty-five feet of inflamed coil. Crying out as the waves came and left, with knees drawn tight to his chest, and a raging thirst he could not slake, he pleaded for a doctor to save his ebbing life. Way beyond medical salvation, on that fateful day in March 1857, at the age of thirty-three, Pierre Emile L'Angelier's life abruptly, and unexpectedly, ceased to exist.

Over the years, he had flirted with death, trying a startling variety of methods, all without success. However, once dead, his demise raised more questions than there were answers.

Had he finally succeeded in ending his own life? If not, had his malicious threats of blackmail caused his young lover, Madeleine Smith, to hasten him to his end? There was, of course, a third option, which was the most disturbing of all. Had Emile, as his friends knew him, tried to frame Madeleine in an elaborate scheme for revenge, but inadvertently died while trying?

The illicit love affair between Pierre Emile L'Angelier and Madeline Hamilton Smith, blossomed in the spring of 1855, but was doomed to end before it had even begun. In an age when daughters unquestioningly obeyed their fathers and married within their class, headstrong Madeleine, socialite and eldest daughter of an eminent architect, was torn between two men - the man she loved who was not of her class, and a father who demanded complete submission.

In the end, poor choices would lead to calamitous consequences from which there would be no escape.

*

Six years earlier, on a cold December morning in 1851, Emile L'Angelier stood in the front room of one of Edinburgh's many lodging houses. He had come to view a room but was not yet aware the rent the landlady was asking was far in excess of what he could afford. He was also blissfully unaware that within a few weeks, he would be indigent and on the brink of homelessness.

He observed the room. It looked smaller than it was. Heavily embossed olive wallpaper, chosen to hide the soot from the coal fire and grime from the oil lamps rather than any aesthetic beauty, drew the walls in. He stepped over the highly polished wooden floor onto a large patterned rug in greys, blues, greens, and reds. It sprawled to all four corners of the room but came up short by a foot.

Last night's coal fire could not mask the smell of naphthalene that hung on the air; mothballs, he presumed, hidden under the chintz cushions, and stuffed down the seats of the high-backed couch upholstered in rich, maroon velvet.

An exotic green and blue parrot was perched on a branch on a side table. Head tilted, it regarded Emile with beady eyes. Beside it, a canary also gave him a penetrating look. On closer inspection, encased in the spotless glass dome, he found them stuffed, and perfectly dead.

He walked towards the numerous portraits and pictures in elaborate frames that lined the walls. Eyes of dead ancestors stared out vacantly from behind the glass.

He checked his pocket watch and wondered where she was. He was in a hurry, and needed to be somewhere soon. He also desperately wanted to smoke his pipe, but decided against it.

Ambling over to the fireplace where a gilded mirror hung at an odd angle above the mantelpiece, he straightened it, and stepped closer. He twirled his moustache, fussed at his tie cravat, patted his wavy hair, and, with a little spit on his forefinger, tamed his unruly eyebrows, then stood sideways to check his profile.

With great reluctance, he detached himself from his reflection and noticed some magazines neatly stacked on a small coffee table. In sheer boredom, he casually picked up the top copy, the latest *Blackwoods* magazine, and started to flip through it.

He was about to set it down when something caught his eye, an article on arsenic, a poison he was familiar with when he lived in France.

'*The Eating of Arsenic. - White arsenic, as is well known, is a violent poison in large doses, but in very minute doses, it is known by professional men to be a tonic.*

'*It is eaten for two purposes: First, that the eater may thereby acquire freshness of complexion and plumpness of figure. For this purpose it will readily be supposed, it is chiefly eaten by the young.*

'*Secondly, that the breathing may be improved, so that long and steep heights may be climbed without difficulty.*

'*In Vienna, arsenic is said to be extensively used for producing the same effects upon horses, especially among gentlemen's grooms and coaching men. They either sprinkle a pinch of it among the oats, or they tie a piece as big as a pea in a bit of linen and fasten it to the bit when the bridle is put into the horse's mouth.*

'*To improve their appearance, young peasants, of both sexes, some no doubt from vanity, and some with the view of adding to their charms in the eyes of each other, take arsenic for this purpose.*

And it is very remarkable to see how wonderfully well they attain their object; for these young-poison eaters are generally remarkable for blooming complexions, and a full, rounded, healthy appearance.

'*Dr. Von Tschudi gives the following case as having occurred in his own practice: A healthy, but thin, milkmaid residing in the parish of Highnam, had a lover whom she wished to attach to herself by a more agreeable exterior. She, therefore, took the well-known beautifier, using the arsenic several times a week. The desired effect was not long in showing itself, for in a few months she became stout, rosy-cheeked, and all that her lover could desire.*'

Sounds of the landlady's footsteps on the staircase interrupted his reading. If time had allowed him to read further, he would have been cautioned against the continued use of arsenic.

'In order, however, to increase the effect, she incautiously increased the dose of vanity. She died poisoned - a very painful death!"

'The number of such fatal cases, especially among young persons, is described as by no means inconsiderable. The practice of taking arsenic, once begun, creates a craving and becomes a necessity of life.'

"Sorry to keep you waiting. Mr. L'Angelier, is it?"

"Yes, it is. Please, don't apologise."

"Are you a man of sober habits?"

"Indeed I am. I seldom drink, although I do smoke a pipe."

"I see. And you want a single room just for yourself?"

"That is correct."

"I don't allow women in my rooms. So any entertaining you do will have to be done elsewhere."

"I perfectly understand. That won't be an issue."

"Well then, I think we'll get along just fine. The room is six shillings a week. That includes one meal a day. However, if you want another meal, that'll be extra."

On hearing the price, Emile's despondency deepened. This was the ninth establishment he had visited in two days. None of which he could afford.

2 SUICIDAL THOUGHTS
EDINBURGH 1851

Emile's financial situation was dire that year, and his misery compounded by a woman. Having left France to chase broken dreams and promises, he soon found himself without a job, with little money for a roof over his head.

The assurance of love and romance turned out to be hollow, and the return was disastrous. Within days, the young woman from Fife confessed she no longer loved him and was to marry another. The fruitless journey left him angry, hurt, bitter, depressed, and worse, impecunious.

The rejection by the young lady from Fife caused a deep scar on Emile's psyche, and knocked his mental and emotional stability off kilter. On a more practical level, his impetuosity and the lack of planning forced him to abandon the idea of securing rooms in a respectable lodging house. Instead, he resorted to taking quarters above Edinburgh's Rainbow Tavern, sharing an attic room barely accommodating two narrow bunks with a fellow waiter, called Robert Baker.

*

One particular night, like many before, Robert tossed and turned. Deep wracking sobs, coming from the new waiter, punctured his sleep. The man wept and wailed as he paced the floor, backwards and forwards, backwards and forwards.

"For God's sake, man. Go to bed so we can both get some sleep!"

Robert turned over to face the wall, hoping his back would block out the lamentations driving him to distraction. He started to drift off when he felt a blast of cold air rush into the room. He turned over and opened his eyes.

What he saw turned him rigid with shock.

A dark silhouette filled the window frame. He watched aghast as his roommate climbed through the narrow opening of the third floor window and balanced on the outer sill. His nightshirt whipped around his pale thighs as the wind swirled and howled.

Robert was voiceless, unable to move. Images flashed before him when seven days prior he had physically manhandled this waiter, Emile L'Angelier, away from Leith Pier as he threatened to hurl himself into the grey, murky waters below. The incident had left Robert Baker emotionally fraught.

Looking at a second suicide bid, so soon after the first, caused Robert's heart to thrash against his ribcage wildly, sound waves of strangulated cries pushed upwards and outwards, his throat pulsated as he held his breath. He watched with increased horror as his colleague shuffled further forward, teetering on the edge, and peering into the abyss below; one small step between stability and finality.

As time froze, Robert watched Pierre Emile L'Angelier remain inert. He wondered what was going through his head. *Was he contemplating that soon his short life would be over? That he had had nothing to live for? That he no longer cared?*

Getting over his initial shock, Robert made his way to the window ledge and grabbed a handful of cotton cloth, yanking Emile backwards. The pair ended up entangled in a heap on the floor.

"Jiminy Crickets, Emile! What the hell were you thinking?"

Emile started to cry hysterically. He just wanted to die.

Robert rolled out from underneath him, his heart still beating wildly, and he felt nauseous. He swallowed hard to hold the contents of his stomach as the bile pushed upwards. Sweat broke out on his upper lip and his teeth began an involuntary chatter.

Emile remained on the floor, curled into the foetal position while Robert sat next to him hugging his trembling knees. For a long while the two of them sat there, perished with cold, but unable to muster the strength to staunch the icy air which fed in from the open window.

Eventually, Robert stood up and pulled down the casement. He returned and sat on his haunches, the balls of his feet making contact with the roughly hewn floorboards. Placing a hand on Emile's shoulders, he spoke to him in gentle tones, coaxing him to share his dark, brooding thoughts.

"Emile, surely nothing could be so dreadful that you would continually try and kill yourself. For days you've been pacing the floor and crying yourself to sleep. You have to tell me what's troubling you. Perhaps I can help."

Emile's fresh young face was deathly pale. Moonlight previously masked by the dark clouds streamed through the undressed window. Moonbeams illuminated his large, pale blue-grey eyes, now red-rimmed, dull, and lifeless. He shook his head sadly.

"You won't understand. No one does."

"I'll try and understand. Tell me!"

After a long silence, Emile finally spoke in a flat, monotone voice.

"I've never been so unhappy in my life. I wish I'd the courage to blow my brains out."

"Hush, Emile, it's a sin to speak so. You don't mean it."

"Oh, but I do, every word. I loved her, I truly did, my lady from Fife. For years, we exchanged affectionate letters whilst I was away in France, but now she tells me she prefers someone else, someone who will be a better provider. I no longer have the will to live. She meant everything to me."

"Why would you want to kill yourself over a woman? You're still young, with a lifetime ahead of you to find someone else."

"I'm tired of this existence, Robert. I want out of this world. I've no money of my own. I'm working for your uncle here under his bounty. No woman wants me because I have no money. What's the point in carrying on when I know my situation is hopeless?"

"Because situations change, Emile, they always do. I promise, in time to come you'll meet someone more worthy of your affections. One day you'll have a better position in society, and better prospects."

Emile thought about it for a moment and smiled faintly.

"Perhaps you're right, Robert. I guess, in any case, I don't have the courage others have to finally end it all. I want to end my life because I'm such a failure, and yet I fail even at this. What a disappointment of a man am I. I cannot live, nor can I die."

The irony of Emile's ineptitude did not escape Robert as he picked himself off the floor and climbed back into bed.

3 BETTER PROSPECTS
DUNDEE 1852

As the weeks passed, Emile's broken heart mended, he found a new love interest, and a new job. Robert Baker was right, Emile later reflected, situations do change.

Emile heard of a vacancy existing with a nursery in Dundee. It came with far better wages and prospects than those of a waiter at the Rainbow Tavern. Due to Emile's strong references and experience in the field, it was no surprise when they offered, and he accepted, the position. Thus it was, on auld Hansel Monday, the first Monday of the year, 5th January 1852, Pierre Emile L'Angelier accepted employment with William Pringle Laird.

When he was a young boy, Emile's father had died, and the event had unsettled him. It left him feeling discontent, for after that, he seemed to drift from place to place, searching for something of which he was never sure. He was hoping this position would bring him the stability and happiness he desired.

Over the months, Emile proved himself to be a reliable, hardworking employee. However, despite these good qualities, it did not take William Laird too long to recognize Emile's fragile state of mind. He was particularly perturbed by regular demonstrations of flux, intense periods of excitement followed soon after by long cycles of depression. It was during one of these periods Laird became alarmed, when he realised there was a strong possibility Emile wanted to do himself harm.

For months, Emile had spoken about a new woman in his life. She was his beautiful fiancée, and they were soon to be married. In fact, he spoke of little else, *ad nauseam* to most. Initially, this was a welcome diversion from the numerous adventure stories of his time in France, where he postulated about his part in the Paris Revolution of 1848. What he failed to divulge was the real extent of his National Guard duties. They had lasted less than a month, and his sole responsibility had been standing guard at a railway station on the outskirts of Paris.

Laird politely listened to the accounts of bravery and action, of rubbing shoulders with powerful men and carrying out duties of great responsibility, but took whatever Emile said with a pinch of salt. Perhaps Laird's attitude was not so much that the stories seemed too grandiose to hold much water, but that, coupled with Emile's claims to be French, when Laird knew he had been born on the British Channel islands, made believing much of his stories difficult.

Of late, Emile's cheerful chatter regarding his fiancée had taken on a negative tone. Recent weeks had seen him withdraw from general conversation, becoming morose and distracted, until one day, he became rather agitated.

"Emile, is something bothering you?" asked William Laird, as Emile repeatedly paced the office floor, whacking a rolled up newspaper against the flat of his hand.

Emile approached him with an expression which made plain he was the receiver of devastating news. He unfurled the rolled up newspaper and spread it out on the desk. In doing so, the pages sprang back, curling in on themselves. With increased frustration, he tried again, and stabbed at an insertion in the classifieds with an indignant, outstretched finger.

Laird silently read the marriage announcement, shocked to see the name of the woman in print was none other than the same fiancée of whom Emile always spoke so highly.

"I don't know what to say, Emile. What dreadful bad luck!"

"I don't understand why this keeps happening to me. This is not the first time."

"Oh, double bad luck! You poor chap!"

"Why do they agree to marry me and then marry another? It can't be because I am unattractive, can it?"

"Not at all, Emile, not at all."

"Women notice me, Laird. When I walk down the street, I see them casting their admiring glances. There was once an occasion when a lady and her companion stopped me in the street and commented on my pretty feet. I've had many a fair lady declare their love for me. In fact, at one time, I was intimate with two beautiful ladies, of considerable wealth, both at the same time. But this!"

He snatched the paper off the desk, enclosed it in a clenched fist, and shook it repeatedly, anger interrupting articulation. Bubbles of spittle foamed at the corners of his mouth. They clung there for a moment before his next explosion released them in a powerful spray as he repeated, "This?"

Emile's agitation increased. He rushed around to the same side of the desk where William stood and snatched up a sharp, short, curved bladed knife used for cutting twine.

Laird stepped sideways, but the knife was not a threat to him. Emile held it melodramatically to his breast, the tip of the blade pressing hard against his chest. Then, just as dramatically, he started to weep.

Visions of her beauty swam before him of the day he had proposed and she had accepted. The weather had been glorious, the water like glass. They had sat at either end of the hired rowing boat, neither noticing they had spent twenty minutes going around in circles. He could still hear her peals of laughter when the boat almost capsized when she had said yes to his proposal and he had leaped off his wooden seat to scoop her up in his arms. It had been a perfect day.

The tears continued to course down his cheeks.

"I wish to be out of this world as soon as possible. There's nothing to live for now she's crossed me and married another. We were pledged to each other. Pledged! How many more times must this happen to me? Oh, I'll end it all now!"

Laird stood transfixed, unclear quite what to say or what to do. Emile held the knife to his breast for a brief moment longer, his shirt still remained crisp white. As quickly as the tears sprang up, they died. He placed the knife back down on the desk and calmly walked away.

"I'm going to throw myself over the Dean Bridge," he said, speaking over his shoulder. "What's the point in living after this?" He stopped abruptly as a fleeting thought arrested his intention. He turned, slowly, to add, "But, if I decide not to then I shall exact revenge. See if I don't! What's happened to me is unforgivable. I'll never allow this to happen to me again, for as long as I live. Never!"

*

Emile recovered slowly from being jilted for the second time. He stewed over his situation, not knowing of any other man so badly treated by women. Twice engaged and twice abandoned for someone else.

The following months saw him drawn down into a dark vortex of revenge plots, self-harm scenarios, and self-loathing. When his thoughts cleared, he blamed his lack of position within society as the impetus of the fickleness these women displayed.

On reflection, he reasoned, it had nothing to do with what he looked like, nor his personal qualities. These women went on to marry men who were simply more eligible than him, wealthier, of a higher social standing. After this revelation, he decided to embark on a quest to climb out of the social class into which he had been born, in order to gain the wealth that kept eluding him.

*

Tonight Emile was looking forward to the Dundee Floral and Horticultural Society's monthly meeting. His duties included preparing Laird's backroom for the gathering.

As he brought out chairs and tables, his pulse raced with the excitement for the evening ahead. With numerous well-bred women attending this was an opportunity he never passed up. All of them were the type of woman he felt he deserved to be allied to, on the level of society he aspired to attain.

While his thoughts of the various ladies jockeyed for position, William McDougall Ogilvie, assistant bank teller by day and secretary of the society by night, arrived early to make sure the tables and chairs were set up in good time.

"Ah, Emile my good laddie, how nice to see you again. Is everything under control?"

"Good evening Mr. Ogilvie. Yes, everything's going according to plan. The room should be ready shortly."

"Looking forward to the meeting then?"

"Oh yes, as always. I so enjoy mingling with the ladies afterwards."

"Um, yes, well, I'm looking forward to the talk on Aspidistras tonight. Fascinating plants! And they grow so well indoors. Do you grow any yourself?"

"I wonder if Miss Chatham will be coming this evening. I do hope so. I hear her father's an excellent surgeon. He's made quite a name for himself in Dundee, apparently. I think she rather fancies me."

"Oh, it must be your French accent women find so attractive, L'Angelier."

"Perhaps. I've been thinking of late I should secure myself a wife who'll help me elevate my position within society. A good marriage is all it'll take."

"Quite possibly, but such a marriage would be almost impossible to secure. I wouldn't advise it. The matters of the heart are complicated enough, without trying to jump class, laddie. Rather stick with the breed you know."

To Ogilvie's relief, the conversation turned to safer ground. Emile embarked on an anecdote concerning a journey to France with a person of some distinction. How they had given him charge of all their luggage, carriages, and horses, when he experienced trouble with the horses *en route*.

"Oh, the journey was quite arduous, actually, especially for the horses. But I found a simple solution which worked exceedingly well," said Emile as he started setting out the water glasses on the table.

"What was that?" enquired Ogilvie, sounding rather intrigued.

"Well, some of the horses were really knocked up and I gave them some arsenic which made them accomplish the journey."

"Arsenic? Good Lord! What effect did this have on the horses?"

"It made them long-winded and enabled me to complete the arduous ride with ease."

"Yes, but weren't you worried you would end up poisoning them?"

Emile laughed and casually flicked off some imaginary lint from the tablecloth.

"Oh no, not at all. You see, I take it myself."

"You take it yourself? Laddie, that cannot be true. I certainly wouldn't like to try it."

"I'm not suggesting you do, Mr. Ogilvie, but I've been taking it for years now, and I've suffered no ill-effects at all. It improves the complexion, you know. I used to have pains in my back for many years, and shortness of breath at times from asthma, but that's all gone now."

"Really? You can't ingest it then, surely?"

"I take it a number of ways, but mainly I drink a few grains from time to time in my tea. Here, I'll show you."

He walked back to his office, and after a few moments came back with a small envelope to prove his point. He opened it up carefully, and inside was a small amount of brilliant white, crystalline powder.

He closed it up again making sure the arsenic grains stayed well contained.

"I take handfuls of poppy seeds too, quite regularly," he went on to admit. "I eat them in such large quantities it makes me quite lightheaded, but all rather enjoyable. It does help in this miserable world of ours, don't you think?"

"Well, I'm surprised you don't seem to have suffered any ill-effects, if what you say is true. From the arsenic, that is," said Ogilvie.

"Ill effects? None whatsoever. I recommend it, Ogilvie. Perhaps you should try it, after all."

The first members started drifting in and the conversation dried up.

Emile left Ogilvie and crossed the room to welcome the first arrival of ladies who had all heard his limited repertoire of stories several times before. Few believed him, but it was fun, nevertheless. His French accent was rather charming and they saw him as the dapper young fellow who fawned and listened to their every word, unlike their busy husbands who worked long hours and whom they seldom saw. For this reason alone, he was a pleasant, harmless diversion tolerated, and for some, even encouraged.

Despite the pleasant start to the evening, Emile was a little on edge. His constant namedropping had caused him some embarrassment during the previous meeting.

He had experienced rather a difficult time explaining why Lieutenant-Colonel Robert Fraser, whom he talked so freely about as being a good friend, attended last month's meeting for the first time and completely ignored him. When asked about his connection to L'Angelier, Lieutenant-Colonel Fraser publicly humiliated Emile by declaring in his normal booming voice that he had never set eyes on the man in his life.

Such was Emile's level of distraction that he was not giving the ladies nearly as much attention as they expected. Instead, he scanned the room each time someone new appeared at the entrance and hoped desperately it was not the Lieutenant-Colonel.

4 A TOUCH OF SOMETHING
GLASGOW, CHRISTMAS DAY 1853

Before Emile knew it, another year was coming to an end. He had now moved from Dundee to Glasgow and while there, an acquaintance, William D'Esterre, invited him to partake in a meal at his home over the festive season.

William D'Esterre, like most Scots, preferred to celebrate Hogmanay, rather than Christmas. However, as Christmas fell on a Sunday this year, he decided to concede and have a small gathering to celebrate the occasion.

The invited guests sat around the merchant's table, a babble of voices interspersed with merry laughter filled the room. The table groaned with food presented on blue and white china transferware platters, to match the dinner plates before them. No one noticed the odd chipped plate as they tucked into their generous meal of oyster soup followed by roasted goose, roast potatoes fried in goose fat, colcannon, parsnips, carrots, peas, and gravy.

When they thought they could not possibly eat another morsel, out came a steaming cloutie dumpling with jugs of custard few could refuse.

Emile ate heartily and while he did so he disengaged from the surrounding conversation to admire the festively decorated room with its ivy ribbon swags, painted pine cones, and cheerful red berries.

His attention came back to his meal. He could not remember when last he enjoyed a meal as fine as this one.

Not being a big drinker, he passed on the ale and wine, and a heady rum and cognac punch being ladled out, up and down the table. It was already having its effect on the women. Raucous laughter and unsuppressed giggles erupted at staccato intervals, despite surreptitious glares from their menfolk whenever they occurred.

Eventually, the gaggle of women retired to the front room much to the relief of the men who eagerly escaped to another area of the house where they swiftly produced packs of cards, along with boxes of cigars. They had not been playing too long, perhaps an hour into their game, when Emile felt ill and excused himself in search of a bathroom.

D'Esterre showed him the way and re-joined the men, thinking nothing of it. A good few minutes passed, perhaps ten or fifteen, when the host became concerned for the guest whose chair had remained empty for quite some time, and left to search for him. At the toilet door, he was about to knock when he heard low moans coming from the other side. He then heard Emile vomiting violently.

"Emile, are you alright? Can I get you something?"

"I need a minute. I'll be out shortly," he managed to reply, after some delay.

He hardly succeeded in finishing his sentence when another portion of oysters and roast goose reversed up his burning oesophagus and ended up in a sloppy mess at the bottom of the toilet bowl. No sooner had his stomach settled than a vicious force gripped his bowels forcing him to sit down to expel whatever was upsetting him. At one stage, he was unsure whether to sit or stand.

*

D'Esterre left Emile and rushed back to his guests, fearful there was something wrong with the oysters. He checked on the women who were all fine, as were the men, much to his relief.

Emile's illness continued. It lasted some time until D'Esterre felt compelled to send for a trusted bottle of Dr. J Collis Browne's Cholorodyne. He administered it to Emile, who by now was lying prostrate on the couch. D'Esterre continued to hover.

"Have some more, Emile. You need to make sure the medicine takes effect."

Emile complied and fell back onto the cushion as if the effort of sipping from a spoon was exhausting.

Cholera was no stranger to the town having swept through in '83 and '84 killing thousands, and leaving others weakened for life. Knowing how contagious this pernicious disease was, D'Esterre was hoping none of his guests would be affected, or any of his household either, for that matter.

After a time, the medication's combination of chloroform, Indian hemp, and opium began to work, and Emile rallied.

"Perhaps we should call a cab for Emile and take him home. I'll go with him," offered one of the guests.

"That's an excellent idea, Matthews, and very genteel of you."

With a horse and driver found, both remained patient as the men helped bundle Emile into the cab with some difficulty. Those who came to help stood on the pavement in the cold evening air, vapour escaping in ghostly plumes as they spoke of the night's strange events and watched on as some continued to fuss and make him as comfortable as they could.

They raised their voices, trying to be heard, as the Hansom clattered across the cobblestones and sped off around the corner. After stamping their feet and shaking their coats to brush off the early snow, they resumed their interrupted game, and tried to enjoy the rest of the evening.

"I do hope the old boy will be alright. Mighty peculiar that he should take ill like that," commented one of the guests as he returned to his seat and picked up his hand of cards.

"Well, at least the ladies will be safe tonight!" replied another, as guffaws rippled round the table.

5 THE ENCOUNTER
GLASGOW, FEBRUARY 1855

Emile's move from Edinburgh to Glasgow was now permanent. Being employed as a packing clerk for Huggins & Co., the first cotton commissioned business in Glasgow, was a step up from working at Laird's seed nursery. Emile, never ignoring those ambitious callings constantly nagging him to better himself, felt his life was finally turning a corner.

This particular morning, he crossed the yard to check on some newly delivered cotton bales, when he stopped short. It was not every day the yard was visited by women, especially exceptionally well-dressed women. They were deep in conversation with young Robert Baird, younger brother to one of his new colleagues. He took advantage of a nearby stack of bales to hide behind, in order to appraise the two women.

One of the young women in particular, caught his attention. She seemed to be the elder of the two. Not handsome girls, he thought, if he were honest. The younger sister was plain and rather dumpy. The elder sister was a better version, and it was she to whom Emile directed his attention. What she lacked in classic beauty, she made up with vivacity that Emile found captivating.

She continued to chat animatedly to Robert, who at seventeen was urgently trying to coax a sulky moustache and beard to hide his spotty skin. While he blushed and stammered his way through the conversation, Emile's focus lingered over their waists and fashionable hooped dresses made from yards and yards of sumptuous fabric and lace in delicate hues of lilac, blue, and cream.

When the exchange of pleasantries ended, the women departed, and Emile wasted no time in approaching the young man.

"Well, I see you're starting to attract the ladies these days, young Robert."

"N...no! N...no! It's nothing like that." He blushed some more. "They're friends of the family."

"They are? Interesting. Who was the vivacious young lady doing all the talking?"

"Oh, that's Madeleine, Madeleine Smith and her sister Elizabeth, whom they call Bessie. They live on India Street. Their father's quite well-known around here. He's the architect, James Smith."

"Is that right? An architect?"

Emile deliberated for a few moments before saying, "Do you think I could secure an introduction to her, Robert? I'd be interested in meeting Mr. Smith, too. See what you can arrange, won't you? There's a good lad."

Robert started to laugh, but stopped short when he realised Emile was serious. How could he explain the Smiths moved in very different social circles to those of Emile L'Angelier? Despite his youth and naiveté, he was certain Madeleine Smith, recently returned from one of London's top finishing schools, 'Miss Alice Gorton's Academy for Young Ladies', would not be interested in mixing with packing clerks.

"I may be able to organise something, but I can't promise," he mumbled, moving away.

Emile reached out and grabbed Robert at the elbow.

"I must meet her, Robert."

"I'll…I'll speak to my aunt and uncle and see if they can organise an introduction. But I can't promise they'll agree to it."

*

Robert Baird hoped Emile would forget about wanting to meet Madeleine Smith. He did not. Emile's constant bombardment of requests became insufferable until finally, under intense pressure, he broached the subject with his aunt and uncle one evening at dinner.

Robert cleared his throat.

"I've a friend who'd like to meet Madeleine Smith. He wonders if you'd help arrange it."

"Well that depends, dear," replied his aunt, briefly looking up at him before daintily manoeuvring her spoon around her bowl. "How old is he?"

"Difficult to say, perhaps ten years older than Madeleine. I think he's about twenty-seven or twenty-eight."

"I doubt he's established at that age, unless he comes from good money. Do we know him?"

"I don't think you do, Aunt."

"Well why not? Who is he?"

"His name is Pierre Emile L'Angelier, but his friends call him Emile."

"Ah, a Frenchman, that sounds intriguing, Robert. Is he part of the diplomatic corps?"

"Um, no, he isn't. His parents are French, but actually he was born on the island of Jersey."

"Well, there's money in Jersey. What does he do?"

Robert stirred his soup for the twentieth time. Sweat bloomed on his neck. He could feel the small beads trickling down under his stiff shirt collar despite being seated nowhere near the fireplace.

He drew in a deep breath, avoided looking at his aunt before he managed to say, "He's a packing clerk at Huggins."

Robert's uncle, unusually mute during the entire conversation, roared. Robert involuntarily jumped. The silver spoon in his hand jerked too, ejecting tomato soup in a far-reaching arc over the crisp damask tablecloth. He stared in horrified fascination as the orange-red droplets beaded, sank and spread into the woven fabric leaving behind unsightly blotches.

"The audacity of the man! Doesn't he realize who she is? What man of his position would dare ask to meet a young girl such as Madeleine? A packing clerk? This is preposterous, Robert! I forbid you to raise this topic ever again in my company or your aunt's. I will not entertain this conversation a minute longer, and you should know better than to have raised it."

"Yes, Uncle."

"You can go back and tell this scoundrel, Pierre or Emile, or whatever he calls himself, that Madeleine Smith is a young lady of good social standing and he should rather look to his own for female company. If he doesn't, he will have me to answer to. A good whipping should soon settle this."

*

The following morning mortification dominated as Robert conveyed the message, omitting the promise of a whipping. Emile smarted at the response but remained undeterred. The more Emile heard an introduction to the young Madeleine Hamilton Smith was impossible, the more resolute he became in orchestrating a meeting.

Finally, fate intervened. He and Robert ambled down Sauchiehall Street one Saturday afternoon, enjoying a break in the weather, when Madeleine and her sister serendipitously approached from the other direction.

Emile, who had been anticipating just such a happenstance meeting, recognised her immediately. He adjusted his top hat, scrutinized his shoes, and glanced quickly at his broken reflection in a shop window with panes too small to do his image justice. He hastily smoothed his necktie before nudging Robert.

"Isn't that Miss Madeleine Smith and her sister coming out of Paterson's Draper's Shop?"

By this time, Madeleine and Elizabeth were drawing level with them. Robert refrained from answering. Instead, he raised his hat as they approached, with Emile doing the same.

"Robert, it's a pleasure to see you again," gushed Madeleine. Robert answered with a deep blush and an awkward grin, shifting his weight from one foot to the other and looking like a dunderhead.

She glanced over at Emile and flashed him a dazzling smile, looking at him coquettishly from under her thick eyelashes. She quickly assessed his physical appearance, and thought him rather handsome. He looked much older than Robert and she was immediately taken with his waxed moustache. Curiosity consumed her to learn who he was.

"F…F…Forgive my manners, ladies. May I present to you Mr. Emile L'Angelier? Emile, Miss Madeleine Smith and her sister, Miss Elizabeth."

Emile bowed deeply. The two young women inclined their heads in return.

"I am at your service, ladies. It's an honour to meet you both," replied Emile emphasizing his French accent.

Madeleine put her French lessons to the test.

"Il est un plaisir de vous rencontrer aussi, Monsieur L'Angelier."

"The pleasure is all mine, Miss Smith." He lifted his hat and bowed again. "And may I congratulate you on your accent? It's *magnifique.*"

"Why thank you. You are too kind."

She turned to Robert.

"I'd love to stay and talk, Robert, but Mama has sent me on an urgent quest for some migraine powders and I've already tarried too long. Can we expect to see you at the MacMillan party, week after next?"

"Y...y....yes I am." He inwardly cursed as he listened to his stumbling articulation. He had no idea why he always felt so tongue-tied in front of the Smith sisters.

"Would you like to join us, Mr. L'Angelier? I hope you don't think us terribly provincial. I know it's not quite the Season yet, but that shouldn't stop us having some fun now, should it?"

"Not at all. I'd be delighted, Miss Smith."

"Well, that's settled then. I'll arrange it. Good day, gentlemen."

Robert was as stunned as Emile was elated. Not only had he finally met the elusive Madeleine Smith after months of trying to orchestrate it, but she had formally invited him to enter an inner circle of society he had only ever watched from afar.

6 GROWING UP FAST
GLASGOW, MARCH 1855

Madeleine could hardly contain her excitement.

"Well, then miss, which dress would you like to wear?"

"Oh, I can't make up my mind. Help me, Christina! I want to look pretty tonight. I need something that won't make my skin look sallow. I don't know why mama insists on buying me yellow silk dresses. They look positively frightful against my skin."

"What about this cream dress?"

Madeleine looked at it critically.

"No, not tonight. It looks too ...." Her voice trailed off. She had wanted to say, 'virginal' but didn't want to shock. Instead she said, "I think I'll try on the rose-pink taffeta."

After wriggling into layers of petticoats and hoops and finally the outfit, it had taken more than twenty minutes to dress.

"By the looks of it, those eyes are shining brightly all on their own. No need for belladonna drops tonight. You look lovely, Miss Madeleine."

"Oh, do I? I do hope so! I want to look my very best tonight."

*

Having arrived early with Bessie, to ensure being there before Emile and Robert, her eyes were now fixed on the entrance, waiting impatiently. She shifted her weight from one foot to the other each time the doorway darkened. The agonising wait was finally over. Emile really was handsome, she confirmed, as she rushed over to greet him.

"Robert, Mr. L'Angelier."

"Miss Smith, wonderful to see you. Please, call me Emile."

"Please, call me Madeleine." She turned her attention to Robert who was looking around awkwardly.

"What have you been doing with yourself Robert, since we saw you last? Are you looking forward to the new opera season?"

She noticed Robert's eyes darted everywhere, until they were finally forced to meet her gaze, a deep blush rising from his cheeks.

"I...I'm n...not really fond of the opera. Would you mind terribly if I excused myself? I've just seen Sam Shepherd and need to see him about something."

"Not at all, Robert."

Madeleine steered Emile away from prying eyes and headed for an isolated corner of the room, partially hidden by an overhanging staircase, affording them privacy in a room quickly filling up with people.

"Please tell me you like opera, Emile. I'm so looking forward to the new season starting Monday next. Madame Caradori is performing. Do you like her?"

"I can't say I've heard of her," confessed Emile. "To be honest, I don't visit the opera halls that often. Do you mind if I smoke?"

Madeleine shook her head as she watched him fill his pipe. She hid her disappointment well, for she had hoped that they would go to the opera together this season. She did not press him further knowing opera was not for everyone. What Madeleine did not know was that after paying his tailor and his landlady there was scant left over for anything else, including visits to music halls and theatres.

Madeleine's emotions soon turned to delight as she listened to fascinating stories of the French army and his many travels abroad. She hung on every word, riveted. To her he was a man of the world, one with an adventurous spirit who had seen and lived life. Oh, how she envied his life so different from her own cloistered upbringing.

To the more astute and worldly-wise, his stories, riddled with half-truths and exaggerations, clearly lacked veracity. Madeleine, neither astute nor worldly-wise, knew no better. At nineteen, recently released from the protective cocoon of boarding school and ill-prepared for the wide world, she was easily bedazzled and beguiled by his tales.

*

Madeline was so enamoured with Emile, and so totally engrossed in their conversation, she failed to notice an acquaintance, Blake MacDonald, or anyone else, for that matter. He, however, had noticed her.

He lounged up against the mantelpiece, trying to look nonchalant despite, ten minutes earlier, failing to impress several ladies seated around him. He gave up his weak efforts to ingratiate himself and focused his attention instead on Madeleine, and the stranger in their midst.

Blake MacDonald continued to watch them engaging in animated conversation, as only Madeleine knew how. He turned to the notorious gossiper in the group, Jemima Stapleton, seated next to him.

"Miss Stapleton, who is the gentleman Miss Smith seems so enamoured with this evening? Do we have a name?"

"I'm afraid not. I've been trying to find out since he arrived. All I've managed to find out so far is that he's French."

"Ah, a frog. What does he do?"

"I haven't been able to find that out yet either. Most distressing! It's not like me to be unable to ferret these things out. If you beat me to it, you will let me know, won't you?"

She smiled and batted her eyelids to encourage the sharing of information. Blake MacDonald was already moving away and crossing the floor.

He sauntered up to Madeleine and Emile whose bowed heads signified deep conversation, and with no apology barged straight in.

"Well, then," he boomed, "what brings *you* to Glasgow?"

Emile cleared his throat, hesitated for a moment, and skirted around the issue.

"Have we met? I don't believe we have."

"MacDonald. Blake MacDonald."

"Pierre L'Angelier. My friends call me Emile."

"So, what are you doing in Glasgow, L'Angelier? Is it work or pleasure?"

"I heard Glasgow had a reputation for beautiful women and I'm not disappointed."

He stole a glance at Madeleine who started to blush. No one ever called Madeleine Smith beautiful. She bent her head and smiled sweetly.

"Ah, well that we can't deny," said Blake, looking over Madeleine's head and taking in some beautiful faces of women scattered around the room.

"So you're French, L'Angelier?"

"Yes, I'm very proud of my French heritage. We pride ourselves on our manners and sophistication."

Blake missed the barb and carried on the interrogation.

"As a Frenchman in Glasgow, what do you do for a living?"

"I'm in the textile industry. Cotton, actually."

Emile wavered between honesty and inventing a more prestigious career. The thought was tempting, but fleeting.

"Ah, a merchant for the French?"

"No, actually, I'm a clerk, at Huggins & Co."

MacDonald guffawed.

"You mean an accountant, surely?"

"No, I'm a packing clerk."

"You're a packing clerk?" roared Blake incredulously. "Don't make a stuffed bird laugh!"

The conversation in the room dried to a trickle, then stopped. Noise emptied, silence rushed in.

"Are you telling me you grovel around on your hands and knees in dusty warehouses counting cotton bales?"

He watched Emile squaring up to him. He noticed too how the dapper little man dug a finger under the newly starched collar to loosen it. They maintained eye contact as Blake continued to size him up, waiting for a different answer.

Tension broke when MacDonald thumped him on the back with such force he jolted forward. MacDonald broke into deep guffaws.

"Lord, man, I almost believed you! Love a good yarn!"

After more back slapping he returned to reclaim his spot by the fireplace and immediately Jemima Stapleton set upon him.

The small circle of people who had previously gathered around Emile and Madeleine retreated and remained distant for the rest of the evening. Even Robert made himself scarce. People tittered and glanced their way. Where some felt it impossible a common packing clerk could be in their midst, others began to wonder. Unwittingly, the couple became the topic of conversation and speculation for the rest of the night.

*

Despising gossip, Madeleine turned her back and ignored the whispers. Tonight she aimed to enjoy herself with one of the most handsome men in the room, and she was determined to have some fun.

"Please ignore Blake MacDonald and his ilk. They are not my friends, and are incredibly rude. We are not all like that."

"My dear Madeleine, I have no expectations for this evening. I am here solely to enjoy your company."

"Tell me more about yourself, Emile. Have you been in Glasgow long?"

"Not very long. I arrived to take up my current position at Huggins & Co."

"So you do work in cotton then?"

"Yes, I do."

"As a..?"

"As a packing clerk."

Madeleine was devastated. How was it possible a man of his dress and impeccable manners was not of her class? The knowledge cut deep for she knew seeing him again was out of the question. Sadder still, as the evening progressed, she realised that there were strong feelings of attraction on both sides, but futile to act upon, considering his social standing.

For the rest of the evening she battled shifting emotions as they oscillated between reason and the heart. Towards the end of the night their hands briefly touched; it was electric. She wondered if he felt it too. When asked if he might see her again, the rebel in her swiftly stamped out sense. Reason tried to speak, but her heart won the day.

*

Madeleine lay in bed the following morning stretching and yawning, a smile playing on her lips as she remembered the dashing man from the night before. Her heart did a little somersault as she remembered him as attentive, kind, and funny. She recalled fond memories of him taking her hand and kissing it gallantly as they said their goodbyes. Papa would disapprove of this man, but instead of it worrying her, it deliciously pleased her.

She was tired of always having to accept what Papa dictated. She had found his sternness, and his lording over them, demanding respect and complete obedience, suffocating of late. He was often beastly to poor Mama. No wonder she kept to her bed for long periods of time and became indisposed to those around her. His rulings remained unquestioned, unchallenged. She pouted as she lay there. She hated Papa sometimes.

Her thoughts turned to Emile, setting her heart aflutter all over again. She admitted the social inequality between them would be problematic if a romance developed in the future. However, she glossed over this important detail, pushing it into a far corner of her mind. Instead, she focused on his confessions of being a clerk within a hostile circle and thought him brave and endearing.

Her thoughts came back to her friends and family. Mama and Papa would probably never accept him, nor would her friends. She flopped back on her pillows in despair.

What made people so dreadfully beastly, judging according to wealth and status? Why could Emile not be her friend, just because he was from the working classes? They were people, after all, no different to her parents' set, except for the size of their purse.

With Madeline being of marriageable age, Papa and Mama constantly discussed potential suitors, always favouring those with a larger bank balance. She cringed at their idea of the perfect husband, which in no way matched her own. Several of the men were bald or greying, toadying friends of her father's, aging widowers looking for younger wives. She shuddered involuntarily at the thought of having to share a marital bed with them.

Those proffered who were younger, either possessed the personality of a sloth, or were brash and boorish, like Blake MacDonald. None were to her liking.

She decided, on brief reflection, that it did not bother her in the slightest if her family disapproved. She was not terribly fond of her family, and she did not need the consent of her friends.

She stretched and yawned again before settling back onto the starched, lace pillows. She found the Frenchman exciting and attractive, and felt compelled to explore the new relationship, and to follow where it led. A faint smile played upon her lips as she began to think about this new man in ways no respectable young Victorian lady should.

7 A BLOSSOMING RELATIONSHIP
GLASGOW & ROW, MARCH 1855

A fortnight had passed since the party, and Madeleine had thought of nothing else except the well-dressed, flamboyant man with the charming manners who had been to France to fight bravely in the 1848 Revolution.

One day she could hardly contain herself when he managed to send word to her. He asked if she could be in West End Park just before midday in order to casually bump into her. Madeleine felt giddy, and all sixes and sevens. Choosing the right outfit took an unconscionably long time.

She looked critically at her reflection, believing her cheeks were losing their blush. No amount of pinching produced the desired effect. Instead, they soon returned to their usual alabaster white.

She eased her hair into her favourite lavender bonnet, several tones darker than her plaid-patterned, cotton dress, and tied the ribbons under her chin into a bow. To complete the look Madeleine found her favourite cream tasselled parasol, and went in search of her sister.

Taking Bessie with her, on the pretext she needed fresh air, they chattered amicably about this, that, and nothing in particular. As they entered the park, Madeleine's heart sank; it was crowded. She would never find Emile in this throng. They forged their way ahead, avoiding darting children and mothers pushing perambulators. Horses, pulling carts and carriages, choked the avenues. Crowds milled aimlessly, gathering in small groups to greet one another. Their path was blocked at every turn.

They had to move out of the way as a policeman chased two little urchins who had just picked a gentleman's pockets. The policeman, red-faced, blew his whistle and waved his truncheon, but pulled up short as they disappeared into the masses leaving him fuming.

"Well, that was a bit of excitement for the day! I cannot believe the crowds. I think everyone has had the same idea. Oh, look at those gorgeous bulbs, Bessie, aren't they a picture?"

They strolled over to admire a thick carpet of bluebells under a grove of beech trees whose leaves were yet to emerge. The sea of tiny purple bells, arched on spring-green stems, nodded in the breeze.

"Shall we go to the lake and look at the ducks?" asked Madeleine.

"Oh, yes, let's. They do so make me laugh."

They stood for a while watching the birds. A few people threw bread into the water, enticing them closer. While some came to investigate, others ignored the food, preferring instead to search for their own. Diving, bottoms up, they disappeared deep beneath the surface while they snacked on worms, small fish, and the occasional frog. Madeleine, the artist, watched with interest as they re-emerged, droplets of water forming glasslike beads that rolled off their feathers, and back into the lake.

She broke her observation and craned her neck to the right, looking to see if she could see Emile. Her stomach somersaulted and filled with butterflies as she watched him hasten towards them. He strode with confidence and purpose, his right hand clasping the knob of his silver-topped cane that swung in unison with his long strides.

Again, he was immaculately dressed. He wore a black frock coat with a deep shawl collar, black and grey striped twill trousers, and a blue jacquard waistcoat with bright metal buttons. As he drew nearer she noticed a small, pearl pin secured his silk cravat. It seemed impossible from his dress, thought Madeleine, that he could come from any class other than her own.

He tipped his top hat and bowed deeply to both of them.

"Miss Madeleine, what a delightful surprise. May I compliment you on your outfit? You are a vision to behold."

He bowed again, and taking her hand in his he casually rubbed his thumb against the back of it before brushing his lips across her cool skin. The touch was electrifying, a palpable thrill coursed through her. She looked into his eyes and as he straightened his expression told her, this time, he had felt it too. She withdrew her hand and turning back to Bessie, laughed a little nervously.

"And Miss Elizabeth, you too are looking exceedingly handsome today." He clasped her sister's podgy hand and bowed over it, but did not kiss it as he had Madeleine's.

Madeleine glanced at her sister and immediately recognised the signs of jealous disappointment. She had an inkling that Elizabeth, too, liked the dapper Frenchman with the twirled moustache and slightly Bohemian beard.

"Walk with me ladies. It's heartening to see the sun out so early this spring, and shame to those who prefer to spend the day indoors."

Madeleine laughed again, this time coyly as she looked at him from under her lashes as they fell into step.

"Why, the very same thing I said to Bessie this morning. Wasn't it, Bessie?"

Bessie nodded eagerly, unaware she was part of a ploy, and happily fell into step. Both young women vied for his attention as the afternoon unfolded.

Emile L'Angelier was pleasant, as usual. He was quite the raconteur, and Bessie was sorry when they needed to leave. There was no hesitation in agreeing to another meeting the following week, weather of course permitting.

After he had taken his departure Bessie turned to her sister and said, "What a charming man he is, Madeleine."

"He is rather charming, isn't he?"

"I still think he likes me."

"You do?"

"Yes, I do."

"Perhaps he likes me better," replied Madeleine.

Bessie walked on in silence for a while longer before she said, "Madeleine, you have to introduce him to Papa. It wouldn't be right if you didn't."

"Oh, Bessie, don't be silly. He's merely a friend. I'm not going to marry him!"

She laughed at the notion and drew her sister closer. In order not to complicate matters she did not tell Bessie why she could not introduce Emile to Papa. They continued walking arm-in-arm to the end of the park before emerging onto the street and heading for home. It was an unusual sight, to those who knew the Smith sisters, for they were not what one called 'close', however, this was not an ordinary day, and for Madeleine this was a new beginning.

*

Within weeks of their first meeting Emile L'Angelier and Madeleine Smith grew from being friends to becoming sweethearts. Their relationship developed quickly, and they eagerly arranged to meet as often as possible, but not nearly as often as they liked. This was the one dark cloud in their blossoming relationship; it had to be conducted in secrecy. Madeleine told Emile that meeting her father, or introducing him to the rest of her family, was a delicate affair. It would need careful orchestrating.

"I don't understand, Madeleine. What is it about me that would offend your father? Am I not good enough for you?"

"Don't be silly, Emile. In my family, when young women are courted, both parties either grow up together, or they are introduced to one another by family members, or friends of the family. No one knows you, and so therefore it is more difficult. I have to think of a way of bringing up your existence with my papa without him forbidding me to see you again. You wouldn't like that now, would you?"

She pouted a little, and he couldn't help but smile.

"It really is not as simple as I would like. Please leave this in my hands. I will find a solution soon, I promise."

*

The situation was far more complicated than she cared to admit. Papa's talk of late was how he expected her to marry well, and how he and Mama were actively looking for suitors.

There was no misunderstanding - to marry a man beneath her social class was inconceivable. Social position was everything to her father, and just why this was especially so was revealed several weeks later, after Madeleine was let into a family secret that surprised her.

She was told her Papa had started his life a crofter's son. When he had met Mama he too had been on an unequal social footing. His saving grace, however, was his education. In addition, his father's rise from crofter to construction business owner, and the then young James Smith being a talented architect, had helped pave the way to him marrying the daughter of David Hamilton, architect extraordinaire.

Yet, instead of this inside knowledge helping her, Madeleine knew it only made matters worse. She now fully understood why social status was so important to her father. He had achieved so much in his lifetime. No one spoke of him as James Smith, the crofter's son. He was James Smith, the brilliant architect, readily accepted within the middle and upper social circles he moved. He enjoyed an excellent reputation and standing within his profession and the community at large.

He would never allow her, as his eldest child, to drag him back down from where he had struggled so hard to rise.

*

The dining room was quiet. Madeleine sat at the long table with no one for company except the ticking of the grandfather clock standing sentry at the far end of the room.

Where others in the household preferred to have their breakfasts in their rooms, Madeleine favoured having hers in the dining room. This morning she was late in rising, and was surprised to find, despite the hour, her breakfast still edible. She relished the hearty plate of kippers and scrambled egg. After that, she lifted a corner of the linen napkin to retrieve a slice of toast which she generously spread with orange and brandy marmalade. The ham, potted beef, and other cold remnants remained untouched.

She pushed her plate back ready to leave when Agnes McMillan poked her head around the open door.

"Oh, begging your pardon, miss, I wasn't expecting you still to be here. I've come to collect the dishes."

"Come on in, Agnes. I've just finished. I overslept this morning."

Madeleine was in no hurry so she continued to sit for a while watching the young woman bustle about collecting the discarded crockery and cutlery. She couldn't help noticing, at such close quarters, what a beautiful complexion the girl had.

"You've a good complexion, Agnes."

Agnes blushed. She looked up briefly and bobbed at the compliment. "Thank you, miss."

"Do you use anything special on your skin?"

"No, miss, only soap and water. I can't afford nothing else."

"Well, soap and water doesn't work for me. I've heard, however, arsenic can do wonders for one's complexion. Perhaps I'll try it. What do you think?"

"No, miss! Arsenic is only used for killing vermin. Who'd want to use that on skin? Oh aye, it sounds horrid. Besides, miss, if you don't mind me saying, you have a lovely complexion."

"Well it's very kind of you to say so, Agnes. However, I don't agree. It could be better. I've read arsenic makes the skin ever so soft.... Oh, before you go, Agnes, can you please make sure my ink well is full and I have a few sheets of writing paper ready? I'll be writing a few letters later on today."

*

Letters and notes became the vehicle through which Madeleine and Emile could reveal their growing feelings for one another. Snatches of stolen time, built around clandestine meetings, were never satisfactory. These missives opened the way for them to communicate at length. However, even this was problematic, for receiving letters to the Smith house without them being noticed by other family members, was impossible. A devious plan was needed.

Like many wealthy Glaswegians, the Smith family spent part of the Scottish spring and summer at their country house, while occasionally travelling back to Town, as Glasgow was referred, for meetings and social gatherings.

'Rowaleyn' was the Smith's new country retreat. A Baronial-style mansion on the outskirts of the pretty village of Row, it was a mile and a half west of Helensburgh, designed and recently built by James Smith himself. It was a solid house built over three storeys. Its situation - on a hill - and its double and triple aspect mullioned windows, commanded expansive, picture-perfect views over Gareloch and the Firth of Clyde beyond. The façade was adorned with ornamental turrets and crow-stepped gables. The house had presence. It was an irrefutable symbol of her father's status.

The interior was cavernous with seven thousand feet of habitable space and fourteen rooms. Each of the children had a bedroom to themselves; a luxury they did not have in Glasgow. Despite their age, they spent many a rainy day inside playing hide-and-seek. The place was perfect for such an activity.

Madeleine loved the house. It was a chance to swap grimy Glasgow for country air and summer fields filled with cheerful wildflowers and alive with bees, and butterflies, grouse, lapwings, deer, and the occasional rabbit.

Rather than enjoying her first year at Rowaleyn, though, she did not. Instead, she yearned for Emile and his company. Each day's passing seemed to stretch into eternity, and he occupied her thoughts from the moment she woke until she drifted off to sleep. She longed to have him there, and her spirits were dampened because of it.

The first time she wrote to Emile she was still at Rowaleyn but she agonised over what to say. She sat at the desk for several minutes, sucking on the end of the dip-pen her brother Jack had given her for Christmas last. She looked out over the sprawling lake looking for inspiration. Chips of sunlight danced and bounced off the water and a small, red-sailed skiff skimmed across, into and then out of, her view. With the weather mild and the windows open she heard the sheep calling to one another as the shepherd moved them onto new pastures. She pondered a while longer before finally dipping her pen back into the ink well, carefully wiping off the excess, and wrote the first line.

Emile L'Angelier Esq., 10 Bothwell Street, Glasgow

My dear Emile,
I do not feel as if I were writing you for the first time. Though our intercourse has been very short yet we have become as familiar friends. May we long continue so. And ere long may you be a friend of Papa's is my most earnest desire.

We feel it rather dull here after the excitement of a Town's Life. But then we have much more time to devote to study and improvement. I often wish you were near us we could take such charming walks. One enjoys walking with a pleasant companion and where could we find one equal to yourself?

I am trying to break myself of all my very bad habits; it is you I have to thank for this, which I do sincerely from my heart.

Your flower is fading.

> *I never cast a flower away*
> *The gift of one who cared for me*
> *A little flower, a faded flower,*
> *But it was done reluctantly.*

Bessie desires me to remember her to you. Write on Wednesday or Thursday. I must now say adieu. With kind love,
Believe me.
Yours very sincerely
Madeleine

Pierre Emile L'Angelier
Image courtesy of Martha and Steven Boyd
www.amostcuriousmurder.com

8 DECLARATIONS OF LOVE
GLASGOW, 1855

Whenever Madeleine thought about her predicament she was overcome by sadness and despair. She pushed the issue to the back of her mind, because she could never find a workable solution acceptable to all parties. All she wanted was her family to accept the man she was falling in love with, yet she knew deep down they never would.

She had allowed the relationship to go on far too long without trying to secure an introduction for Emile with her parents, or finding a suitable time to discuss the issue with her mother. For what was the use? She already knew the answer. Emile was from the working class, her family from the upper-middle class; the divide unbreachable.

Worse still, Emile failed to understand why an introduction to her father was a delicate affair, or why it was she needed to meet him in secret. These social mores were a mystery to him, for they did not exist within his own class structure. It often strained their relationship and stole the joy she felt whenever they spent time together. However, despite these differences, and the inability to be alone other than a handful of times over the months, the pair had grown exceedingly close.

Today the three of them sat in Mary Perry's tiny parlour, a place Madeleine enjoyed visiting. Mary was incredibly kind to them, and sympathetic to their plight. This was also the only place where she and Emile spent time together in a social setting where their relationship felt completely normal.

Mary Arthur Perry was a few years older than Emile, and unmarried. Despite her relative youth, Miss Perry looked every inch the old maid, her glasses perpetually perched on the end of her nose. She possessed an intelligent looking face, but was plain in looks and, unfortunately, readily forgettable.

She lived on her own and, expediently for Emile, opposite the very offices James Smith occupied for his architectural business. It had been here in the past where Emile often sat, sipping tea and nibbling on homemade biscuits, as Miss Perry prattled on about the church they both attended, and her weekly news.

However, it was neither the biscuits nor the company for which he came. It was to look at the young Miss Smith as she came and left from her father's premises, in the company of her sister, Elizabeth in the weeks before he had managed formal introductions through young Robert Baird.

Mary Perry excused herself, saying she needed to go into the garden to look for some mint for their tea. This left Emile and Madeleine conveniently alone together for a few moments. Mary often made pretexts for leaving them on their own, especially after hearing from Emile how difficult not being able to meet freely made their relationship. Mary felt it was the least she could do. She was a romantic at heart and felt sorry for the young lovers.

No sooner was she out of the house when Emile stood up, grabbed Madeleine by the hands, and pulled her out of her seat. He drew her closer to him kissing her passionately and leaving her breathless.

"Oh, my dearest Madeline, I cannot keep it to myself a moment longer. I love you!"

Madeleine's heart beat faster on hearing his words. The speed at which the relationship had evolved was unexpected, considering they had only known each other a few months. She had not dared to hope he loved her, as much as she loved him.

"I know it may all seem a bit sudden, my dear, but I've wanted to tell you for some time now. I cannot think of living without you. I want to marry you, Madeleine. I want you to be my wife."

A giggle that initially escaped Madeleine's lips was soon suppressed when Emile instantly frowned. This was her first real relationship, and her first proposal. At twenty years old, and not long out of boarding school, she was inexperienced when it came to men.

"Oh, Emile, this is all a bit sudden. I don't know what to say," she said, stalling for time as a thousand reasons flooded her thoughts as to why her answer should be no.

"Say yes, Madeleine. It's all I need to hear. But think very carefully before you give me your answer. Having been disappointed in love, twice before, I don't intend for it to happen again. Such a promise should never be made lightly, Madeleine. Once made, it can never be undone."

Madeleine was swept away by the moment. She was giddy with rampant emotions. The man she fantasised about, day in and day out, wanted to marry her. This was the moment she dreamed about, hoped for, planned for. And yet, she felt totally unprepared. How did she feel? Did she really love Emile enough to go against her parents' wishes? Did she want to be his wife? She looked at his face, knowing he was eager for her answer.

And then it was out, before she thought things through thoroughly.

"Yes, oh yes, Emile! I want to be your wife!"

A look of incredulousness turned to pure joy as he picked her up and, in a most undignified manner, swung her around the parlour narrowly missing a table cluttered with china ornaments, that had they smashed, would have had Miss Perry arriving back in an instant.

Madeleine giggled, and finally managed to say, "Emile, set me down before Miss Perry sees us."

On releasing her he cupped her face in his hands and kissed her gently again.

"Marry me, Madeleine. Marry me tomorrow! We'll go to London, or Australia! I don't care where we go, as long as we're together and you'll be my wife."

Madeleine smiled. Her mind was buzzing with a multitude of thoughts. Marriage would be so exciting. She would be the lady of her own house. She could escape Papa's stern looks, and unfair discipline. She could host her own tea parties, have dinner parties, and …

And then, she stopped.

Would it be possible to convince her father that Emile made her happy? Might he bestow on them a small legacy to allow them to live comfortably? She could only hope, as time passed, James Smith would want to help his daughter continue to live the life to which she was accustomed.

9 EXPOSED,
GLASGOW, JULY 1855

Unfortunately for Emile and Madeleine, their numerous covert meetings had not gone unnoticed by the town's gossipmongers and matchmakers. Despite Madeleine being short on looks, her father was not short in pocket. A marriage to Madeleine, for any young man, would be considered a profitable match. An interfering matronly-type, who was a family friend of the Smith's, made it her duty one day to enquire about Madeleine's new gentleman friend.

Madeleine noticed the atmosphere was tense when she entered the dining room for the meal that evening. She uttered the usual polite greetings and shuffled onto her seat. She did not look at her siblings for fear of giggling and enraging her father further. Instead she managed a sly glance down the long table towards Papa who returned a stare leaving no room for doubt she was the target of his fury.

She looked over at her mother's seat. It was empty. The rest of the seats were occupied by her younger siblings: Elizabeth, John, James and Janet. Their eyes were fixed on their empty dinner plates waiting for the maid to dish up their food so they could escape as quickly as they could. Madeleine did not bother to engage in conversation. It was better not to, under the circumstances.

The silence of the meal was broken only by metal cutlery screeching across porcelain as the family carved their meat and speared their food. Finally, the ordeal was over and she sighed audibly as she watched her father finish his last mouthful. As she stood up to leave, his cold voice stopped her in her tracks.

"Madeleine, I need a word with you. The rest of you may go." He dismissed them with a flick of his hand, neglecting to notice that some of them were still eating. Her father's command went unchallenged. Her siblings pushed back their seats, abandoned their half-eaten meals, and left demurely.

Her heart raced. She had no idea why she was about to incur his wrath. She sat back down and watched as he slowly dabbed at his mouth with the corner of the starched napkin. She waited an eternity for him to fold, and then re-fold it meticulously and place it next to his side plate. There was no noise except for the tick-tock of the clock. She had never noticed how loud it could be. It seemed to be in competition with her heart thumping against her ribcage in unison.

And then it came.

"Madeleine, are you seeing a man?"

"A man, Papa?"

"Do not play games with me, Madeleine," he warned in a slow, measured voice, cold and veiled in an implicit threat. He fixed his gaze on her, boring into her soul.

"I asked a simple question, Madeleine Hamilton, and I expect a simple answer."

"I don't know what you mean, Papa."

James Smith raised his large fist and brought it down with such force that cutlery and crockery lifted off the surface and danced briefly before settling again.

"I will ask you again, Madeleine, and I *will* expect a straight answer from you. I've been told you've been regularly seen with a man in Glasgow's parks and on the high street. Someone I haven't even been introduced to, I believe. Is this true?"

Madeleine drew in her breath sharply in order to clamp down on any potential quiver, where fear might play upon her vocal cords, like bows on violin strings.

"Who told you this, Papa?"

"That is none of your concern, Madeleine. Answer the question. Is it true?"

"If you're referring to someone I met with Bessie in West End Park, then he's a friend. I was sure you'd been introduced, Papa and therefore saw no harm."

She tried to sound glib but it soon transpired that her father knew far more of the relationship than he had first intimated.

James looked at her, his eyes narrowing.

"Madeleine, please listen very carefully. I forbid you to meet this man again. Do I make myself clear?"

Madeleine nodded, purely through habit, but said nothing.

"I've done some investigating, and I don't like what I hear. This man, a Frenchman I believe, is paying you attention. He moves in different social circles, he has no education, no prospects, no money, and as such, he is entirely unsuitable. Do you hear me, Madeleine? And even if he were suitable, the way he has conducted himself is less than impressive. What man would dare court another man's daughter without being introduced to the family first and asking permission?"

"He really is a very nice man. If you haven't met him yet, please say when you will, Papa. He's a gentleman. You'd like him. We'd like to marry one day, Papa."

Madeleine's heart was thumping. There! She'd finally said it. She felt brave but quaked, waiting for the response. It came quietly. There was no raised voice this time.

"If he has intentions of marrying you, forget it. I will never give my consent. Never!"

"Please. Papa, I ..."

He put his hand up to stop her from continuing.

"I am appalled. Firstly, since I'm learning about this relationship for the first time, and from what you're telling me, if there is talk of marriage, it's been going on behind my back for quite some time. And secondly, your actions have encouraged a great deal of gossip. What were you thinking, Madeleine?"

"I'm sorry, Papa."

She was crushed.

"You'll end this relationship immediately! And I don't want to hear any more pointless talk of marriage. I will have your complete obedience and compliance in this matter. I don't expect to raise this conversation with you again. Do I make myself perfectly clear?"

James Smith pushed back his chair, wood scraping against wood.

"On your word and honour, Madeleine?"

"Yes, Papa," replied Madeleine meekly. She remained seated with her head bowed, hands folded on her lap. Her father left the room, closing the door firmly behind him.

*

Madeleine remained seated. She sat in stunned silence for several minutes before flinging her folded arms onto the table and burying her head into them. She sobbed uncontrollably.

Her sobs filtered through closed doors, but no one came to comfort her. The servants returned to the kitchen, her siblings tip-toed past and scurried away. Her mother, still upstairs in her bed, was oblivious to the distress of her daughter, and too preoccupied with yet another migraine. Her father remained in his study.

After several minutes Madeleine reached for her handkerchief and dried her eyes. She headed upstairs to her room and stood gazing out into the wide open spaces before her, contemplating her plight. What was she supposed to do? She knew she should obey her father. Her father demanded it. He expected it. It was just how it was. Papa's word was law. But an older Madeleine resented his treatment of her. She loved Emile, and he loved her. She was no longer a child. Why did Papa not realise this?

She did not want to be like her mother; always agreeing with Papa. It made her angry to watch her mama having no opinions of her own, only those Papa allowed her to have. Mama was constantly apologising for her silliness if she crossed him, and telling him he was always right, even when he was not. No, she would not be like Mama. She wanted to be herself. She wanted to express her opinions, to make her own decisions. And why not? She would be of age in a couple of years' time and Papa would not be able to stop her then. She would make sure of that!

In addition, there was Emile. What was she to tell him? That her class was made up of bigoted snobs who automatically discriminated against those who were not educated or moneyed? Her cheeks burned with shame, and the rage of being part of a class she was beginning to despise.

A knock at the door interrupted her flow of thought. It was Bessie. Madeleine stood at the open door, barring the way into her bedroom. She did not want to have to deal with her younger sister, as well as Papa. One was often as bad as the other.

"What brings you here, Bessie?"

"I heard Papa yelling this evening, Madeleine. I did tell you to tell him about Emile."

"It was you, wasn't it? You told him about Emile?"

Despite not being the bearer of the news Elizabeth intimated she was, with a hint of a smile, she said "I hate to tell you, Madeleine, but you brought this upon yourself. You should never have encouraged Emile, knowing he's not like us."

"Bessie! You've met Emile, and you liked him. And now, because Papa is displeased, you tell me you no longer like Emile? How fickle you are."

"I didn't say I didn't like him, Madeleine. That's entirely untrue. However, if you remember, I told you when we first met Emile, to make sure Papa knew about him. This you failed to do. Papa has every right to be angry with you, Madeleine. You've brought this all upon yourself."

"If all you've come to do is gloat, then I think you should leave before I say something I'll regret. But one thing I will tell you now. You're a jealous, spiteful cat!"

Madeleine closed the door just as Bessie began to open her mouth to say something else. Her heart was pounding. She hated confrontation, especially with Bessie for whom, at this moment, she felt an intense dislike.

*

Madeleine, who answered to a variety of names - Minnie, Mimi, or Mini, as Emile often called her, spent several days giving thought to her position with her family and her relationship. The situation was complex, and for the first time she felt trapped.

After her father's reaction, knowing how he felt about Emile, clearly he would never be welcome in their home, not as a friend, even less as a suitor. For days she agonised over her dilemma. With no one to talk to, the burden was hers alone to bear. She felt as if the relationship were a growing millstone around her neck.

Yes, she loved Emile. Although at times, she found him unfathomable. One moment he was kind and confident, always rushing about doing this and that, and the next, he was angry and irritable. He was constantly finding fault with her, urging her to improve herself, being jealous of whom she was seeing, and wallowing in self-pity and black thoughts.

Her life had changed. She used to be a social butterfly, but she could no longer ignore Emile's frowns when she mentioned whom she had danced with at the latest ball. His face darkened with jealousy if she mentioned men who had shown her attention. He had started to curtail her outings, demanding she spend more time at home. She had to promise him she would stop flirting and think only of him.

Despite all this, deep down, she still loved him.

And then there was Papa. He was not an abusive father. He was, however, a strict disciplinarian who loved her, wanting only the best for her.

As much as she wanted to break free from the shackles of convention, in the end, she needed Papa's protection and a roof over her head. With great reluctance and much sadness, she decided it would be best to break off the attachment with Emile. She promised her father she would. She had sworn on her honour. There was no going back now.

With a heavy heart she penned several letters the following day.

Farewell, Dear Emile,

My Papa will not give his consent. I've given my word of honour I will have no more communication with you.

Get married. You will never get one who will love you as I have done. I must banish your image from my heart. It almost breaks my heart to return to you your likeness and chain. I must not keep them. Write me a parting note. It will be the last one I can ever receive.

As a parting favour I ask that you will burn all my letters the day you receive this. Do it.

Be happy. Forgive me and may she whom you call your wife be a comfort unto you. May she love and esteem you.

Fare thee well,

Madeleine

*

On the same night she wrote a quick note to their mutual friend Mary Perry whose friendship she valued and would always be grateful to her for allowing them to meet in her home in Regent Street.

Dearest Miss Perry,

Many, many kind thanks for all your kindness to me. Emile will tell you I have bid him adieu. My Papa would not give his consent, so I am in duty bound to obey him.

Comfort dear Emile. It is a heavy blow to us both. I had hoped someday to have been happy with him, but alas! It is not intended. We were doomed to be disappointed.

You have been a kind friend to him. Oh! Continue so. I hope and trust he may prosper. Think my conduct not unkind. I have a father to please and a kind father too.

Farewell, dear Miss Perry, and, with much love, believe me.

Yours sincerely,

Mimi

*

Emile was enraged when he read her latest letter. He was incensed at her dismissiveness and the constant reminder he was unworthy of her family. He was also hurt that Madeleine could cast him off so readily. He felt she toyed with him; betrayed his affections.

After reading her note he crumpled it up and had almost thrown it into the fireplace. For days it lay on his small table, a constant reminder of yet another failed relationship.

Finally, one wet afternoon, more than a week later, his emotions were under control, well enough to respond. Time, however, had not blunted his feelings. His reply dripped with vitriol.

Glasgow, 10 Bothwell Street, 19th July 55

In the first place I did not deserve to be treated as you have done. How you astonish me by writing such a note without condescending to explain the reasons why your father refuses his consent. He must have reasons, and I am not allowed to clear myself of accusations.

I should have written you before but I preferred waiting until I got over the surprise your last letter caused me, and also to be able to write you in a calm, and a collected manner, free from any animosity, whatsoever.

Never, dear Madeleine, could I have believed you were capable of such conduct. I thought and believed you unfit for such a step. I believed you true to your word and your honour. I will put questions to you which answer to yourself.

What would you think if, even one of your servants, had played with one's affections as you have done or what would you say to hear that any lady friends had done what you have – or what am I to think of you now? What is your opinion of your own self after those solemn vows you uttered and wrote to me? Show my letters to anyone, Madeleine. I don't care who and if any find that I mislead you, I will free you from all blame.

I warned you repeatedly not to be rash in your engagement and vows to me, but you persisted in that false and deceitful flirtation, playing with affections which you knew to be pure and undivided, and knowing at the same time that at a word from your father you would break your engagement.

You have deceived your father, as you have deceived me. You never told him how solemnly you bound yourself to me. If you had, for the honour of his daughter, he could not have asked to break off an engagement as ours.

Madeleine, you have truly acted wrong.

May this be a lesson to you never to trifle with anyone again. I wish you every happiness. I shall be truly happy to hear you are happy with another you desire. And now you are at liberty to recognise me, or to cut me just as you wish – but I give you my word of honour, I shall act always as a gentleman towards you.

Think what your father would say if I sent him your letters for a perusal. Do you think he could sanction your breaking your promises? No, Madeleine, I leave your conscience to speak for itself.

I flatter myself he can only accuse me of a want of fortune. But he must remember he too had to begin the world with dark clouds around him.

I cannot put it into my mind that yet you are at the bottom of all of this.

Emile

Madeleine was shocked at his cruel attacks, and his lack of understanding of a situation out of her control. She felt despondent at his inability to see that obedience to her father was not a matter of choice. She reread the letter now with smudged ink and fading words, awash with tears.

10 A TOUCH OF CHOLERA
HELENSBURGH, 1855

Auguste Vauvert de Mean answered the door to his new home in Helensburgh one Saturday morning and welcomed Emile into the house. De Mean was the chancellor to the French Consul in Glasgow, where he had met Emile through his colleague, Amadée Thuau, Emile's fellow lodger at 11 Franklin Place. Convenient for Emile, De Mean also knew Madeleine Smith and her family.

"Nice to see you, L'Angelier. Do come in! Tell me all your news. You'll have to tell me what's been happening in Glasgow. I can't believe I would ever say this, but I actually miss the sooty old town."

De Mean, so busy talking and ushering his guest into the hallway failed to notice his friend was ill. After hanging Emile's coat and hat on the coat rail next to the door, he bolted up the stairs to his rooms, expecting Emile to follow. Except he did not. De Mean retraced his steps and ducking his head under the overhanging landing, peered down into the hallway.

"Are you coming up then?"

"I'll come up in a minute." The voice was feeble, unlike the cocksure tone he was used to. De Mean frowned and descended the stairs.

Whatever's the matter? Are you ill?"

De Mean, taking one look at his friend's deathly pallor, guided him into his landlady's front room, and sat him down on the settee. He settled into an oversized chair a few feet away and listened to Emile discussing his illness. De Mean had always suspected his friend to be a bit of a hypochondriac, but this was different.

"I've been dreadfully ill. I've been vomiting for days. It's stopped now, but at the time the nausea came in waves, even now it won't leave me. The gripes in my stomach are still excruciatingly painful."

"Have you seen a doctor?"

"No, not this time. A while ago I experienced a bad bought of cholera and I'm suffering from the same symptoms."

He pulled out a small phial, undid the cork and took a draught, his hand trembling slightly. Noticing De Mean watching him, he saluted him with the bottle, before replacing it in his waistcoat pocket.

"Laudanum," he said, without De Mean having to ask.

"Emile! You cannot take laudanum like that. You'll kill yourself. Do you know how dangerous it is?"

Emile shrugged.

"It helps with the pain. I couldn't function without it."

They sat conversing for well over half an hour before Emile raised the subject of arsenic, much to De Mean's surprise.

"I wonder how much arsenic one would have to take before you were injured by it?"

"I wouldn't like to guess, nor would I like to try." He laughed, believing Emile was joking.

"I'm being earnest, De Mean."

"Ah… well… I'm sure any amount would be injurious, from grain to a drachm. Perhaps you should put that question to the thousands of rats poisoned in cellars and sheds around Scotland, every day of the year. Isn't that proof enough?"

"That's where you're wrong, De Mean. Arsenic eating is quite safe in small doses. It also has a number of health benefits. It has cured my asthma and my back pain. However, I only ever ingest small amounts. It's really is quite beneficial. For stamina too, as long as you don't overdose yourself. Which brings me back to my original question, I wonder how much is too much?"

11 WILLIAM HARPER MINNOCH,
GLASGOW, 1855

Servants rushed from room to room sprucing up the place. A flick of a duster there, a flower turned around in a vase there. The Smith household was expecting an important visitor.

"Madeleine, do hurry up! Mr. Minnoch will be here soon! I want you to look your best for him. Wear that pretty silk lemon and lilac dress we made for you last week. I think it suits you admirably."

"Mama, why is it so important I look good for Mr. Minnoch? No doubt he's short, fat and balding, and well past his prime. Just like the rest of them."

"Madeleine Hamilton Smith! Hold your tongue. How dare you be so impudent! Do you want to remain a spinster all your life? Because if you do, you're certainly going about it the right way! I'm finding you extremely disrespectful of late, to the point of exasperation. I'm surprised at your attitude. Many girls your age can't wait to marry and start a family of their own. However, you, you seem to think there's no one good enough."

"Perhaps I might be more enthusiastic if I had a choice in the matter."

Her mother ignored the retort.

"Now, you'll be polite this evening, and don't you dare let us down. Your papa tells me Mr. Minnoch is an amiable gentleman whom he has known, on a business level, for several years. He's a man of means, and a nice looking gentleman at that. He may be a little older than you, Madeleine, by about fifteen years, but you need a strong man to keep you in check. It's time, Madeleine, and I won't hear another word about it. Now go and change, and do as you're told for once!"

Madeleine fled the room, tears stinging her eyes. Mama seldom spoke in this vein, but when she did, it hurt.

When she reached her bedroom she found the dress and petticoats already laid out on the bed. It seemed she did not have a choice about anything these days, not even what she could wear.

Christina helped her dress, and styled her hair as she remained sullen throughout the ordeal. An ordeal was exactly how she saw it. She knew she would not enjoy this Mr. Minnoch's company. All potential suitors, so far, had turned out to be entirely incompatible. This one would be the same, no doubt. She did not want an additional swain. The only man she wanted was Emile, whom she could not have.

Meeting Mr. Minnoch was another way in which her family were stifling her. She was the shoe too small. Her family was the shoehorn; forcing into her their desires without taking into consideration her needs.

With a final glance in the mirror, Madeleine looked critically at her hair pulled back off her face, parted in the middle, and done in full bandeaux. The rest of the hair was fastened back with an ornate pearl comb. It would have to do, she thought. She picked up the flounced skirts of her dress with both hands, and descended the stairs. On arriving at the landing she heard talking coming from the drawing room. Mr. Minnoch had arrived.

She hovered outside the half-opened door, listening to his voice, trying to imagine what he looked like. For a few minutes all she heard was Papa, and then she heard Minnoch's reply. It was delivered in a rich baritone; masculine and modulated, easy on the ear. She was intrigued and moved closer to the threshold.

"Madeleine, there you are. Come on in! I have someone here I would like you to meet."

William Minnoch was standing with his back to the door when Madeleine entered.

"William, may I present to you my eldest daughter, Madeleine. Madeleine, this is Mr. William Minnoch."

William enclosed her gloved hand in his, and Madeleine held his gaze far longer than was necessary. She looked at him critically. He was slim and not overly tall. His complexion was fair, making him a lot younger than his proposed thirty-four years. She thought his face pretty, rather than handsome, and his eyes were a hazel brown. What was immediately apparent was the fine cut of his clothes. They were exceptionally fine, making him perhaps one of the best dressed men of Glasgow. He was the first to break the gaze, much to her amusement, and he bowed deeply.

"It's a pleasure to meet you, Miss Smith."

She returned the greeting and curtsied to her parents.

"Mama, Papa."

"Your father tells me you like to paint. Do you?"

"Oh, I do, but watercolours only. I'm afraid I'm not good at all. I dabble really, but I'd like to take up formal lessons one day. I'm told my work could do with some improvement."

"You're too modest, Madeleine. For it's entirely untrue. William, come over and you be the judge."

James Smith guided his guest to a framed piece of artwork hanging above the settee. There hung a picture of 'Rowaleyn,' painted the previous summer. It was one of her best works, and James loved it. He had wanted to take it and hang it in his office, but in the end decided to have it hanging in the drawing room, for wider enjoyment.

William studied the painting extensively before he turned and said, "Miss Smith, your father is right. This is a charming composition, and you have enormous talent. I am a great admirer of art, and this is exceptional."

Madeleine bowed her head, smiled sweetly, and thanked him. She was genuinely surprised to see how much he liked it.

Once, when Mama and Papa were away for the day, she had sneaked Emile into the house and brought him into the drawing room. When she showed him the painting and said it was her work, his response had left her disillusioned.

"It's not quite what I was expecting, Madeleine," was what he had said. "You told me you had artistic talent. Of course, you can always improve, if you so desire, by taking some lessons. In fact, I would strongly urge you to do so."

Her thoughts were dragged back to the present as her father said, "Madeleine is an accomplished pianist too. Perhaps she will play and sing for us after dinner, Minnoch."

"I'd enjoy that very much indeed. In fact, I look forward to it."

The rest of the evening passed pleasantly enough. Madeleine found William Minnoch agreeable to talk to and as the evening progressed she was surprised to find they shared a number of similar interests. As their night together drew to a close, slightly after eleven o'clock, Madeleine Smith was already looking forward to spending more time with William Minnoch and knowing him better. However, as soon as she did, her thoughts turned to guilt as she remembered Emile.

Emile was someone she loved, but not being able to go to balls together, or to the opera, William Minnoch would fill that role. Moreover, she had been forbidden to see Emile again. Perhaps it was time for a new beginning.

12 PLEASE STAY
GLASGOW, SEPTEMBER 1855

Emile had taken time off work to spend a few days on the island of Jersey with his family, where he had been born. After Madeleine's final letter, breaking off her engagement and telling him her family wanted her to cease the relationship, he felt thoroughly depressed. Three months had passed, and with no further communication between them, he decided to visit his mother, and to seek her advice on what he should do.

While he was home, Bernard Saunders, the man to whom he had once been apprenticed, told him of some news that would help improve his financial situation.

He knew of a man, he told Emile, with a market-garden outside Lima, Peru, looking for a dependable person to manage and oversee the business. A fine house and a good salary came with the offer. He suggested Emile apply for the position.

Emile was elated and asked Saunders for a recommendation which he readily agreed to do. Emile saw this as an opportunity he couldn't refuse. It would give him time away from Madeleine to think more clearly. It would also allow him to earn a good wage and improve his position further, possibly returning with the money and elevated status he so desperately craved.

However, when he shared his plans with his mother, she was appalled. Having lost several children and her husband over the years she really couldn't bear to lose Emile to Lima.

News travelled fast. Even Madeleine heard the rumours that Emile was going to Lima, and that he was leaving directly from Jersey. She, too, was devastated. It was unbearable to think that he could be away for so long. The months apart had been agony. The thought of these extending to years, was unimaginable.

She broke her word to her father as soon as she heard the news and sent Emile smuggled letters, begging and pleading for him to stay.

*

Addressed to Emile L'Angelier at Jersey,
September 4, 1855

My Dearest Emile,

How I long to see you. It looks an age since I bade you adieu. Will you be able to come down the Sunday after next? You will be in town by the 14th. I do not intend to say anything 'til I have seen you. I shall be guided by you entirely, and who could be a better guide to me than my intended husband?

I hope you have given up all idea of going to Lima. I will never be allowed to go to Lima with you; so I fancy you shall want to get quit of your Mimi. You can get plenty of appointments in Europe - any place in Europe. For my sake, do not go. It will break my heart if you go away. You know not how I love you, Emile. I live for you alone; I adore you. I never could love another as I do you.

Oh! Dearest Emile, would I might clasp you now to my heart.

Adieu for today. If I have time I shall write another note before I post this. If not, I shall have a letter at the garden for you.

So dearest, love and a fond embrace. Believe me, your ever-devoted and kind,
Mimi

*

Two weeks passed and the channels of communication between them remained silent. She wondered daily if he had gone. Had he left as he threatened, without even saying goodbye? Her heart ached at the thought, her spirits depressed. Eventually, she made herself quite ill. Finally, it came. She received a note from Emile.

He asked to see her, if she could arrange it.

*

18th September, 1855

Beloved Emile,

I have just received your note. I shall meet you. I do not care though I bring disgrace upon myself. To see you I would do anything. Emile, you shall yet be happy; you deserve it.

You are young; you who ought to desire life not wishing to end it! Oh! For the sake of your once-loved Mimi, desire to live and succeed in this life.

Everyone must meet with disappointment. I have suffered from disappointment. I long to see you and speak to you.
Mimi

*

Their brief, forbidden meeting did not go well. Although Emile had not set out to upset her, he had. They faced each other, longing to touch, but the moment was spoiled by feelings of recriminations that brewed and simmered. A talk in Mary Perry's garden highlighted the issues.

"You say you love me, Madeleine, but I am beginning to wonder that it is only for my looks, rather than for who I am."

"That is not so, my pet. I adore you, inside and out. Yes, you are handsome, and I do love the way you look, is that so wrong?"

"Perhaps not, however, if you really loved me you would fight for me. You gave in far too easily this time around. You were too quick to break off the attachment, with little thought to me or my feelings."

"Pet, that is unkind. I didn't have a choice. When will you see that?"

"Choice?" he sneered. "What choices do I have? I wanted to go to Lima, to improve my position, earn more money, to be someone. Someone you would be proud of. I wanted to finally prove myself worthy of your family. But, you begged me to stay, which I did. I gave it all up and for what? You offered me nothing solid in return. You trifle with me, Madeleine, and the thought upsets me. The strain of this relationship has turned me upside down. If I can't go to Lima, and if I can't marry you, what's the point of it all? I'd be better off dead, that's what. Maybe if I ceased to exist everyone would be happy!"

"Emile! Don't you dare talk like that! You know I would be devastated if something happened to you. I love you! Please don't talk so. If you were to take your own life, because of me, I'd never survive that on my conscience. Promise me you'll do nothing rash. Please, my love, I beg you! Don't give up hope. One day these dark times will be behind us and we will be together."

Despite her reassurances, a follow up letter reaffirmed his suicidal threats, and he continued his attack against her for not loving him for who he was.

19th October, 1855.

Beloved Emile,

Your kind letter I received this morning. Emile, you are wrong in thinking I love you for your appearance. I did and do admire you, but it was for yourself alone that I loved you. I can give you no other reason, for I have got no other. If you had been a young man of some Glasgow family, I have no doubt there would be no objection to you. But because you are unknown to him, Papa has rejected you.

Dear Emile, explain this sentence in your note "Before long I shall rid you and all the world of my presence." God forbid that you ever do. My last letter was not filled with rash promises. No; these promises written in my last letter shall be kept must be kept. Not a moment passes but I think of you.

Mimi

13 FORGIVENESS, AT A PRICE
GLASGOW, DECEMBER 1855

As much as Emile wanted to punish Madeleine with his silence, he did not carry out his thoughts. Despite it all, he still hoped there would be a future for them. On the one hand, he cursed his situation. On the other, if he could persuade her father to allow them to marry, he would enter social circles previously denied. He needed to find a way to make this relationship work.

*

Recent times were tumultuous times for Madeleine. First, she had mourned her loss for Emile after she had been forbidden to see, or contact him. After breaking that promise in October, and begging him to stay, with Emile hopeful for the future, more covert meetings followed. Soon, they were back seeing each other as often as they could.

After the renewed relationship, however, the reunion was strained. He wasn't the same Emile she knew, and loved. He had returned to her with a different attitude. Before, the last break, they had enjoyed learning more about each other, exchanged sentimentalities and dreams. Now, he was fixated in securing an introduction to her family, and pressuring her to make it happen. She felt trapped by the situation, continually struggling to divert his obsession away from her family to safer waters. Sometimes, successfully, other times, his persistence ended up in an ugly quarrel.

Madeleine hated disagreeing with Emile. He would sulk for days and his comments were caustic, and hurt to the quick. She found herself apologising first. She loathed herself for it. She was turning into her mother. The mother she despised for being so weak against Papa, and yet, she found herself doing the same thing with Emile.

One way she could change his mood, was if she allowed him to fondle her. She used the weapon, with growing frequency, to bring much needed peace to their turbulent liaison. On the few times they were alone without a chaperone, he took full advantage of familiarizing himself with her body. He tested her resilience to his advances, and found her weak.

In some ways, he told her, he found her openness to his advances rather thrilling. Afterwards, he said, he was annoyed with himself for pressing her to do things that placed her reputation at risk. Moreover, he scorned her for being weak, unable to resist him. He cursed her family for forcing them into a situation they need not be. If they were married by now, he reasoned, their behaviour would be perfectly acceptable.

*

Emile stood under partial shelter in the rain waiting for the family to go to bed. He was ill yet again, and he worried about standing around in the cold and damp. Madeleine had sent word. Cook was ill, and if he wanted to see her, he should do it tonight.

In agitation, he watched the lights burning in the drawing room, wondering what was keeping the family from retiring for the night. He drew his pocket watch from his waistcoat and under the pale, yellow gaslight saw it was already ten minutes past eleven. There was no option but to continue to wait in the wet and plummeting winter temperatures. He would have to wait until the last lights were extinguished if he wanted to see her tonight, albeit for a short while. Resentment seeped through every sinew and bone as the minutes passed; he outside, them inside.

At long last, the lamps were turned down and the house was in darkness. He impatiently waited a further fifteen minutes before he approached the back door, knocking ever so softly before it opened.

Madeleine placed a finger to her lips as she led the way down the passage to the kitchen. She placed the candlestick on the well-scrubbed table and turned towards Emile.

"Oh, pet! Look at you! You're soaked to the skin. Take your coat off and come and stand next to the range for warmth. You cannot stay in those wet clothes. You'll catch your death."

Emile shook off his coat, heavy with rain and placed it over the back of the kitchen chair closest to the range that was still radiating heat.

"I was thinking your family were never going to retire for the night, Madeleine. Where is Cook? Are we safe to be here talking like this?"

"Cook took ill, and retired early, which was why I could see you tonight. Oh, my love, it's so good of you to come in this weather. Would you like some cocoa to warm you up?"

"Thank you, my dear, I would. I have to say, the weather is perfectly frightful out there. I haven't been feeling particularly well again, I'm afraid. I do hope the night air won't cause another bout of whatever I have."

"Emile, how often have I told you to stop doctoring yourself and to go and see a real doctor? Promise me you'll do so this time. Ignoring these symptoms is foolish. It might be serious."

Emile watched Madeleine make the cocoa and as she approached he couldn't help but notice the seriousness on her face. He smiled, and receiving both cups from her, placed them on the table.

"Mimi, why are you so solemn sometimes? Come and give your Emile a kiss. You haven't even given me a hug yet."

Madeleine stepped forward as he reached for her hands. Instead of kissing them, he examined them, turning over one hand, and then the other. Madeleine tried to retrieve them for she knew what was coming next. She bit her lower lip.

"I see you're still chewing your nails, Madeleine. How many times do I need to ask you to resist this disgusting habit? Why is it you always seem to go out of your way to ignore everything I ask of you?"

"I'm sorry, Emile. It isn't as if I do it on purpose. I've been worried about you, that's all. Please don't be cross with me. I promise I shall try better to please you, Emile. I really shall."

He continued to look sternly at her and then he wrapped his arms around her and drew her closer to him. She lay there for a moment with her head on his chest, listening to the steady beat of his heart and she allowed the strain of the day wash over her. She always felt safe in his arms.

She snuggled closer.

He kissed the top of her head, and then bent down to kiss her mouth. His tongue sought hers as his hand moved into the top of her gown, and cupping her breast with one hand, he undid the buttons of his trousers with the other, and brought himself to climax.

*

3rd December, 1855

My own darling,

I am afraid I may be too late to write you this evening, as all are out I shall do it now, my sweet one. I did not expect the pleasure of seeing you last evening; of being fondled by you, dear, dear Emile.

I think you should consult Dr. McFarlane; that is, go and see him. Get him to sound you - tell you what is wrong with you. Ask him to prescribe for you, and if you have any love for your Mimi, follow his advice. And oh! Sweet love, do not try and doctor yourself; but, oh, sweet love, follow the M. D.'s advice. Be good for once, and I am sure you will be well.

My own sweet beloved, I can say nothing as to our marriage, as it is not certain when they may go from home - when I may, is uncertain. My beloved, will we be required to be married in Edinburgh, or will it be here? You know I know nothing of these things.

I fear the banns in Glasgow; there are so many people who know me. If I had any other name but Madeleine it might pass; but it is not a very common one. But we must manage in some way to be united ere we leave town.

Much, much love; kisses tender, long embraces - kisses, love.

I am thy own, thy ever fond, thy own - thy Mimi L'Angelier

*

Madeleine was setting her pen down when her brother Jack, home for the term holidays, hovered at her door.

"Aren't you going to invite me in?"

"Since when do you need an invitation silly boy? Come in! Tell me how are things going at school? Are you on the cricket or rugby teams this term?"

"I don't want to talk about school while I'm on holiday. Horrid place! I'd much rather be here with you and everyone else."

"Well then, let's talk about me then. Let's talk about the one person in the whole wide world I love."

"L'Angelier?"

Madeleine punched him softly on the arm. "No silly. Not L'Angelier."

"Good, I'm glad about that."

"Why's that?"

"Well, because for a while I was ashamed of you."

"Ashamed of me? Why were you ashamed of me?"

"Do you know he's only a clerk at Huggins?"

"Yes, he's a clerk, but when you love someone, it should be enough."

"Papa expects you to marry a rich man, not some clerk. You could never marry him, Maddie. You have to stop thinking about him, because if you don't, Papa will be really angry, very angry. And so will I."

14 A DANGEROUS FAD
GLASGOW, JANUARY 1856

Peter Guthrie was the manager for the Frazer & Green establishment at 469 Sauchiehall Street.

Frazer & Green was well-known in Glasgow. They were the pharmaceutical chemist to the Queen, and specialised in catering for the wealthy. They had several other establishments scattered around Glasgow, but their two main shops were on Sauchiehall Street and another at 127 Buchanan Street.

Their shops were the finest in the city. Inside, were extensive counters, with elegant fittings and glass showcases to display their large stock of the very best in pharmaceutical emporia, including the leading patent medicines, proprietary articles and toilet requisites, with a complete stock of the best and newest drugs and chemical preparations. In addition they had, a thriving trade in supplying medicine chests, both for family, Colonial, and sea-going use. They also sold arsenic.

One slow afternoon, a woman in her mid-forties with a fading beauty, but one who still carried herself well, entered the shop. One could see from her clothing she was clearly well-to-do.

"Good afternoon, madam. How can I assist you?"

"Good afternoon, sir. I've come to show you these."

She proceeded to unfurl two different copies of the *Blackwoods* magazine, with the pages turned down at certain places, which she now proceeded to spread open on top the wooden counter. One was dated, June 11, 1853, and the second publication was more recent, January 9, 1856.

She turned them around so he could read them, waiting a few minutes before asking, "Have you seen these articles?"

"I have indeed, madam."

"Well, I would like to purchase some arsenic, too. I really do need something to improve my complexion. Old age is a terrible curse."

"Madam, I cannot sell you arsenic for this purpose. The encouragement of using arsenic as a beauty product in these magazines is, in my opinion, irresponsible journalism."

"Well, sir, with all due respect, it's merely your opinion. I'd still like to purchase some. Would sixpence be enough?"

"Madam, with the greatest of regrets, I cannot sell you arsenic for cosmetic purposes. My conscience wouldn't allow it."

"But surely…"

"Madam, arsenic is a poison. I'm really sorry, but if you wish to purchase this, you'll have to do so from another establishment. Good day to you, madam."

15 SEEKING MAMA'S HELP
GLASGOW, 4 MARCH 1856

For once Janet Smith was not convalescing in her bedroom, but was up and about. She sat with her back to the window to ensure enough light was illuminating her needlework.

"Mama, it's nice to see you up. Are you well?"

"For the time being. I hope to finish this tapestry for your cousin's wedding next month. Another week and it should be accomplished."

"Mama, can I ask you something?

"Of course you can, child. What is it?"

"I need your help."

"It depends on what you want help with. If I can, I will. You know that."

"It's Papa."

Janet set her needlework aside. He eyes narrowed.

"What about Papa?"

"Do you think you could talk to him and tell him how much I like L'Angelier?"

"Madeleine, I thought you had banished this man from your thoughts months ago, as you promised your papa you would. You know how he feels about this man. The man is a lowly clerk and has no money. Forget about him! You have to aim higher than this! He is a grubby little nobody who's only after your money!"

"What proof do you have? That's very unfair, Mama. You don't even know him."

"I've proof enough to make those comments. To say nothing of what people would say!"

"I don't care what people say. I intend to be Emile's wife one day. When I am of age, I can do whatever I please. I love him, Mama. Don't you understand? I love him!"

"Love doesn't come into it. I'm ashamed to hear you talk so."

Janet started to weep.

"I beg of you, Madeleine. Stop this madness. Your papa would rather see you in your grave than as this man's wife."

"I cannot, Mama. I'll never give him up. Never!

"Let me tell you, young lady, you'll never marry this man with our consent. Your papa and I are in complete agreement on this. A marriage to this man would be a complete disaster. Do not go against our wishes. And let me remind you that you are still forbidden to see him, or correspond with him."

"Once I'm of age I shall have all his letters delivered to the house."

"If you were some sort of heiress, you may talk so, Madeleine, but you're not. You shall not receive his letters. I will make sure the postman does not deliver any of them to you from this man. And he should be ashamed of himself if he is still trying to press himself upon you. Especially, when he knows we don't approve and the relationship has been forbidden. I think even less of him, if that's possible."

She sniffed into her hanky before she continued.

"If your father hears that you're still carrying on with this relationship behind his back, after promising him months ago that it would cease, his anger will be fearful! Even I would be afraid at his ire. Give him up, Madeleine, please! I beg of you! Nothing good can come of this!"

"I cannot and I will not."

"You are an obstinate, disobedient, wilful young woman with no sense between those ears of yours. If you take this attitude I'll make sure you're watched again at all times. You'll not go out of this house without a chaperone, and all letters now will be sent to my room on arrival. You have proven to be totally untrustworthy. Don't think you can outsmart me on this matter, Madeleine. I may be ill at times, but there is nothing wrong with my faculties! Now go to your room and stay there until you're called for dinner. I cannot tell you how angry and disappointed I am at the moment. Your behaviour and attitude are despicable!"

*

4 March

Dearest Emile,

What a lecture I have had, I cannot tell you dearest, what I have suffered this day. I was told by Mama – Papa is not at home and knows nothing of it – that she knew Papa would rather see me in my grave than your wife. You were called all that was bad.

I am now never to be allowed out by myself this summer.

Dearest, one thing I shall propose. I know you won't like it. But I must do something to have a little peace and happiness. Would you consent to drop our correspondence till September when we shall be married?

"You must think this cool of me. But if you wish me to live, I must have some happiness. If I continue to correspond, I shall be dead with misery, ere September. This is a horrid plan, but darling, what must I do? Can you trust me till then? The time shall pass quickly - Emile, I shall be thine in September.

I promise I shall not play billiards. They have been playing cards tonight - one or two of Jack's friends were in. But I was in a state of mind to be in the drawing room. I have not touched a card since you asked me not to do it.

Mimi

*

When Emile heard about Madeleine wanting to break off the relationship yet again, he flatly refused to consent to it. Somehow, some way, he assured her, they would find a way to be together. In the end they did find a way, allowing their correspondence to continue, but the solution to their problem had arrived serendipitously, rather than being connived.

One evening, Madeleine was padding barefoot towards the kitchen to fetch some hot water for her cocoa, when she heard a man's voice. As she neared she came in full view of Christina Haggart and a strange man engaged in a passionate clinch. Madeleine's first thoughts were to raise the alarm and have her dismissed. However, just as quickly, she realised that what she was witnessing was advantageous to her situation.

Madeleine cleared her throat and the two of them sprang apart looking like deer facing a pair of crossbows. Christina, her cap in disarray, pushed escaped tendrils of hair back under the cloth as best she could. She battled to rearrange her dress to resemble something more respectable.

"Oh! Miss Madeleine! I'm so sorry. Please don't tell the mistress. This is my fiancé come to tell me some news that couldn't wait."

"Yes, I saw," replied Madeleine dryly.

Christina blushed as the young man grabbed his cap from the table, and made a hasty retreat.

"I'll not say anything, Christina. However, you'll return the favour by taking and receiving notes on my behalf, whenever you are asked. If you don't, or if you try to cross me, I will tell my mama what I witnessed this evening. If you think, after that, you will receive a reference, you will be gravely mistaken."

"Yes, miss. Anything you ask, miss. Thank you, miss."

*

Mr. L'Angelier, 10 Bothwell Street, Glasgow
Tuesday, 29th April, 1856

My own beloved Emile,

I wrote you Sunday night for you to get my note on your birthday (today) but I could not get it posted. Disappointment it was to me – but, "better late than never."

My beloved may you have very, very many happy returns of this day – and each year may you find yourself happier and better than the last – and may each year find you more prosperous than the last.

I trust, darling, that on your next birthday I may be with you to wish you many happy returns in person. May you dearest, have a long life. My constant prayer shall be for your welfare and continued good health. I hope you continue to feel better.

I wish I were with you alone, that would be true happiness. Dearest, I must see you. It is fearful never to see you - but I am sure I don't know when. Papa has not been a night in town for some time, but the first night he is off, I shall see you. We shall spend an hour of bliss. There shall be no risk, only Christina Haggart will know.

Dearest, how I picture our marriage day. Where would you like to go the day we are married? I don't fancy a place in particular, so you can fix that when the time comes. I hope it may yet turn out to be September.

I asked Papa if I were to be married if the banns would be in Row church, but he said no, we had nothing to do with the Row Parish. I did not belong to it. So, darling, it would not require to be here – it could never be here – it would not do.

I don't in the least mind if they won't give their consent, for I know they will be the first to give in.

I have got my 'Chambers Journal' for this month and the article you mention is not in the April number so it must be in the May volume. I have been reading, 'Blackwood' for this month. 'Blackwood' is a favourite publication of mine. In fact, I think it is the best conducted monthly publication.

Now this is a very long letter tonight. Must conclude with a fond, fond embrace, a dear, and a dear sweet kiss. I wish it to be given, not sent. A kiss. Another. Oh, to be in thy embrace, my sweet Emile

Love again to thee from thy very fond, thy loving and devoted Mimi

16 THE SEDUCTION
ROW 6 MAY, 1856

It was Tuesday night, and all occupants within the house at Row were in bed. Madeleine feigned a headache, telling Mama she thought she was coming down with a migraine. Excusing herself early from the evening reading session, and making sure no one was about, she slipped out of the kitchen and into the garden in search of Emile, whom she had promised to meet.

For once, there was a clear night and a full moon, allowing her to navigate her way around the shrubs and trees until she finally came to the secluded steps, singled out as their meeting point. When she arrived no one was there.

She stood waiting for a few more minutes, wondering if he were coming. Perhaps he had changed his mind. She fiddled nervously with her necklace, speculating where he could be. She chewed her nails as she waited. Then, without a sound, he stepped out from behind a large yew tree where he had been standing all along, watching her.

Madeleine was startled by his sudden appearance.

"Oh! Emile! You startled me!"

He wrapped her in his arms, and kissed her chastely on the forehead. Madeleine drew Emile closer to her. She giggled, and he placed a finger to her lips to silence her.

Placing both hands on either side of his face she said, "Oh, my darling pet, Emile. How I love you! I've missed you. It's so good of you to come all this way to Row."

"And why would you think I wouldn't come, my love? Did Emile not promise in his last letter that he would?"

"Oh, my sweet! Life here in Row is so tedious without you." She pouted a little and he stroked her cheek with the back of his hand.

"I am here now, my love, but not for long as I need to return to De Mean's house in Helensburgh. How are things?"

"Dreadfully dull without you, pet. How are you keeping? Are you well? It seems like an age since I saw you last."

"I had one of my bilious attacks last week. I took to my bed once more, but dear Mary Perry was good enough to come and bring me some grapes, and look in on me from time to time."

"Please go and see a doctor, Emile. You cannot go on like this without knowing the cause. Promise me you'll go and see Doctor McFarlane. I hear he's a skilled physician."

She placed her hand on his chest and he reached out and caressed it gently before kissing the tips of her fingers.

"Stop fretting, I shall be fine. Have you told your papa about us yet, Madeleine?"

"You know he doesn't approve. I'm hoping to find the right time to persuade him to have a change of heart. After the last conversation with Mama, it has become impossible for them to agree to anything."

She could see he was angry. His voice was cold when he responded.

"Madeleine, you have been promising to do this since last summer. You know I want to marry you and we cannot carry on meeting in secret like this. I have needs and urges. Each time I see you I want to love you, all of you. I need you, Madeleine. Do you not want us to marry?"

She hated it when she made him angry. She felt so young and silly sometimes. Her inexperience with men made her unsure of how she should act. Emile had told her he had enjoyed relationships with other women of his own age in the past. He confessed to having been intimate with them. She felt the panic rising. Emile should know what was right. He was so much older and wiser than she was. She looked to him for guidance.

"Emile, you know I love you, but should we not be careful with expressing our physical feelings? We need to wait until we are married, and yes, I do want to marry you."

"How can we continue like this? Waiting and waiting for your family to accept me, to even acknowledge me? I cannot carry on like this; the furtive glances, the secret meetings, the covert love letters. Madeleine, we've been doing this for over a year now. Things have to change. Perhaps it would be better for us to stop seeing each other. I shall take a job in Australia or Lima, anywhere, but here. Being here with you and not being able to have you is torture to my soul.

"And, Madeleine, if I do go abroad, I hope you will at least make an effort to know how much a letter costs to post. I'm tired of having to pay for your letters. You never pay enough for the postage. You really are a silly girl, Madeleine. Never thinking of others, it's always about yourself. You treat me cruelly. All I've ever wanted was to be your husband. Is that not what you've always wanted too? Tell me, Madeleine! For if it is not, than we can end this now, as hard as it will be. I need the truth from you, now!"

Madeleine felt ensnared like a spider in a sticky web. How could she prove to Emile she loved him but still remain true to Papa? The fact that she was seeing Emile behind her father's back was giving her pangs of guilt. She despised the circumstances they were in.

On the other hand, she thought of Emile wanting to leave Scotland to live so far away from her, wanting to escape her, and it caused her high anxiety. How would she survive without him? He had threatened before, and not gone. Perhaps this time he would.

"I want to be your wife, Emile. I've never loved anyone but you. I want to please you, pet and I know I'm often a disappointment to you. You think me young and foolish. Let me prove to you that it's not true. If you want to love me, love me. Take me as your wife."

Her response caught him off guard and then she kissed him passionately, as a way of confirmation.

The argument was forgotten as he feverishly pressed her face to his, kissing her closed lids, the tip of her nose, before finding her mouth with his tongue and pushing it gently inside her parted lips.

Her lips had opened readily, for she was eager for his love and caresses. But she was frightened too by his sudden ardour and roughness, and again she pulled back.

This time, Emile did not stop. He undid her cape, allowing it to drop to the grass, and moved his hands to the pert breasts which pressed against the thin material of her nightgown. He knew they were aching to be stroked and kissed. He slowly undid the six pearl buttons to expose her nipples. He bent down to kiss them, teasing them to attention as he ran his teeth up and down, gently sucking on each in turn.

He watched in the moonlight, with great satisfaction, as her rosy nipples enlarged and stood erect. He heard her groan and felt her arch her back.

She felt a strange sensation between her legs aching; tension building. She did not stop him when he lowered her onto the grass and moved his hands from her breasts to under her gown. His hands moved deftly between her legs. Repeatedly touching her as she kissed him and whispered, urging him on.

Their ardour and passion overtook reason and responsibility. He pushed himself into her and she winced at the fire of pain. She wanted to love him, but was surprised at how much it hurt.

He pushed a little deeper and then he was moving inside her. He was trying to be gentle, but in the end passion overcame consideration. She waited for him to finish; wishing for it to be over. It was nothing like she had expected. The speed at which he moved inside her increased, until he managed to withdraw before collapsing and quivering on top of her; it was over in a matter of minutes.

She lay there quietly, not knowing quite what to say, or what to do. Instead she caressed his head and ran her fingers through his hair as she felt his pounding heart against her exposed skin.

As she hugged him to her she heard him say, "Oh Mimi, what have we done?"

Madeleine only knew she had wanted to please the man she loved. And she had not regretted any of it, even though she had not taken much pleasure from it.

"You must return to the house, Madeleine, before you are missed, and I need to return to Glasgow. We will correspond tomorrow. We've a lot to talk about and much to think about."

He stood up, extending a hand to help her up, and placed her discarded cape around her shoulders. They walked back to the house in silence. She was bitterly disappointed at his wanting to depart so soon. When they arrived at the edge of the garden he planted a chaste kiss on her brow and vanished into the darkness, leaving without a word.

*

The following morning she sat down to pen a quick letter to Emile. She wanted to make sure he understood her intentions last night, with no misunderstandings.

Emile L'Angelier Esq., 'No. 10 Bothwell Street, Glasgow

7th May, 1856
Wednesday Morning, 5 o'clock.

My own, my beloved husband, I trust to God you got home safe and were not much the worse for being out. Thank you, my love, for coming so far to see your Mimi. It is truly a pleasure to see you, my Emile.

Beloved, if we did wrong last night, it was in the excitement of our love. Yes, beloved. I do truly love you with all my soul. I was happy; it was a pleasure to be with you. Oh, if we could have remained never more to be parted. But we must hope the time shall come.

I must have been very stupid to you last night. But everything goes out of my head when I see you my darling, my love. I often think I must be very, very stupid in your eyes. You must be disappointed in me. I wonder if you like me the least. But I trust and pray the day may come when you shall like me better. Beloved, we shall wait 'til you are quite ready. I shall see and speak to Jack on Sunday. I shall consider telling Mama. But I don't see any hope from her - I know her mind. You, of course, cannot judge my parents. You know them not.

I did not know (or I should not have done it) that I caused you to pay extra Postage for my stupid cold letters - it shall not occur again.

Darling Emile, did I seem cold to you last night? Darling, I love you. Yes, my own Emile, I love you with my heart and soul. Am I not your wife? Yes I am. And you may rest assured after what has passed I cannot be the wife of any other by dear, dear Emile. No, now it would be a sin.

They cannot keep us from each other. No! That they never shall. Emile beloved, I have sometimes thought, would you not like to go to Lima after we are married? Would that not do? Any place with you, pet.

I did not bleed in the least last night - but I had a good deal of pain during that night. Tell me, pet, were you angry at me for allowing you to do what you did, was it very bad of me? We should I suppose have waited till we were married. I shall always remember last night. Will we not often tell of our evening meetings after we are married?

Why do you say in your letter - 'If we are not married'? I would not regret knowing you. Beloved, have you a doubt that we shall be married some day?

I shall write to dear Mary soon. What would she say if she knew we were so intimate - lose all her good opinion of us both - would she not?

Adieu again my husband. God bless you and make you well. And may you yet be very, very happy with your Mimi as your wife. Kindest love, fond embrace, with kisses from they own true and devoted Mimi

Thy faithful,
Wife

*

Emile was her heart, her soul, her lover, her husband, her friend. From his response to her letter it was clear he found her lacking. He proportioned blame. Madeleine was distraught.

My dearest and beloved Wife Mimi,

Since I saw you I have been wretchedly sad. Would to God we had not met that night, I would have been happier. I am sad at what we did. I regret it very much.

Why, Mimi did you give way after your promises, my pet It is a pity. Think of the consequences if I were never to marry you. What reproaches I should have, Mimi. I never shall be happy again.

If ever I meet you again, love, it must be as at first. I will never again repeat what I did until we are regularly married. Try your friends once more - tell your determination - say nothing will change, that you have thought seriously of it - and on that I shall firmly fix speaking to Huggins for an increase in September.

Unless you do something of that sort, heaven only knows when I will marry you. Unless you do, dearest, I shall have to leave the country. Truly, dearest. I am in such a state of mind I do not care if I were dead.

We did wrong. God forgive us for it. Mimi, we have loved blindly. It is your parents' fault if shame is the result. They are the blame for it all.

I got home quite safely after leaving you, but I think it did my cold no good. I was fearfully excited the whole night. I was truly happy with you, my pet, too much. for I am now too sad.

I wish from the bottom of my heart we never had parted. Though we have sinned ask earnestly God's forgiveness and blessings that all the obstacles in our way may be removed from us.

I was disappointed, my love, at the little you had to say, but I can understand why. You are not stupid, Mimi, and if you disappoint me in information, and I have cause to reproach you of it, you will have no one to blame but yourself, as I have given you warning long enough to improve yourself! Sometimes, I do think that you take no notice of my wishes and my desires – but yes for more matter of form.

Mimi, unless Huggins helps me, I cannot see how I shall be able to marry you for years. What misery to have such a future in one's mind? Do speak to your brother, open your heart to him and try and win his friendship. Tell him, that if he loves you, he should take your part.

Mimi, dearest, you must take a bold step to be my wife. I entreat you, pet, by the love you have for me, Mimi, do speak to your mother - tell her it is the last time you ever shall speak of me to her.

You are right, Mimi, you cannot be the wife of anyone else than me. I shall ever blame myself for what has taken place. I never, never can be happy until you are my own, my dear, fond wife. Oh, Mimi! Be bold for once! Do not fear them. Tell them you are my wife before God. Do not let me leave you without being married, for I cannot answer what could happen. My conscience reproaches me of a sin that marriage can only efface.

I can assure you, it will be many days before I meet such nice people as the Seaverights, especially the daughter. I longed so much to have introduced you to her to see the perfect Lady in her, and such an accomplished young person.

My evenings, as you say, are very long and dreary. We must not be separated all next winter, for I know Mimi you will be as giddy as last. You will be going to public balls and that I cannot endure. On my honour, dearest, sooner than see you or hear of you running about as you did last, I would leave Glasgow myself. Though I have truly forgiven you, I do not forget the misery I endured for your sake! You know yourself how ill it made me. If not, Mary can tell you, my pet.

Dearest Mimi, let us meet again soon but not as last time. See if you can plan anything for the Queen's birthday. I intend to be in Helensburgh some night to cross over with Miss White to Greenock.

My dear Wife, I could not take you to Lima. No European woman could live there. Besides, I would live three or four thousand miles from it, far from any white people, and no doctors if you were ill or getting a baby. No, if we marry, I must stay in Glasgow until I get enough to live elsewhere. Besides, it would cost £300 alone for our bare passage money.

I do not understand, my pet, you not bleeding, for every woman losing her virginity must bleed. You must have done so, some other time. Try to remember if you never hurt yourself in washing, etc. I am sorry you felt pain. I hope, pet, you are better. I trust, dearest, you will not be with child. Be sure and tell me immediately you are ill next time, and if at your regular period. I was not angry at your allowing me, Mimi, but I am sad it happened. You had no resolution. We should indeed have waited until we were married, Mimi. It was very bad indeed. I shall look with regret on that night. No, nothing except our marriage will efface it from my memory. Mimi, only fancy if it were now.

I cannot help doubting your word about flirting. You promised me the same thing before you left for Edinburgh and you did nothing else during your stay there. You cared more for your friends than for me. I do trust you will give me no cause to find fault again with you on that score, but I doubt very much the sincerity of your promise.

Mimi, the least thing I hear of you doing, that day shall be the last of our tie, that I swear. You are my wife, and I have the right to expect from you the behaviour of a married woman - or else you have no honour in you; and more you have no right to go anywhere but where a woman could go with her husband.

Oh, Mimi, let your conduct make me happy. Remember, when you are good how truly happy it makes Emile - but remember this, and if you love me you will do nothing wrong.

Dearest, your letter to Mary was very pretty and good. I thought a great deal of it and I like its seriousness. Fancy how happy I was when Mary told me the other day how Mimi was improving fast. She could tell it by your letters.

For God's sake burn this, Mimi, for fear of anything happening to you, do dearest.
Emile

17 THE INTERCEPTION
GLASGOW, 1856

Janet Hamilton Smith walked into the drawing room to find her daughter bent over the writing desk so engrossed in what she was doing that she failed to hear her mother's swishing skirts, or her soft footsteps approaching from behind. She jumped as her mother spoke.

"Madeleine? What are you doing?"

"My goodness, Mama! You scared me half to death. I didn't hear you coming."

"Who are you writing to?"

"Oh, just a friend," she replied airily.

"You're being evasive, Madeleine. To whom are you writing?"

Her mother stood at the table, while Madeleine obscured the contents of the letter with her left hand.

Her mother stretched out her hand, palm up.

"Give it to me, Madeleine. I fear you are not being entirely honest."

"Mama, please! It is merely a letter to a friend. You remember Mary Buchanan? She wants to visit us soon and I was writing to tell her she could."

"Then, if that is the case, you won't mind me reading the letter, Madeleine."

"Mama, of course you can read it; there's nothing here of interest. And I'm sure Mama has more interesting things to do with her time than to read my silly prattle."

"I don't like your impertinence, Madeleine. Your behaviour of late has left a lot to be desired. I hope that you've not rekindled your relationship with that French scoundrel. I trust you're obeying your papa's instructions."

"Of course, Mama, why wouldn't I be?"

"Because I know you, Madeleine Hamilton Smith. You're wilful, and it'll be your downfall one day, God forgive me if it won't. Now give me that letter."

"I would prefer not to, Mama."

"I'm not asking you, Madeleine, I'm telling you. Now give it to me."

Madeleine was unsure if she was more surprised by the fact that her mother showed more strength of character than she gave her credit for, or whether she should be mortified for being caught out as a liar. Reluctantly, she slid the letter along the desk towards her.

Her mother's hand, skin taut and blue veins pronounced, lifted the letter off the desk and read the few lines written in ink barely dry. A fairly innocuous letter in content but there was much fault with it. She stood for a long time in silence, staring hard at the page; reading the lines, and between the lines. Her free hand unconsciously covered her mouth in a sign of disbelief.

When she looked up, her eyes shone wet with tears. Madeleine swallowed hard, her cheeks burned.

"I'm sorry, Mama. I'm sorry for lying. I didn't want you to know I was writing to Emile. I…"

Her mother cut her off with a flick of her hand.

"I cannot believe you would cross us so, knowing we forbade you to have any further dealings with this man. Why do you continue to be so rebellious, Madeleine?"

Her mother's voice was icy cold; soaked in abhorrence and disdain, a voice foreign to Madeleine. Madeleine remained silent, her eyes fixed on the floor. She felt the heat on her cheeks resurge from the strong and unexpected rebuke.

"You refer to this man as your husband, Madeleine. What's the meaning of this? Please tell me you've not brought further disgrace upon this family? Whatever do you mean by this? Tell me the truth, I implore you!"

Madeleine looked up.

"No, Mama. I swear. It's my pet name for him. That is all. I love him, Mama. We love each other. We want to be married. He's a gentleman, Mama. Emile would never to do anything to bring my name into disrepute. I wish you would try to know him. Give him a chance. Please, Mama! I beg of you! Meet him, for my sake. Help me with Papa. I'll never be happy with another."

"Now listen here, Madeleine Hamilton, marrying this man is out of the question. If you continue to see him your father will be quite within his right not only to disinherit you, but also to disown you. Is this what you want? To be cast out of the house like a fallen woman? Is this man worth forsaking everything - monetary comfort, losing your family, your friends? It has come to this now, Madeleine. You need to give your actions serious consideration. What about William Minnoch who has started paying you attention?"

"I care not a fig for my friends, or money, or for William Minnoch! If I could marry Emile I know I would be happy," cried Madeleine between sobs.

"Don't talk like a child, Madeleine! You have to start showing some maturity in this matter. Running off and marrying this penniless skilamalink will bring you nothing but financial ruin and a lot of personal misery. Your suggestion is unconscionable. Your father will have to hear about this. Your disobedience has tested me, and I cannot hide this from him. I cannot vouch for his reaction because not only will he be deeply saddened, Madeleine, he will also be exceedingly angry, and rightly so!"

"Yes, Mama."

"Now remove yourself. I do not want to see you, or hear from you until dinner time. Is that understood?"

"Yes, Mama."

"And if you think it is only your father who is disappointed, it is not. I cannot tell you, Madeleine, how deeply distressed and unhappy you've made me feel this afternoon. I feel as if I don't even know you."

*

Madeleine wondered if Mama ever told Papa. She was sure she had because he was cold and distant towards her. For weeks he ignored her. When he conversed with the rest of her siblings it was evident she was not included. The letter was not mentioned despite it being two weeks since the incident. Each day she expected to incur his wrath, but it never came. In some ways she wished it would. At least then, it would be over.

Everyone was now watching her, yet again. She was no longer allowed out on her own, not even with Bessie or John. She was only allowed out with Mama. She was also told she would no longer be allowed any writing material.

Madeleine was quick to remind Christina a favour was owed, and she smuggled in what was needed to continue her correspondence. Any writing now was done in her room, late at night by candlelight, away from prying eyes, and well after her little sister Janet had fallen asleep.

She daren't write to Emile and they did not see each other for a good while. However, she knew if she wrote to Mary, he would receive the news, via her.

Dearest Mary,

Mama has discovered the correspondence. I am truly glad that it is known; but strange to say a fortnight has passed and not a word has been said. I cannot understand it.

Now that it is known, I do not mean to give way. I shall state in plain terms that I intend to be dear Emile's wife. Nothing shall deter me. I shall be of age soon, and then I have a right to decide for myself. Can you blame me for not giving in to my parents in a matter of so serious importance as the choice of a husband?

I had been intended to marry a man of money; but is not affection before all things? In marrying Emile, I will take the man whom I love.

I know my friends will forsake me, but for that I do not care. So long as I possess the affection of Emile; and to possess and retain his affection, I shall try to please him in all things, by acting according to his directions, and he cures me of my faults.

I am sorry not to be able to see you, as we are going to Edinburgh in a week or ten days.
Madeleine

18 NUMBER 7 BLYTHSWOOD SQUARE
GLASGOW, 1856

James Smith's family life may have been in turmoil, but his business was thriving. As the current director of the North British Insurance Company, and as a member of the Council of Glasgow Fine Art Association, he had not done too badly for a crofter's son. He was enjoying the fruits of his success, and the time had come to move his family from 16 India Street to a more fashionable address in Glasgow. He finally settled on a newly built townhouse at Number 7, Blythswood Square.

Number 7 was a handsome house befitting the eminent Glaswegian architect, James Smith. The block of townhouses stood firmly rooted, exuding an air of grandeur. Occasionally, when the sun shone on the shell-pink sandstone façade, it lifted the spirits of those in the neighbourhood suppressed by the steel-grey skies and dreary Glaswegian weather.

Leading up to the grand front door was a sweeping flight of stairs edged with ornate wrought-iron railings. At the top of the stairs, protecting its occupants from the relentless Scottish rain, was a grand portico supported by four Ionian columns. As soon as James Smith saw the house, he knew he had to have it, even before seeing the interior, or knowing the price. Not only did it have the address, it oozed money and success.

With great pride he turned the key in the lock and opened the house to the family for the first time to show off his new acquisition.

"Oh, Papa, what a delightful house!" enthused Madeleine as she picked up her skirts and glided from room to room, examining each briefly before turning out into the passage and looking into the next. The rest of her siblings rushed around doing the same. Voices and footsteps were amplified by the bare floors and cavernous spaces.

"Do you like it, dear?" James asked his wife, who managed a weak smile. She had left her sickbed to see the new house on his insistence.

"It's beautiful, James. It's rather grand, compared to India Street. How will the servants manage?"

"Well then, we shall just have to employ some more, won't we now?" His eyes twinkled as he placed her arm on his and escorted her around the rest of the house.

Madeleine passed the drawing room and the dining room and then explored the three bedrooms upstairs. On her return, she decided to explore the stairs leading to the floor below ground level.

She descended the wooden stairs and found herself in another long passage. She turned left and entered a small room at the far end, with a door opening out onto a narrow lane. There was a downstairs toilet, pantry, wine cellar, and a kitchen. Downstairs was also the largest bedroom in the house. Along with the generous space, it boasted a fireplace and two windows below street level looking out onto Main Street. She moved across the floor and stood at the windows. She could not help giggling at glimpses of trouser legs and buttoned up boots peeping from under voluminous fabric, belonging to headless people passing by.

Coming out of the large bedroom, and turning left along the passageway, she passed the kitchen again. She came to a door which opened onto a small courtyard leading up to Main Street via a small flight of steps. This area was cordoned off with the same wrought iron railings seen when approaching the house.

Her heart raced a little when she saw the layout downstairs, and she returned to the large bedroom for another look. Correspondence between herself and Emile had never been easy with the chance of letters being intercepted. Now he could pass by and drop the notes directly through her bedroom window from the street outside. She could leave hers to be picked up during an arranged time. It couldn't have been a more perfect situation if she had orchestrated it herself. Her mission, now, would be trying to contact, or see Emile, to set it up. Something that had been impossible, of late.

Returning to the rest of the family she said, "Papa, do you think I could have the room downstairs?"

"You can, but you'll have to share with either Bessie or Janet. There are not enough rooms in the house for you to have one on your own."

"I don't want to share with Madeleine, Papa," said Elizabeth, pouting a little. "I want my own room. You know how untidy Madeleine is. She can share with Janet."

"I don't mind sharing with Madeleine, Papa," said thirteen year old Janet, enthusiastically. She was holding on to her mother's thin arm, looking up at her father with her large, innocent eyes that allowed her to get away with far more than she should.

"Well, that settles it. Madeleine, you can have the room, as long as you share it with Janet."

Madeleine nodded, but said nothing.

She cast a critical eye around the house once more, and despite the setback of having to share this below stairs room with her younger sister, and having the servants on the same floor, she thought the new bedroom may well turn out to be a blessing in disguise. Yes, she thought, a blessing indeed!

7 Blythswood Square, Glasgow. Madeleine's windows being shown at street level right corner of the building covered in white blinds. William Minnoch, Madeleine Smith's betrothed, lived above the Smith family. His entrance can be seen to the right, on Main Street.

19 ROMANCE RESUMED
GLASGOW, 1856

Had it not been for a chance meeting one day in Regent Street, Madeleine and Emile may never have resumed their fractured and forbidden relationship, despite moving to the new premises.

Occasionally, she wrote to their mutual friend Mary Perry, but any letters between her and Emile had stopped. Madeleine was once again the dutiful daughter she was expected to be, yet all the while dreaming of Emile, and longing for his warm embrace.

Madeleine had no option but to be complicit in remaining obedient. There was no other choice, for she was only ever allowed out whenever Mama left the house, which was not very often.

As time passed, and her family was satisfied that the relationship was over, her actions were no longer under heavy scrutiny. Their hold on her eased to the point she was allowed out with her sister, Bessie. Mama had come down with a series of migraines, and on this particular day she needed them to run errands for her. The two girls were walking along Regent Street, during one of these chores, when Emile spotted them from across the road. He was almost run over by a horse and carriage in his eagerness to greet them.

Madeleine, although delighted with this opportune moment, did not say anything for a while. Her heart was beating uncontrollably, and knowing she would do a poor job of hiding her excitement when she spoke, she also felt it prudent not to show any of the enthusiasm bubbling away inside. Instead, she allowed Bessie to do all the talking. It gave her time to compose herself.

"Mr. L'Angelier! What are you doing here?"

Bessie scanned her sister's face as she spoke, but was satisfied to see Madeleine was equally as surprised to see him.

"I do hope you are keeping better than the last time I saw you," continued Bessie.

"I'm not in good health at the moment, Miss Smith. I'm recovering from an illness that keeps coming back. However, I'm finally regaining my strength, and today is the first day I've been out for a while. Of course, I feel better already after seeing both of you. Where are you going?"

"We're just off to Frazer and Green, Mr. L'Angelier. Anyhow, we need to be off. It was lovely to see you," replied Bessie, taking command of Madeleine's elbow and steering her away.

He hurried after them.

"Oh, I do hope you won't mind if I walk with you?"

Bessie turned to her sister, who still was yet to speak. Finally, she said, "You are most welcome to join us, Mr. L'Angelier. That is, if you would like."

"I would indeed, Miss Madeleine."

He tipped his hat to her, and walked between them. During this time, he directed all his conversation to Madeleine who was petrified someone she knew was watching them, and would report her to her father, once again. She deviated from the main street and slipped down a side alley to avoid prying eyes. Once there, she started to relax as she listened to dear Emile talking away, oblivious to her anxiety and concerns.

"Bessie, do you think you could give me a few minutes on my own with Emile?" Madeleine suddenly blurted out.

Her sister looked horrified.

"Madeleine, Papa…"

"Only a few minutes, Madeleine. I really don't want to be in trouble for something you've done. It has to be just a few minutes."

Bessie walked away, but not far enough. Madeleine was sure she was still within earshot and so lowered her voice as she spoke.

"Oh, pet! I have so missed you. Not being able to see you or write to you has almost killed me! Have you missed me, my love? Please say you have?"

"Of course I've missed you, Madeleine. Not a day goes by when I don't think of you. But I've heard nothing from you, Madeleine! Not a word! How cold-hearted you are to have ignored me for all these weeks? Do I mean nothing to you?"

He grabbed her elbow, and moved away from Bessie who was straining to hear the conversation. His grip was like a vice, and she winced.

"Emile, please! You have to understand! I've no choice in the matter. I wanted to write, honestly, I did! But my parents have been watching my every move. They even removed my writing equipment. I persuaded Christina to smuggle some in, which she did, and I wrote to Mary, hoping she would tell you all my news. But I could not risk writing to you, Emile. Please understand."

"I don't understand you, Madeleine. You have to start growing up and tackling this situation like an adult. How can you allow your family to keep us apart like this? Perhaps I need to go to your father's place of work and tell him how things are between us, seeing you are unwilling or unable to do so."

"Emile, I beg of you, please don't. I have to wait for the right moment. But I will, my pet. I promise. I will talk to Papa and Mama again. Soon you will be my husband."

She glanced over at her sister looking into a milliner's window. Madeleine could see Bessie was using the reflection of the glass to see what they were doing. She was careful to place some distance between herself and Emile.

"My love, take heart, for there is some good news for a change. We have moved from India Street. We now live at 7 Blythswood Square. It's a corner townhouse opening onto Main Street."

She could see Bessie walking towards them.

"We don't have too much time, Bessie's on her way back. I have the basement room, Emile. White blinds. Drop me a note tonight, and leave it on the window ledge. I'll leave one out in return, outlining a schedule, so we don't get caught."

He was about to reply when her sister said, "Madeleine, Mama will be getting worried. We need to return to the house. A pleasure to meet you again, Mr. L'Angelier!"

"Ladies."

Before Madeleine could reply, Bessie linked arms with Madeleine and steered her firmly towards Blythswood Square.

*

In her naiveté, Madeleine thought moving to Blythswood Square would make things easier in corresponding with Emile. Although he could drop letters in at her window, he often did so when she was not there to receive them, ignoring the times she had suggested. It made it difficult to reply, especially as she was still being watched.

Emile's lack of sympathy to her predicament manifested itself through his notes and letters, when they found their way to her. The tone oscillated between sarcastic derision, and the melodramatic. She never knew which mood he was in when she opened his letters, nor how her reply would be received.

The reality of the situation was the opportunities for corresponding were simply not there. Spending the summer at Rowaleyn did not help matters either. However, nothing placated Emile's disgruntlement, no matter how often she explained her predicament.

He increased his threats to take up employment in some far flung, distant land. Madeleine was frantic. *How can he possibly think of leaving me now? Now that we are married under Scottish law?* He had taken her virginity, which bound her to him, as husband and wife. She lamented his attitude, and wept at the hopelessness of it all.

*

Helensburgh, 15th July 1856

My sweet, beloved and dearest Emile,

I shall begin and answer your dear, long letter. In the first place, how are you? Better, I trust.

You know I feel disappointed at our marriage not taking place in September. But, as it could not, why then, I just made up my mind to be content and trust that it may be ere long. We shall fix about that at our next meeting, which I hope won't be long.

So do not weep, darling fond husband. It makes me sad to think you weep. Do not do it, darling; a fond embrace and dear kiss to you, sweet and much-beloved Emile.

Our intimacy has not been criminal, as I am your wife before God - so it has been no sin our loving each other. No, darling, fond Emile, I am your wife. I shall cease to be childish and thoughtless. I shall do all I can to please you and retain you, truly, dear, fond love.

You shall, dear love, have all your letters back. Emile, love, you are wrong. If I did feel cool towards you in winter, I never gave thoughts of love to any other.

No other image has ever filled my heart since I knew you.

*

Envelope addressed--" Mr. L'Angelier, 10 Bothwell Street, Glasgow." [Posted at Row; Helensburgh post-mark, day not legible, July, 1856 ; reached Glasgow July, 1856.]
[LETTER.]

Saturday Night, 11 o'clock.

Beloved and darling husband, dear Emile,

I have just received your letter. A thousand kind thanks for it. It is kind, and I shall love you more for writing me such a letter. Dearest, I do love you for telling me all you think of me.

Emile, I am sorry you are ill. I trust to God you are better. For the love of heaven, take care of yourself. Leave town for a day or two. Yes, darling, by all means, go to Mrs. M' Lan's. It will do you much good, only come back to me.

Yes, Emile, you ought, in those sad moments of yours, to consider you have a wife. I am as much your wife as if we had been married a year. You cannot, will not leave me, your wife. Oh! For pity's sake, do not go. I will do all you ask, only remain in this country. I shall keep all my promises. I shall not be thoughtless and indifferent to you.

On my soul, I love you and adore you with the love of a wife. I will do anything, I will do all you mention in your letters to please you, only do not leave me or forsake me. I entreat of you, my husband, my fondly loved Emile, only stay and be my guide, my husband dear. You are my all, my only, dear love.

Have confidence in me, sweet pet. Trust me. Heaven is my witness, I shall never prove untrue to you I shall, I am your wife. No other one shall I ever marry. I promise I shall not go about the streets Emile, more than you have said. We went about too much. I shall not go about much.

But one you must promise me is this, that if you should meet me at a time in B/ Street or S/ Street you will not look on me crossly. For it almost made me weep on the street last winter sometimes when you hardly looked at me.

I shall take lessons in watercolours. I shall tell you in my next note what I intend to study. It will rather amuse you.

I hope, dear Pet Emile, you will get nice lodgings. I always thought the Gardens were too far away from your office. How nicely the 12/. would suit us at Billhead. I hope we may meet soon.

Now, Emile, I shall keep all my promises I have made to you. I shall love and obey you. My duty as your wife is to do so. I shall do all you want of me. Trust me, keep yourself easy. I know what awaits me if I do what you disapprove - off you go. That shall always be in my mind Go, never to return. The day that occurs I hope I may die. Yes, I shall never look on the face of man again.

You would die in Africa. Your death would be at my hands. God forbid! Trust me, I love you, yes, love you for yourself alone. I adore you with my heart and soul. Emile, I swear to you I shall do all you wish and ask of me. I love you more than life. I am thine, thine own Mimi L'Angelier.

Emile, you shall have all your letters the first time we meet. It may cost me a sigh and pang, but you shall have them all.

Minnoch left this morning say nothing to him in passing. It will only give him cause to say you did not behave in a gentlemanly manner. Do not do it. He said nothing to me out of place, but I was not a moment with him by myself. I did not wish to be alone with him.

I shall answer your letter the next time I write. Love, my pet, my husband, my fond and ever dearly beloved Emile, good night. May God grant you better health. Be happy. I will do all you wish, I shall keep my promise, this I swear. Be happy. Weep no more. Adieu, sweet one. I am thy wife, thy own fond pet,

Madeleine Smith, alias Mimi L'Angelier

20 BROKEN PROMISES
GLASGOW, 1856

Emile watched the house from across the street. It was close to midnight and the building was shrouded in darkness. He crossed over and ran his cane along the bars, not loud enough to wake the occupants of the rooms on the other side, but loud enough to announce his presence to the immediate occupant.

There was no response. Emile bent down and peered into the windows covered with thick, white blinds, hoping to see something through a narrow chink.

Police Constable Thomas Kavan was on his beat that night, which covered the north and east sides of Blythswood Square, including James Smith's house. When he saw the man loitering outside the house, he recognised him as the same man who had been standing under the lamppost opposite, and had been for some time.

"Can I help you, sir?"

"Good evening, policeman. No, I'm just waiting for a friend."

"What sort of friend would that be, sir? You do know what time it is, don't you?"

Emile cleared his throat, stalling for time, as he watched the policeman strike his baton menacingly onto the open palm of his hand.

"Ah, this is a little delicate, you see, sir. It's a lady friend."

The policeman pursed his lips together in a smirk, winked, and lowered the baton.

"Well, hopefully she still has some energy left over for you once she's finished her daily duties, working for them lot!"

"I'm beginning to wonder, because I've been waiting quite a while." Emile laughed and the policeman joined him.

"Cold night, policeman. Do you smoke?"

"Yes, sir, I do."

Emile reached into his breast-pocket and pulled out two cigars, giving both to the policeman.

"That's generous of you, sir. Goodnight, and enjoy your evening."

The copper left and Emile ran the cane along the bars once more. Finally, the blind rose and Madeleine came to the window wearing her night attire.

"Emile, what are you doing here?" she whispered fiercely, glancing back at Janet, who remained fast asleep.

"Why, I came to see you, my love. Did you not receive my note to say I was coming by this evening?"

"No, pet, I did not. Would you like some cocoa to warm you up? You look frozen! How long have you been waiting?"

"A while. It's bitterly cold outside. I was wondering if I could come in, Madeleine. Please?"

"The servants are all in tonight, Emile. It would be a great risk."

"I need my little Mimi tonight. Are you going to deny me that, my love? Please? What if we used the laundry room?"

Madeleine thought about it for a moment. If Papa caught her with Emile, he would be exceedingly angry. Luckily, he had gone to Edinburgh on business, and Mama had the vapours, so she saw no harm in it.

She lit a candle so she could find the oil lamp. After several failed attempts the wick caught, and she made her way to the back door. She heard the gate squeaking on its hinges as Emile entered the courtyard, and she held her breath. Finally, she exhaled. No one stirred.

Placing her finger to her lips, she held out her free hand and led him past the servants' rooms, past her room where Janet was still fast asleep, and entered the laundry room at the end of the house.

Shutting the door behind them, Madeleine was overcome by a fit of nervous giggles. However, Emile's thunderous expression soon quashed them.

"Do you want to wake the whole household, Madeleine, with your childish giggles? Stop it at once!"

Madeleine instantly regretted her innate response.

"I'm sorry, my pet. I wasn't thinking. I'm so silly sometimes. I don't know why you're so patient with me. Come my, love. Take off your hat and let me look at you. How are you feeling now? Are you better?"

He sniffed before answering, "Well enough, I suppose."

She smiled at him and patted his arm as she placed the lamp on the nearest flat surface. She turned the wick up high so she could see him.

Emile's anger dissipated. He moved towards her.

"Oh, Madeleine! If only we didn't need to conduct ourselves like this. I've so missed you."

He held her hands and kissed the palms of each. For once he did not inspect her nails. Instead, his kisses moved from her palm to the full length of her arm, and he nuzzled into the nape of her neck. She loved the smell of him so close; the smell of tobacco, mingled with rosemary, and the thyme from the Pears soap she knew he used.

"Emile, sometimes I wish you were with me every minute of every day, and other times, I wish you were so very far away. I yearn not to be tortured so."

He stopped and looked at her. His face had darkened.

"Perhaps I should go away. You never seem to want me these days. I'll leave Huggins and go far away. There is that position in Australia I may take. Would that be far enough for you?"

She could see he was angry once more. She had said the wrong thing, yet again.

She wound her arms around his neck, trying to soothe his anger.

"That's not what I meant at all, my pet. I love you so much my heart aches to breaking point because of the position we find ourselves in. I only meant that if you were far away, I may not suffer so. It's my love for you that is so great it hurts."

She snuggled closer to him and he frowned over the top of her head. Pulling away, he looked at her, searching her eyes for answers that kept eluding him.

"Do you think it's easy for me? Why am I always tetchy these days? If only you'd speak to your father. It is you keeping us apart. You I long for, constantly!"

"Shhh… Let's not spoil the moment. Come here, my love."

She allowed him to unbutton the pearl buttons on her nightdress and to fondle her breasts. Momentarily, the quarrel was set aside. He cupped each breast and kissed her nipples until they stood hard. His hands travelled south, lingering on her skin. She moved back from him as he lifted her nightdress, and tried to feel her between the split of her cotton drawers.

"No, Emile! Please! You promised. Not before we are married."

"But we are married, are we not, my pet? The deed was long done. Once more won't hurt, will it?"

He lifted her chin, and looked into her eyes for a signal to proceed. Instead, she dropped her gaze and shrank from him. The light from the lamp cast her face in a soft glow, throwing highlights off her chestnut brown hair, now falling out of its long braid. She backed into the washing table where she felt safer, except he followed.

"Lie back on the table, Madeleine. If I cannot make love to you, at least show me what you have underneath that nightgown of yours. Show it to me, Madeleine. It's a husband's right."

She didn't want to disappoint him, start another row, nor risk being discovered through raised voices. She complied.

Lying down on the table, she pulled up her knees, undid the drawstring and allowed the two halves of her drawers to fall open. With her nightdress hitched up to her waist, she was fully exposed.

She lay studying the water stains on the ceiling, while she felt him move her legs apart, for a better look. Her checks burned hot with the shame.

When they first made love, darkness had hidden any evidence of shame. It had seemed different. But it was not dark now. Nice girls did not do such things. Papa would kill her, she thought, if he could see her now.

She stayed like that for a while as he trailed his fingers up and down her inner thighs, brushing the back of his hand over her mound several times. Instead of it being sensuous, she focused on the rough calluses she felt, rather than the soft hands she was expecting. She wondered if the touch was accidental, but there was no mistake when he repeated the action. He bent down and kissed her there, his lips hovering, his breath licking her skin, waiting for her to weaken. Determined not to succumb she sat up abruptly, pushed him away, and started redressing.

"I think it's time you were going, my love." Her voice cracked, quivering vocal cords unable to come together. She was trembling and fumbling with her buttons.

"It's late and the air is damp. I wouldn't want you to fall ill just because you came to see me."

He smiled, replaced his hat, and picked up his cane.

"Well, my love, if you're going to eject me into the cold night so early, I shall wish you sweet dreams. You'd better show me out."

Mr. L'Angelier, 10 Bothwell Street, Glasgow.

Beloved & ever dear, Emile,

I am all by myself. So I shall write to you, dear husband. Your visit of last night is over. I longed for it. How it passed - it looked but a few minutes ere you left me. You did, my love, look cross at first, but thank Heaven you looked yourself ere you left - your old smile. Dear fond, Emile, I love you more and more.

I am your wife. You cannot leave me forever. Could you, Emile? I spoke in jest of your going last night. For I do not think you will go very far away from me, Emile. Would you leave me to end my days in misery?

But sweet love, I do not regret that - never did and never shall. Emile, you were not pleased because I would not let you love me last night. On your last visit, you said, "You would not do it again 'til we were married."

I said to myself at the time, 'well I shall not let Emile do this again.' It was a punishment to myself to be deprived of your loving me. For it is a pleasure no one can deny. It is but human nature. Is not everyone that loves of the same mind? Yes. I did feel so ashamed after you left of having allowed you to see my .... I blush, feel free to add any word here, but as you said at the time, I am your wife.

Emile, you must consider about leaving me. I do not think you need expect to get the Australian situation - there are always people ready to fill such situations, friends of those connected with it. You have given up your situation in Huggins. Get another, you say not in Glasgow. Well try some other town in Scotland, or if you would, go to England, then we might have a chance of seeing each other sometimes. But to go to Australia, never more to come back to your wife, your Mimi - unkind of you to think of such.

Will nothing persuade you to remain in Huggins?

Emile, my husband, I do not intend to make promises as I know you won't receive them or believe them (fearful thing, but it is my own fault). But, I know now pretty well what you would like me to do, and what you dislike, so I shall by actions try and retain your dear love. I shall do all I can that I know to please you. I shall not go out as I did, but I need you to make promises, too.

What made me a little vexed with you last night was this, you went back on last winter, and that you promised me you would not do. I have done all I could do to try and make myself better for you.

I do hope you got home safe - and were none the worse for it. A fond, dear embrace - a kiss dear love, my own, sweet Emile, my best loved husband. Forgive me, and be what we once were.

I shall not wear crinoline as you don't like it. It is off today.

No one heard you last night. Next night it shall be a different window. This one is much too small. I must see you before you go to Badgmore.

I am so glad I have your letters as they are such a pleasure to me. I read and read them over and over again, and I love them so.

I hope you will correct the person who told you of our having been at the Tweedies & Raits. I have seen Mr. Rait in the shop when I was in there with Papa - but that is all. And I have heard Mary say that she has met Mr. Rait at parties, but that is all. I never spoke to Miss Rait. I know her by sight, but that is all. James called at the Tweedies when they were at Stone. I don't like the family, and there is no respect attached to Mr. Tweedie's name. As for Tweedie junior, I don't even know him by sight. So sweet love, you may hear much that is false when you have heard of two such simple things being wrong.

I shall tell Jack someday that you know Miss Dongall the doctor's daughter in Elmbank Place. I remember a long, long time ago seeing you meet that young Lady opposite Aunt's windows, whether by appointment or not, I cannot say. Aunt told me that you were engaged to her.

I must have a letter from you very soon - the beginning of the week, perhaps Wednesday when we will be in Row. Please address it as before; Miss Bruce, P.O. Row. You shall tell me all your arrangements. Mimi, your wife

21 STOMACH PROBLEMS
GLASGOW, SEPTEMBER 1856

Charles Baird, Robert Baird's elder brother, and Emile were colleagues, and friends. Both men frequently socialised together, and it was quite common for Charles to visit Emile at his lodgings. One evening, he decided to visit Emile when the landlady, Mrs. Jenkins, met him on the threshold. She informed him that Emile was unwell but she would show him up to the room, so he could see for himself.

"Good God, Emile, whatever's the matter? You look dreadful!" exclaimed Charles seeing Emile languishing on his bed, and making a feeble attempt to stand up to greet him. He flopped back onto the bed before replying.

"I've been really ill. It attacked me so suddenly, too. One minute I'm on my way home from the office, ordering some tea from Mrs. Jenkins, and the next minute, I'm clutching my stomach doubled up with pain. It hasn't passed me yet."

Almost on cue, another wave of pain gripped his intestines and he whimpered in agony. This scenario continued for more than fifteen minutes. Charles Baird felt at a loss as to what to do. One did not need to be a doctor to see his friend needed medical attention.

"Can I call a doctor for you, Emile? You look like you really need one."

"I think Mrs. Jenkins has done that already. He should be here shortly."

"Well then, if you're sure, for the time is late, and I should be getting home. Don't come in tomorrow, unless you're better."

"I may well take a day off. I'll see how I go."

The following day, Emile surprised Charles by turning up for work, albeit a little late. Considering how bad he was when Charles had left him, he was astounded.

"Good God, Emile! What are you doing back at work so soon? How are you feeling?"

Although Emile stood while he spoke, he used the chair in front of him for support. His beard did much to hide the severity of the yellow-tinged skin that sagged at his cheek bones, but failed to mask the dark circles under the eyes, and the bags beneath that sat puffy and proud.

"I'm a little washed out after last night. I vomited a great deal during the night, but the doctor came eventually, and gave me something for the pain and the vomiting. It seems to have settled down."

"How long have we known each other now, two years?"

"About that."

"Well, for as long as I've known you, you've had this ailment. What do they say it is?"

"They keep telling me I have a bile problem. I'm sure it's nothing serious. If it were, I'd be dead by now."

22 SUBTLE CONTROL
GLASGOW, NOVEMBER 1856

All Madeleine ever wanted to do was to please Emile. His flashes of anger often confused her, for there never seemed to be consistent triggers. However, whatever she said or did of late seemed to displease him. The outbursts frightened her. Last week she had looked at his face, black with rage, the vein on his head prominent and pulsating as he fumed.

Her heart now raced, and her palms dripped with sweat, as she learned she was the cause of his dissatisfaction.

"You disappoint me once again, Madeleine. I heard you were being an outrageous flirt this weekend. Just because we don't socialise together, doesn't mean I don't hear what you have been up to."

Madeleine chewed her nails, and then hid them behind her back in case he had seen her indulge in her 'filthy' habit.

"I don't know who has been telling you stories, Emile, but they simply are not true. Exaggerations at best."

"You are my wife, Madeleine! How dare you flirt and talk to other men. Do you have no shame?"

"Please, darling husband of mine. Let's not fight. I promise to be good when I go out. I shall ignore all offers to dance, and tell everyone who asks that I have a bad leg. Please smile, my love. I hate quarrelling, especially as we spend so little time together."

"Well, modify your behaviour, Madeleine. It is not befitting of a married woman. And I don't like the things you wear. I've told you before; I don't want to see you in crinoline, and keep the necklines modest, unless you want men ogling you."

Looking at the new clothes lying on her bed now, she sighed. She would never be able to wear some of these Mama had ordered because Emile would not approve.

Along with his short temper, she was concerned at his fits of depression which, he said, were caused by her constant socialising and flirting. Perhaps if she sent him a long letter, he might start feeling better about himself, she thought. She really loved him, why couldn't he accept it as being true?

Mr. L'Angelier, at Mrs. Jenkins, 11 Franklin Place, Great Western Road, Glasgow.

Friday night, 12 o'clock.

My own darling, my dearest Emile,

Dearest love, I hope you are more cheerful, and not sad. Oh, for your own wife's sake do not be sad; it makes your Mimi feel sorry to think her husband is sad. Darling, try and not get low spirited.

Did you go to the concert? I did. Jack went, he came in, ordered the cab, and brought me my gloves (he always does that when I am going out with him) so I went and B/. I looked at everyone but could not see my husband. Mr. Minnoch was there with his horrid old sister, but I only bowed to them. I have not seen any of them yet.

I shall send you the likeness some night soon, perhaps next week, but you shall have it.

Sweet love, you should get those brown envelopes. They would not be so much seen as the white ones put down into my window. You should just stoop to tie your shoe, and then slip it in. The backdoor is closed. M/ keeps the key for fear our servant boy would go out of an evening. We have got blinds for our windows.

I saw Robert Anderson the other day. He was speaking of Huggins, but he did not speak of you. I am so fond to hear one speak of my own Beloved Mr. L'Angelier. He fancies I am going to take Mr. Minnoch.

I am sure you won't like me in my jacket. I don't like it both P/ and M/ do. My bonnet is fawn. B/ has a pink one, and M/ wanted me to have pink, but I knew you would think pink very vulgar.

Dear love, when I am your wife I shall require you to tell me what I am to wear, as I have no idea of how to dress myself. M/ and B/ do all that for me. My dress for the winter is to be dark grey tweed. You will like that, I am sure, Emile.

I know you won't look on my likeness with pleasure it is so cross, but love, when it was done, I had been in the horrid man's place from twelve o'clock, and I had it closed at four o'clock. I had no food from the night before, and I was very furious. I am just looking as cross as I did that night at you. I feel so ashamed, dear love, of having showed temper to you. But now you know it, love.

I was at M/ to-day (asking) about painting, and she said, nonsense, I did not require it. I told her she had promised, and then she said, "Oh, well, there is plenty of interval before we go home."

I have been ordered by the Dr. since I came to town to take a fearful thing called "pease meal," such a nasty thing, I am to take at luncheon. I don't think I have tasted breakfast for two months. But T/ doesn't think I can take this meal. I shall rather take cocoa.

But, dearest love, fond embraces, much love and kisses from your devoted wife.

Your loving and affectionate wife,

Mimi L'Angelier

Madeleine Hamilton Smith poses for the likeness she sent to Emile L'Angelier

23 THE INVITATION
GLASGOW, NOVEMBER 1856

When a note arrived from William Minnoch, one Monday morning, addressed to Madeleine inviting her to the opera the following week, she penned her reply without delay. She wrote how delighted she was to have received it, and that she looked forward to seeing him again, and meeting his sister, who would be accompanying them.

Although Minnoch had known James Smith for several years, once formally introduced to Madeleine, he started calling at the house, rather than seeing James at his offices. Janet and James Smith were doing everything in their power to encourage the friendship.

The evening during the previous week, Minnoch had dined with the Smiths. Not only had he enjoyed their company, but at the end of the evening, he had listened to Madeleine give an impromptu, but accomplished piano recital. There was a lot more to this young lady than he first realised and he looked forward to spending time getting to know her.

*

The Smith family gathered around the dining room table for lunch, one day when William Minnoch came up in conversation.

"I thought William Minnoch to be a fine young man, James," commented Janet to her husband as the rest of the family sat in silence. It was a household where people spoke only when spoken to.

Madeleine overfilled her mouth and chewed her food with deliberation, in the hopes she would not be invited to make a response. Her father sipped some water from a crystal tumbler before making his reply. Heavy expectations filled the silence.

"Indeed he is, my dear. Not only that, but he's also a successful business man, and the director of Houldsworth and Co. I don't know if that means anything to you, dear, but they are a most prominent firm of cotton spinners. He is an eligible bachelor indeed, with a healthy yearly income that even surpasses my own, I've been told."

Madeleine squirmed as he turned his attention to her.

"Madeleine, I take it you spent a pleasant enough evening with him the other night?"

She continued to chew, finally swallowing hard before answering. She liked him, but it did not mean she wanted to encourage him, nor lead her parents into thinking she welcomed his attentions.

"He's pleasant enough, I suppose," she said grudgingly.

"Well, that's rather noncommittal, Madeleine. Did you not like him?" enquired her father, sounding a little rattled by her response. He put his head down and viciously attacked the meat on his plate.

Madeleine smiled as he looked up and glared at her.

"I do not know him enough to make a judgment, that is all, Papa."

"Well, I hope to change that, Madeleine. I'm pleased to hear you have accepted his invitation to go to the opera. To refuse would've seemed rather churlish, do you not agree?"

"Oh, I have no intention of refusing him, Papa. You see, I'm rather looking forward to going. I've being wanting to see this particular performance for quite some time. It was all the rage down in London when the cast was performing in Covent Garden. I've heard the tenor is quite extraordinary."

Silence stretched from wall to wall, only broken when Mama said, "Well, we'll have to buy you a new dress for the occasion. Won't we, James?"

James dabbed at his mouth with his napkin, as he was wont to do, and folded it several times over before standing up to make his reply.

"I am sure Madeleine has more than enough dresses in that ever-expanding wardrobe of hers. It's just butter upon bacon, in my opinion. However, if you insist, my dear, I leave these things up to you. Well, I'd better go back to the office and earn some more money, seeing as the two of you like to spend it on yards of silk and ostrich feathers!"

*

One night, after one of Minnoch's visits, and after the family had retired for the night, there was an unexpected visitor. Madeleine had climbed into bed, closed her eyes, and was just dozing off when a rattling noise of tin on iron jolted her back into consciousness. She sprang out of bed, heart pounding, eyes darting around the room to see if Janet was awake too. She was not. She hoped the rest of the house was sleeping just as soundly.

Emile was at the window, grumbling and complaining in a peevish voice about waiting out in the rain for several hours before he could talk to her. She was sorry to see him wet and miserable.

"Oh, Emile, what are you doing out so late? You didn't tell me you were coming."

"No, I wanted to see my Mimi, except when I did, I discovered she was indisposed. Who did you have tonight at the house? Was that the William Minnoch you've been mentioning of late? I thought I saw him leave."

"Yes, it was. Mama and Papa invited him to dine. You know he now lives above us. His entrance is off Main Street."

"Does he often come for dinner?"

"I suppose he does. After all he's a bachelor and Mama always thinks he needs feeding, even though he has a perfectly good housekeeper."

"How do you know that?"

"Know what?"

"That he has a perfectly good housekeeper."

"Because we've been to his house for several meals, and they were rather good."

"I see. You seem to be spending a lot of time in his company of late. Is he paying you attention, Madeleine?"

"No, of course not, pet. He's just a family friend. Now, would you like some cocoa to warm you up before you go home?"

Sunday night, half-past eleven o'clock

Emile, my own beloved, you have just left me. Oh, sweet darling, at this moment my heart and soul burns with love for thee this moment to be your fond wife. My nightdress was on when you saw me. Would to God you had been in the same attire. We would be happy. Emile, I adore you. I love you with my heart and soul.

I do vex and annoy you, but oh, sweet love, I do fondly love you with my soul to be your wife, your own sweet wife.

I never felt so restless and unhappy as I have done for some time past. I would do anything to keep sad thoughts from my mind. But in whatever place, some things makes me feel sad. A dark spot is in the future. Oh, may we be happy - dear darling, pray for our happiness.

I weep, Emile, to think of our fate. If we could only get married and all would be well. But alas, alas, I see no chance, no chance of happiness for me. I must speak with you. Yes, I must again be pressed to your loving bosom - be kissed by you my only love, my dearest, darling husband.

Why were we fated to be so unhappy? Why were we made to be kept separate? My heart is too full to write more. Oh pardon, forgive me. If you are able I need not say it will give me pleasure to hear from you tomorrow night. If at ten o'clock don't wait to see me - as Janet may not be asleep, and I will have to wait until she sleeps to take you in. Make no noise.

Adieu, farewell my own beloved, my darling, my own Emile. Goodnight best beloved. Adieu, I am your ever true, and devoted,

Mini L'Angelier

24 A GROWING DISCONTENT
GLASGOW, 19 DECEMBER 1856

When Madeleine began comparing her liaison with Emile to that of William Minnoch, it emerged just how often Emile criticised. It never occurred to her that his behaviour was anything other than normal. After all, her father criticised her. She thought it something men did, that was until she met William.

William was kind and supportive. He never once took her to task. When she confessed to having ragged fingernails one day as they sat under a spreading wych elm at Row, he had smiled and said, "Madeleine, that's what gloves are for. No one, but I, will know what they hide."

He also appreciated and praised her artistic ability. Where Emile had ridiculed her style and suggested lessons, William admired her work enough to ask for several pictures to grace his office.

Doubts began to surface. Did Emile love her for who she was? He seemed discontent, wanting a better version of herself, but each time she tried, she came up short. Earlier in the day, when the rest of the family was out, she had prearranged for Emile to come to the house. This was a rare treat. They had sat in the sitting room sipping tea out of thin china cups, and nibbling on oatmeal cookies she had Cook make, knowing how fond he was of them.

She smiled as she extended her hand to offer him another biscuit. She pictured them sitting in their own front room one day, just like this.

"Madeleine, are you interested in pleasing me?"

"Of course, my love, why would you ask?"

"Well I feel that I talk, but you ignore my requests. Did I not ask you the other day to change the style of your hair?"

"Yes, you did, Emile, and Christina is learning how to do it. But she hasn't quite mastered it yet, so we are left with this one for the moment."

"Well, that won't do. Please ensure she learns it, before I see you next."

"Yes, dear."

Further into the conversation Madeleine laughed heartily at something he said.

"Can you modulate that laugh, Madeleine? It sounds coarse, and you are often shrill. I am surprised, considering your upbringing."

His tone and words left her feeling crushed. A scathing note followed his visit accusing her of lying about Minnoch, and once again of being a flirt. For the first time in their relationship, she was annoyed. She needed to highlight his treatment of her. Perhaps, he was unaware of how his sarcastic denigrations cut to the quick.

However, even though she admonished, it came with difficulty, such were her overwhelming feelings of love and adoration.

*

Mr. L'Angelier, 10 Bothwell Street
[Posted Glasgow, Dec. 19, 1856; deliverable between half-past one and three same day.]

Thursday night, 11 o'clock

My beloved, my darling,

Do you for a moment think I could feel happy this evening, knowing you were in low spirits and I am the cause? Why was I ever born to annoy you, best and dearest of men?

Do you not wish oh, yes full well I know you often wish you had never known me. I thought I was doing all I could to please you. But no! When shall I ever be what you wish me to be? Never! Never!

Emile, will you never trust me, she who is to be your wife. You will not believe me. You say you heard I took Minnoch to the Concert against his inclination; I forced him to go. I told you the right way when I wrote. But from your statement in your letter of to-night you did not believe my word. Emile, I would not have done this to you.

Every word you write or tell me I would believe. I would not believe every idle report. No, I would not. I would, my beloved Emile, believe my husband's word before any other. But you always listen to reports about me if they are bad.

But you will think I am cross. I am not, but I feel hurt. Yes, ah, yes! You, my only love, the only being I love with my soul, should doubt my word and believe a stranger's. I know I talked to him. I could not sit still without talking a whole evening, but I did not flirt. I gave up flirting some time ago. There is a difference between flirting and talking. He was not with me last night; he had a second-rate looking girl with him of the name of Christie. John M'Kenzie was engaged to her for two years.

My beloved, my dear, dear husband, I am truly sorry you are ill. God grant you may soon be well.

Emile, my beloved, perhaps I am wrong to write you as I have done. Sweet love, a kiss. Oh! Would to God we could meet. Oh, darling! Do not think of dark clouds; they may pass away, and all will be sunshine. Oh, Emile, you do not look on the bright side of the picture. I do. I cannot look on the dark. Love, do not give way to such sad, dark thoughts. All will end well.

My love will repay you, Emile. If ever woman loved a man I do love you. Yes, many a sigh I heave, many a tear I shed, that we are so placed. I love you with my heart and soul. Never do I cast a thought on any other man living. My thoughts are all of my beloved, my darling husband. My sweet, dear, little pet, Emile darling, I love you. A kiss, sweet one.

Emile, Emile, my beloved, my darling, I would love your child, could I help it? No. Sweet love, I would adore, I would be to it a fond mother. I would forget the suffering, knowing it was a pledge of our love. Thank you for saying you would love me more if I had a child, and that I need not be jealous. I would rather a son, as he might have a greater chance of doing like his father. And when you were away from me I should have him to look at. When will that happy day be? Oh! Yes, my beloved, we must make a bold effort. I shall do it with all my heart, if you will.

I should so like to be your wife ere they leave here end of March. Oh! These horrid Banns. I will go to Edinburgh for twenty-one days if that will do. I am so afraid of Glasgow people telling P/, and then there would be such a row.

I see, darling, we would have a greater chance of making up if we were off than if he found it out before we were married. Have you not two friends that would do as witness? Sweet love, we have much to contend with.

Emile, darling, I think I can promise that I shall not be in Sauchiehall Street on Saturday. I shall go out in the forenoon, come in about half-past one o'clock and not go out again; it will please you if I do so, so I shall do it, sweet love. A kiss, a fond embrace.

Mama has been very ill all day and in bed. She is very ill to-night. P/ has come home. He could not stay away, she was so ill.

We shall meet. Cheer up, beloved, adored, my love, my husband. I am thy fond, loving wife, thy own dear, faithful, true and loving little wife, thy Mini L'Angelier.

I do so like to write Mini L'Angelier. It is such a dear, pretty name. I love it so. A kiss. Another. Monday evening, six, eight, or ten o'c.

25 INSURMOUNTABLE PROBLEMS
GLASGOW, JANUARY 1857

Madeleine had promised Emile they would be married by last September. However, September came and went, and they were no closer to securing an official union. She just could not find a way around marrying without her father's consent. She was still not of age, and as such, marriage without permission was impossible.

The thing that worried her most was that if they pushed ahead without her father's consent, the Banns would be read in the parish service over three consecutive Sundays. She was petrified someone would notify her father of the proposed nuptials before they happened. After all, he knew so many people, from different walks of life, and the thought terrified her. It was this, more than anything else that delayed the plans they spoke so much about.

After September passed she proposed a new wedding date for March. Madeleine began to fret yet again about the Banns as the time drew near. She expressed her concerns to Emile, but she already knew his response would not be what she wanted.

Mr. L'Angelier, 10 Bothwell Street, Glasgow

Sunday morning, one o'clock

Beloved and best of husbands, my love, a fond embrace for thy letter of this evening.

Oh, how glad I am to get such letters from you, the man I love and adore. My love, my own darling Emile, my husband, ever dear.

Don't fear Minnoch watching, he won't know. I wish we could meet sooner. Christina H. has promised she shall be happy to put all my things out of the house. I shall see them off before I go. P/ and M/ would not let them go if I left them. It will be very easy to just put them out at the back gate people may fancy some of the servants are leaving. But I shall manage all that.

About those horrid Banns, love. I wish we could do without them, for if they go on Friday, why my old father will be there at church on Sunday to stop them. And then, sweet darling, how could you trust two witnesses?

Emile, my sweet love, I have often heard of clergymen in Glasgow marrying people without banns, &c. Just go to their house, and ask them to marry us. They would never refuse. If not that, sweet love, why not the J.P.? And you say that a marriage by a J. of Peace is binding, why not do it? So as we are married we need not mind how, dear love of my soul.

I knew, sweet love, you would dislike my jackets. I tell M/ and P/ I look a fright in it, but they like them. If I had known it was your pipe in my window, darling love Emile, I would have taken it in, but I fancied it was some man's. You, sweet dear darling, a kiss, a fond dear embrace, a kiss, my love, my life, my beloved husband.

I hope, darling, your excuse to Lane and D. E. in the spring will be that you have your wife at home, and cannot leave her. I will be so happy if that is the case. I should so much like to be your wife. My love, I long for it. I sigh and wish I were near you, dear love. I do most sincerely love you with my heart and soul. I adore you, you dear little love of a husband.

Emile, my husband, my love, you dear, sweet love, I would like to have a child, because I know you are fond of children and I would I am sure love the child, you dear love, were the father of. Yes, Emile, I would be very sorry if we had no family, only I would be very jealous of a baby as I would then not get so much of your love. I would envy every loving word or look you bestowed on the child. Emile, I love you much, as much as I can. I dote on you with heart and soul. You will be sure to spoil me. You will pet me far too much. I have not been accustomed to much petting, so will be spoiled by you, I am sure, dear love, my truly dear love, my Emile.

Everyone is asking why Bessie and I are not walking in Sauchiehall. St. in the afternoon. Mama was quite annoyed we did not go out several times this week in the afternoon. You don't mind when Mama is with us. When we go with her, she always comes home by Sauchiehall. St.

Dearest love, I am doing all I can to be good. Considering the way we walked every other winter I am behaving very well. But, sweet Emile, you don't think so. I fancy I see by your look.

Again love, a kiss for your darling letters, dear kind Emile. A fond dear, dear embrace, much love and kisses, my best wishes. Heaven be kind to you, my husband.

I am thy fond, thy loving wife thy own ever dear devoted Mini L'Angelier

P.S. Thursday Evening, six or eight o'clock. A letter, my love, my pet, my ever fond one. And, Emile, love, in your next letter please fix the next night you will give me a letter you may be engaged the night I fix, and I would rather you would fix the night always. If I cannot take in your note, C. H. will do it for me. Adieu, my love, my pet, my husband. Good night, dearest love, a kiss.

26 THE TURNING POINT
GLASGOW, 1857

Madeline stood at the foot of Emile's iron cot, and braced herself as he laced up her corset. Since the night at Row, and despite promises of wanting to wait, they weakened and were intimate several times. This time, she arrived with Christina on the pretext of going to market, but then sent her ahead, allowing them time alone.

"When are we going to marry, Madeleine? You told me you were saving up enough money to be with me by September. But September has come and gone, and we're still not married. Will we be together this March?"

"I wondered if we could marry somewhere other than Glasgow, Emile. What do you think? I've thought about our situation constantly. If the Banns were read here in Glasgow, Papa would hear about it for sure. I've already mentioned this in my letters. However, if we were to go away, and marry elsewhere, then by the time he hears about it, it will be too late."

"Is that what you want to do, Madeleine? Marry in secret, as if we were some sort of criminals, hiding from everyone?"

"Of course not, pet. But what alternative do we have? I fear when the Banns are read, someone will tell either Mama or Papa, I just know it. Madeleine is not a common name. My surname maybe, but link them together, and someone will recognise the name as being mine. It's too much of a risk. I don't know what to do."

"Why don't you admit you're reluctant to marry me because I'm poor, and I'd be an embarrassment to you and your family. I'm not good enough for the likes of you. I've heard the rumours about you and William Minnoch. I've heard how you and he are spending quite a lot of time in each other's company."

Every sentence was punctuated with hard tugs on the laces, making her catch her breath each time.

"Minnoch means nothing to me, Emile. He's just the family friend who lives above us. It's inevitable I'd see him from time to time. Yes, I've been to the opera with him but there's no need for you to be jealous, my love. It's you, and you alone I love. When are you going to realise money is not important to me, Emile? I'd marry you tomorrow if I could. I'd be happy living in a place like this. I think it's rather delightful."

She waited for him to do up the numerous pearl buttons on her dress before moving away from him. She trailed her fingers over the roughly hewn desk that served several purposes in his one-bedroomed living space, before turning to face him.

"Perhaps we should elope without my father's consent. What say you, my love?"

She grabbed his hand in both of hers and said, "Darling Emile, let's elope. Let's do it soon! I don't know why I didn't think of it sooner. It would solve all our problems. Once we're married, Papa will have to accept you."

He snatched his hand away as if her flesh were glowing coals. His lip curled in scorn as he said, "I expected to marry up into society, Madeleine, I didn't expect to marry down!"

"What do you mean?"

"Do you think you will still keep your inheritance if we eloped? Oh, yes! Let's elope and risk the chance of your father making you penniless with the stroke of a pen. Do you think you could live on my ten shillings a week? Living here in one-bedroom lodgings after where you live?" His laughter followed, devoid of joy, heavy with rancour. The prominent vein on his forehead stood out, indicative of his level of anger.

"You never think things through, do you Madeleine? What a silly, impetuous, vacuous young woman you are!"

She stared at him in disbelief. As he continued to rant, the scales fell from her eyes. How could she not have seen it? She questioned his motives. Had Emile seduced her as a ploy to change his social status? Had he seen her as a marriage of opportunity? Had he used her in the worst possible way? Seconds later, the possibility of it all hit her full force. She felt ill. How could she have been so naïve?

She needed air. She needed to leave. She turned her back on him, and retrieved her bonnet, dangling by its silk ribbons on the brass door hook. Her hands trembled as she tied the bow under her chin with some difficulty. The task allowed her a few moments to compose herself before she was able to face him again.

"Christina will be waiting for me, I have to go."

He reached out to kiss her, but she side-stepped him, and closed the door.

27 MOST DISPLEASED
GLASGOW, 6 JANUARY 1857

Madeleine remained indoors for as long as possible over the winter, fearing she would bump into William Minnoch again. She and Mama had done just that last November. To her horror, not only had he stopped and spoken to them, but he had joined them on their walk down Buchanan Street.

Not that she didn't like William Minnoch, she did. But she was petrified Emile would see them, or someone would tell him she and Minnoch were walking out together. She wrote to Emile in the evening confessing all, letting him know first-hand how Minnoch had ended up walking with them.

She remembered the exchange of hot words between Emile and herself the day after her letter. He had come to the house later that night, fuming.

"I demand to know what William Minnoch means to you, Madeleine!"

"He means nothing to me, my love. I swear."

He grabbed her arm, and loomed over her, speaking to her inches away from her face.

"You're hiding something from me, my dear. Don't let me find out you're telling me untruths."

"Please, my love, calm yourself. It is only you I love."

"Then start showing me. You disobey my orders by parading up and down the streets, causing a stir, and having the local town boys following you around like the Pied Piper! Start behaving like a wife. My wife! Afford me some respect as your husband! I'm fast running out of patience, Madeleine. If you cross me, it will be the last thing you'll do."

She had listened in stony silence, but thereafter refused all offers from her family to walk down the second most fashionable street in Glasgow.

The incident in Emile's lodgings had changed her position on certain matters. For the first time, she began examining her relationship and his treatment of her. She realised she was being forced to be someone she was not. In addition, she was haunted by the thoughts that he saw her as a way of elevating his social position. Something Mama had pointed out some months back, but she had ignored at the time. If this were true, he had ensnared her in an elaborate plan from which she now had no escape.

*

Gnawing doubts followed long periods of introspection. Did Emile love her for who she was or for what she was? Sadly, she did not know the answer, and if it were true that he saw her as a way of bettering himself, the situation was too hideous to contemplate. It was terrifying.

She stood up abruptly and turned to her sister who was reading a copy of *Jane Eyre* in the corner of the drawing room. One of the few books they were allowed to read.

"Bessie, would you like to go for a walk? I need some fresh air. I've been cooped up in this house for months!"

"Well, it isn't for want of asking you, Lena. If you want to go, we can go now. I'll just need to fetch my bonnet."

The two sisters were not close, but on occasion they were known to put their differences aside, and it seemed like today was one of those days.

The two girls sailed down the steps and linked arms as they made their way across the street towards the shops and the excitement of the main town's thoroughfare. The pavements were thronging with people. They skirted around the street doctor selling peppermint cough lozenges from his portable stand, and the shoe shine boy who seemed to have more blackening on his face than on the shoes he was polishing.

Once their path was relatively clear they chatted away, nodded at acquaintances, and flirted harmlessly with a few young men they knew from the various balls and dinner parties they had frequented. The men returned the playful smiles, and lifted their hats in their direction.

Suddenly, Madeleine's smile died on her lips. Emile was storming towards them. She wondered if he would stop and talk. He did not. Instead, he bowed curtly and carried on up the road not giving her a second glance.

She was vexed with herself, Emile, and the whole situation. Of all the times she had remained indoors, and on the one afternoon she had gone out, she was caught red-handed disregarding his wishes of staying off the streets, and remaining at home.

There would be no escaping his wrath. However, she remained defiant and continued her walk. There was no point in closing the stable door after the horse had bolted. She would enjoy the outing and take pleasure in knowing that she was finally regaining her independence.

*

Friday, 3 o'clock, afternoon.

My very dear Emile,

I ought ere this to have written you. hope your hand is better, do take care of it, my own sweet, pet. Try and soon get well. I hope you have no cold.

Well, my dear Emile, you did look cross at your Mimi this afternoon. Why, my pet, you cannot expect I am never to go on Sauchiehall Street?

Sometimes I must. It is not quite fair of you. I have kept off that street so well this winter, and yet when you met me, and the first time you have bowed to me this season that you should have looked so cross. When I saw you, my little pet, coming, I felt frightened even to bow to you.

But I hope the next time I have the pleasure of meeting you, love, you will have a smile, one of your own dear, sweet smiles. The smile I love to see on your face. Adieu, a fond kiss. I am, ever and ever your own devoted and loving,

Mini L'Angelier

28 THE LETTERS
GLASGOW, 22 - 25 JANUARY 1857

Looking at her relationship from every angle, Madeleine knew she had no choice but to end it for the final time. This time, family members did not influence her decision. The choice was hers, and hers alone. The reasons for doing so were many.

The disparity in class had never bothered her. Instead, Emile's numerous jealous rages and his smothering, controlling behaviour had become insufferable. The never-ending cycle of melodrama, and his unreasonable behaviour were emotionally draining. She no longer enjoyed what they had. If she were honest, he had turned out worse than Papa.

The catalyst for her decision, the ugly truth that leaped to mind, still with uncertainty, was that his attentions were not for her, but cast far wider; fixed on her family's status and wealth. Grudgingly, she conceded to the murky revelation, her parents may well have been right, after all. If all were true, his actions had been dishonourable and she deserved better. Unable to see how she could extract herself from this intricate web of subterfuge he had possibly spun; ruining her with the intent of ownership, and staining her virtue, the prospects left her feeling helpless and at the feet of mercy.

*

As the cracks appeared in her relationship with Emile, William Minnoch became her saving grace. He called on the Smith house often, and invited Madeleine to countless social events which she actively encouraged. He even presented her with a gold necklace in order to cement his feelings of a promised future.

As a hopeless flirt, initially it thrilled her to have two men jostling for her affections. After the episode in Emile's lodgings, her encouragement towards Minnoch increased. She was sure it would not be long before he would ask for her hand in marriage.

She gave little consideration to how she was going to end her association with Emile. Impetuosity and a head swimming with romantic notions afforded little room for reason. Only lately had she realised the gravity of losing her virginity and the implications thereof. Would Minnoch ever suspect she had been broken in? Could a man feel or know such a thing? Her inexperience added to her misery of not knowing the answer.

She knew Emile well enough to know he wouldn't give her up so easily. She bitterly regretted everything. His emotional flux and mental fragility meant ending this relationship would have to be done with great care.

*

For Mr. L'Angelier, at Mrs. Jenkins, 11 Franklin Place, Great Western Road, Glasgow.

Thursday, twelve o'clock.

My dear Emile,
I was so very sorry that I could not see you to-night. I had expected an hour's chat with you, but we must just hope for better the next time.

I don't see the least chance for us, my dear love. Mama is not well enough to go from home, and my dear, little sweet pet, I don't see how we could manage in Edinburgh, because I could not leave a friend's house without their knowing of it, so, sweet pet, it must at present be put off 'til a better time. I see no chance before March. But rest assured, my dear love Emile, if I see any chance I shall let you know of it. Yes, my dear love, I shall.

My dear love, I shall have your note to-morrow. How happy it will make me feel, you sweet, dear little pet. You shall have a note Monday morning from me.

I hope Mary is well. We were at Partick today in the rain, in a cab.

Emile, take care of yourself. God bless you, make you happy. Adieu. Good-night. I wish I were with you, I would be happier than I am. Again farewell, with much, much love, and warm loving kisses. I am, with much love, forever your own dear, sweet little pet wife.
Your own fond,
Mini L'Angelier

29 A PROPOSAL
ROW, 28 JANUARY 1857

Madeleine couldn't stop thinking she was a pawn in Emile's elaborate game of social betterment. She replayed the last two year's events in her head, trying to see what she had missed. What signs should she have seen? What had they been, and why had she not seen them?

She felt used, betrayed, angry, and sad. That day, as he had laced up her corset, her love for Emile had died as suddenly as it had sprung up. She mourned for what was lost; a deep love she once had, and for her virginity, given away in blind trust. There was no going back, but what could she hope for? Who would want her now she was ruined, second-hand goods? Her thoughts returned to William Minnoch.

She was no longer keeping him at bay, and she hoped he would free her from a hideous predicament she could share with no one. She enjoyed his company more than she allowed herself to admit. The more time she spent with him, the more she liked him. He was intelligent, witty, and fun to be with. He suited her vivacious personality. More importantly, he never criticised, or made her feel wanting. He was all Emile was not.

She was guilty of toying with Minnoch's affections. This she acknowledged. For months she had given him no signs of encouragement, despite his persistence, until recently.

That afternoon, she wrote the letter to Emile she had dreaded to write for some time. In it she asked for a hiatus, for she needed time to think.

The following day her letter was returned, unopened.

Although not the first time he had treated her letters this way, it gave her opportunity to feel vindicated for her actions. The proverbial millstone fell away.

*

Madeleine embarked on a mission to encourage Minnoch in earnest. The time they spent with each other increased at her invitation. Although she didn't love him as she had Emile, she liked him enough to want to spend the rest of her life with him, if he were to ask. In addition, her decision of accepting him was channeled via the expectations of Mama and Papa, and there was no point anymore in trying to go against their wishes.

Evening after evening they frequented concerts at the City Hall, went to dinner parties with friends and family, both in Glasgow, and in the country. William even bought tickets to Bell's Alliance Circus one Saturday matinee performance, much to Madeleine's delight. Thrupence each gave them access to a spectacular show of tight-rope walkers, gymnastic artistes, and vaulters on cantering horses with flowing manes and flanks of rippling muscle. It was a magical afternoon that Madeleine would remember for many years to come.

Her time with Minnoch was not monitored. Her parents allowed her the freedom to walk with him un-chaperoned. During these times, she focused on what he was saying, without distractions, and realised what a decent person he was. They talked about pressing societal issues; how he wanted to alleviate poverty, how Glasgow's lack of sanitation brought disease to the less fortunate, and the desire to become involved in local politics and business affairs.

Each time they spoke he treated her as an adult and an equal. Despite the age difference between them, he asked her advice, and was interested in her replies. It surprised her more than anything; he valued her opinions, and she liked him the more for it.

She did not deny that she had set her sights on him with an ulterior motive, but there was mutual respect and shared interests, admiration for each other's minds, and for who they were. A love enough, she hoped, built to last.

They walked around the extensive gardens of Row, passing the steps near to where she had been intimate with Emile. Flashes of impropriety were followed by waves of shame as she tried to block out the images. To distract her thoughts she placed a gloved hand in the crook of William's arm and turned to look at the loch; a broad ribbon of blue threading through forests of green.

"It's a beautiful view, is it not, William? I never tire of looking at it."

"It is indeed, Madeleine."

He turned to face her, his eyes probing her soul for surety that he would not be rebuffed. His nervousness showed, wondering if he had read her incorrectly. He grasped both her hands in his, and continued, "But not nearly as beautiful as you. I am only truly happy when I am with you."

He faltered before he continued.

"I haven't spoken to your father yet, Madeleine, but if you would have me, I'd like you to be my wife. I would be a good provider. You would want for nothing."

Although she had been expecting the words, she hesitated before answering. She continued to gaze at the man who wanted to marry her, unwittingly being the knight in shining armour she so desperately needed, all the while her thoughts were of Emile and what they had done. What if William ever found out? What would he do?

William, a man from her own social class, was offering her a way out of her shameful predicament. He was waiting for her answer, and she felt she could keep him waiting no longer.

"I would like that very much, William."

He clasped her around the waist, drew him to her, and planted a chaste kiss on her forehead, before letting go.

"Oh, my dear, I'm the happiest man alive. Let's go and ask your father to give us his blessing. I don't want to wait a minute longer."

The pair arrived back at the house breathless and laughing, having run for most of the way. While Madeleine rushed off to find her mother, William Minnoch needed a few minutes to compose himself before rapping on the study door, hoping her father was on the other side.

The drawing room was a chaotic scene minutes later. Voices masked voices, and laughter was interspersed with squeals of delight coming from the female household. Her parents, elated by the news, did not hesitate to give them their blessing. Janet Smith kissed William on both cheeks, welcoming him to the family. James Smith thumped him on the back, pumped his hand, and congratulated him on an excellent choice of a wife.

*

Inwardly James Smith sighed with relief. His headstrong, wayward daughter was going to settle down to become a respectable, married woman. The day had not come soon enough. He just hoped William was the man to tame her. He had an inkling that he was.

30 MARRIAGE PLANS
GLASGOW, FEBRUARY 1857

Alexander Miller stood in the yard at Huggins & Co. listening to Emile chatting away about his plans for the future. Having heard them all before he was still kind enough to listen to them anyway.

"Well then, Alex! Didn't I say I was to be married?"

"Several times, Emile, but each time you named a date no wedding took place. Dare I remind you, you're still a bachelor?"

"That's true, though through no fault of our own, I might add. Families can be interfering when it comes to matters of the heart."

Miller swung a cotton bale off the wagon as he continued to off-load, large sweat stains marking his shirt, despite the cold weather in the yard.

"Oh, aye, so when is the wedding then, or is this date going to come and go, like all the rest?" teased Alex.

"Not this time, definitely not this time. We will be marrying at the end of the month."

"So who's the lucky lady, Emile? You keep talking about your sweetheart but you've never told me who she is."

"Well, we like to keep it a secret. Her name is Madeleine Smith."

"Can't say I know her. Where does she work?"

"She doesn't work. She's a lady, Miller. She's the daughter of James Smith, the architect."

Alexander Miller dropped the bale at his feet and whistled.

"And her father has agreed to this marriage?"

"Why wouldn't he? Do you think I'm not good enough for her?"

"It's not important what I feel. It's what her father thinks."

"It'll happen. I'm looking forward to finding something better after that."

"What will you do if you can't marry her?"

Emile's face darkened.

"Believe me. There is nothing preventing us from marrying if certain parties were privy to some truths. I couldn't marry her I may as well kill myself."

"You cannot mean that, it's a sin to talk so."

"I don't consider it a sin taking one's life to be out of this world, being tired of it, having lost all happiness. I don't consider it a sin at all."

"I have to say, I don't agree. Your life is not your own. You have no right to do what you choose with it. You can't mean what you say."

"Ah, but there you are mistaken, Miller, my dear man. I mean exactly what I say. I always do."

31 RUMOURS AND JEALOUSY
GLASGOW, FEBRUARY 1857

One Monday night, a few days after her official engagement, Emile rattled the tip of his walking stick across the window bars, metal striking iron in staccato blasts, jolting Madeleine once again out of a deep sleep. Janet turned over, mumbled something, and then fell back to sleep. Madeleine slid out of bed, making as little disturbance as possible. She pulled up the blind and peered out.

Under the cover of darkness she could see nothing. She knew he was there, she had heard him. Or had she? She turned to go when his grey, tan and black plaid trousers stepped into view. He bent down and peered at her in the gloom.

"What are you doing here, Emile? Everyone has gone to bed. I wasn't expecting you," she whispered fiercely.

"I need to talk to you, Madeleine. Now! It cannot wait."

"Emile! For goodness sake! What could be so important? You cannot come here unannounced and risk being seen. Why would you do such a thing?"

"I've something to ask. It cannot wait."

"It's late now, Emile. We'll meet tomorrow in the park, just before noon."

"No, Madeleine. I need to speak to you now. Open up the back door."

Madeleine lit a candle and reached for a night jacket that covered the top of her nightdress. She made sure it was buttoned all the way up to her neck, before opening up the door.

"You cannot come in tonight, Emile. I'm really sorry but ..."

Emile didn't wait for her to finish. Instead he brushed past her and made his way to the kitchen. With little choice she followed, closing the door to muffle their voices.

Her heart sank. She knew the look all too well. The vein on his forehead was throbbing. She waited for the eruption, and it came soon enough. When he spoke his voice was icy cold and he looked at her with disdain.

"It has come to my attention, Madeleine, you continue to spend a disproportionate time with William Minnoch. I have come to find out first hand if the rumours are true."

Madeleine needed to diffuse the situation. She grappled with words she hoped would placate him. She wasn't sure what he had heard.

"Why do you always question who I am seen with?"

"Madeleine, you are skirting around the issue. I've heard from a most reliable source you've been to concerts, recitals, and countless other functions with this man. Do I need to go on?"

"Emile, there's no need to be jealous. I like music, and so does Minnoch. Mama is often sick so she cannot accompany me, and Papa is too busy with his business. Going to concerts is a pleasant diversion one takes from being in Glasgow. Please pet, don't be quarrelsome. You don't expect your Mimi to stay at home all day, every day, do you? I cannot go to parties, or operas, or even take a walk in the street, anymore. Your demands are becoming unreasonable."

"Don't spurn my affections, Mimi. How many times do I have to tell you I love you before you start to believe me? How many? You go out and see other men while I have to look from afar. You are my wife, God damn it! I expect you to act like one!"

His voice was rising, and Madeleine was petrified others would hear them.

She placed a finger to her lips to warn him.

"Hush, my love, calm yourself, you'll wake the household, and then what?"

He dropped his voice, and continued.

"I am nothing to you; a mere diversion, a dalliance, a plaything! You don't love me as much as I love you. You're often so cold to me, pushing me away, and I continue to hear there is another man paying attention to you, attentions you seem happy to receive. How dare you behave so! You make me miserable, Madeleine. I sometimes wish I were dead and we had never met."

Tears coursed down his cheeks as he slumped into a chair, shoulders rounded, head hanging down. Madeleine sympathised for he was in obvious distress. Pangs of guilt softened her stance.

"Please don't cry Emile. I'm sorry if I've made you so unhappy. This was never my intention. Would you like some cocoa, my love? It's cold outside. Let me give you something warm to drink."

She moved to the range to boil some water but before she could he was out of his chair and by her side. His demeanour turning ugly. He spun her around and pinned her arms to her sides.

"No amount of cocoa can make me feel better about myself. I'm warning you, Madeleine. Don't play with my feelings. What we have is not something trivial."

She was frightened by his wrath and moved to the safety of the pantry. However, he followed, looming over her in a threatening manner and grabbing her arm to prevent her from taking a step further.

"Don't you dare walk away from me when I'm talking to you. I command your obedience!"

"Emile, please stop! Let go of me, you're hurting me."

Her pleas were ignored. Instead the grip on her arms intensified.

"I'm telling you this once, and only once. I do not want to hear of you going off with Minnoch like some wanton harlot. You are my wife and you'll behave with propriety. If you don't, I'll be forced to tell both Minnoch and your father about us, Madeleine. I'll tell them how you allowed me to know every inch of your body. How you permitted me to touch you in places only a husband should. How you eagerly engaged in, and might I remind you, enjoyed our sexual encounters. Do you think Minnoch will still want you after that? And what about your father, will he continue to see you as the dutiful daughter you pretend to be? I think not, my dear Madeleine. More likely you will be tossed out onto the streets to join the rest of the whores who ply their wares. You play a dangerous game."

He finished with a sneer and relaxed his grip long enough for Madeleine to free her right arm and strike him hard across his left cheek as quick as a rattlesnake.

He recoiled in shock and then retaliated, knocking her down with the back of his hand.

She lay sprawled out on the cold, stone flag floor. Her body ached more than her pride, but she refused to cry. That would come later.

He stood over her, unmoved.

"Take heed, my dear Madeleine. You are mine, and always will be. There is nothing you can change about what we did, nor what you have become. Unlike you, I did not destroy your letters. I have them all, every single one of them. I will not hesitate to show them to Minnoch or your father. And as for you, God strike me down dead if I ever meet you again!"

*

The night brought little sleep for Madeleine. She tossed and turned, replaying the events hours earlier. How did their relationship end up like this?

There seemed no way of evading an escalating nightmare. Worse still, he had struck her. Papa would never have struck mama. For the first time she was afraid of Emile.

She had to make him understand the affair was over without him resorting to jeopardizing the rapport she had with the two most important men in her life. She felt trapped, and her situation seemed hopeless, for she had no remedy.

If only she had heeded her parents. What would become of her now? She had been certain that after the seduction, marriage to Emile would follow. The possibility that it might not, had never entered her head.

What if Minnoch ever discovered her sordid secret? What would her friends and family say? What terrible gossip would spread to wider social circles? Emile's blackmail threats were real. Her cheeks burned with mortification and she cried into her pillow, muffling the sobs so Janet would not wake up.

For the first time in her life, she cared what other people thought, and what they would say. She would go from being Madeleine Smith, belle of Glasgow, to Madeleine Smith, fallen woman and pariah of polite society. She would be disgraced, and humiliated, by her lustful indiscretions; scandalised by the women, and the centre of ribald jokes by the men. She wished she could turn back the clock, but it was far too late for any of that now.

*

When she left her bed in the morning she moved to the mirror and saw livid bruises on her upper arms where Emile had gripped her. Her body ached all along the left side where she had made contact with the floor. She avoided Christine's questioning eyes as she helped her dress. Instead, her thoughts raced on, trying to think of ways to redefine the conditions of their association.

She needed to tread cautiously, placing distance between herself and Emile by writing letters that were no longer ardent but cool and aloof, yet not too distant to raise his suspicions. She needed to keep his trust. More importantly, she needed those letters back. Without those, he had the power to destroy her. She needed to convince him that her love was undivided and to hand over the letters that could expose her dark and lustful secrets.

Sleep eluded Madeleine that night, and many more to follow. The hours were crammed with tortured thoughts of her plight and possible solutions to putting it right.

*

Mr. L'Angelier, 14 Franklin Place, Great Western Road, Glasgow

Tuesday morning

My Dear Emile,
The day is cold, so I shall not go out - I shall spend a little time in writing you.
Our meeting last night was peculiar. Emile, you are most unreasonable. I do not wonder at you not loving me as you once did. Emile, I am not worthy of you. You deserve a better wife than me. I see misery before me this winter. I would to God we were not to be so near Mr. Minnoch. You shall hear stories and believe them. You will say I am indifferent because I shall not be able to see you much.
I forgot to tell you last night that I shall not be able to spend the happy hours we did last winter. Our letters - I don't see how I am to do. Mama will be watching every post. I intended to speak to you of all this last night but we were so engaged otherwise.
I do hope you got home safe and that you have got no cold – tell me love. I could not sleep all night I thought of your unhappy appearance – you shed tears love, I did not. Yes, you must think me cool – but it is in my nature. I never did love anyone till I loved you – and I shall never love another.
Love, Emile, my sweet darling, causes unhappiness in more ways than one. I know you will quarrel with me this winter. I know it well, sweet love – but God only knows, dearest that I have no desire ever to be parted from you, so Emile, my own sweet Emile, if we should ever part it will be on your side, not mine.
I sometimes fancy you are disappointed in me. I am not what you once thought I was. I am too much of a child to please you. I am too fond of amusement to suit your fancy. I am too indifferent, and I do not mind what the world says in the least – I never did.
I promised to marry you knowing I would never have my father's consent. I would be obliged to marry you in a clandestine way. I knew you were poor. All those I did not mind. I knew the world would condemn me for it, but I did not mind. I trust we have days of happiness before us – but God knows we have days of misery, too.
Emile – my own dear husband, I have suffered much on your account from my family. They have laughed at my love for you – they taunted me regarding you. I was watched all last winter. I was not allowed out by myself for fear I should meet you – but if I can, I shall cheat them this winter.
I shall write you as often as I can – but it cannot be three times a week, as it has been. And speaking of writing you, I intend to change the day – Monday, it is not convenient for me to post

a letter for you on Sunday. I thank you very much, my dear love for being at such trouble to come and see me. I thank you truly from my soul, and do accept a dear embrace. I shall never forget last night.

There is a sentence still in my ear you said about God striking you dead if ever you meet me again. Since my childhood that is a sentence I have shuddered to hear expressed. When I was very young, about five years, a woman made use of that sentence on my Grandpapa's farm, and she was struck dead that hour. It has never left me since. I heard you say it. I do hope you were none the worse of coming out.

Darling Emile, believe me, I love you – yes, I do, and that, most sincerely. I have come to the conclusion that you do not know me. If you were with me long, you would know me better. It is only those I love that I am indifferent to – even to my dog, which I love. Sometimes I hate it, and for no reason – it is only a fancy which I cannot help. To strangers it is different. I do love you truly, fondly.

Do you still wish to show your likeness to a friend? I hope I did not show much temper to you last night. Did I, sweet love?

Adieu for the present. A very fond embrace to you sweet husband. I am ever true and ever loving,
Mimi L.

*

Madeleine's intent of trying to win him over failed for her letters were again returned. She was annoyed he continued to treat her so. She lost her temper, and where she had promised to tread with caution, she wrote a scathing letter to him instead, revealing the full extent of her ire.

*

Mr. L'Angelier, Mrs. Jenkins, at 11 Franklin Place, Great Western Road, Glasgow.

I felt truly astonished to have my last letter returned to me. But it will be the last you shall have an opportunity of returning to me. When you are not pleased with the letters I send you, then our correspondence shall be at an end, and as there is coolness on both sides our engagement had better be broken.

This may astonish you, but you have more than once returned me my letters, and my mind was made up that I should not stand the same thing again. And you also annoyed me much on Saturday by your conduct in coming so near me. Altogether I think owing to coolness and indifference (nothing else) that we had better for the future consider ourselves as strangers.

I trust to your honour as a gentleman that you will not reveal anything that may have passed between us. I shall feel obliged by your bringing me my letters and Likeness on Thursday evening at seven. Be at the Area Gate, and C. H. will (take) the parcel from you. On Friday night I shall send you all your letters, Likeness, etcetera. I insist you may yet be happy, and get one more worthy of you, than I. On Thursday at seven o'clock. I am, etc. M.

*

Mr. L'Angelier, Mrs. Jenkins, at 11 Franklin Place, Great Western Road, Glasgow

You may be astonished at this sudden change, but for some time back you must have noticed a coolness in my notes. My love for you has ceased, and that is why I was cool. I did once love you truly, fondly, but some time back I lost much of that love. There is no other reason for my conduct, and I think it but fair to let you know this. I might have gone on and become your wife, but I could not have loved you as I ought.

My conduct you will condemn, but I did at one time love you with heart and soul. It has cost me much to tell you this sleepless night, but it is necessary you should know. If you remain in Glasgow or go away, I hope you may succeed in all your endeavours. I know you will never injure the character of one you so fondly loved.

No, Emile, I know you have honour and are a gentleman. What has passed you will not mention. I know when I ask you that you will comply. Adieu.

*

Mr. L'Angelier, Mrs. Jenkins, at 11 Franklin Place, Great Western Road, Glasgow.

9th February, 1857

I attribute it to your having a cold that I had no answer to my last note. On Thursday evening you were, I suppose, afraid of the night air. I fear your cold is not better. I again appoint Thursday night first same place, Street Gate, seven o'clock. M.

If you cannot send me or bring me the parcel on Thursday, please write a note saying when you shall bring it, and address it to Christina. H. Send it by post.

*

Where Madeleine grew up knowing men to be honourable gentleman, Emile had not. Her hands shook as she read his curt note, refusing to send back or destroy her letters. These were his to do with what he liked, he told her. He reminded her, yet again, that he would not hesitate to present them to both her father and to Minnoch if she insisted on severing ties with him.

*

Immediately. Mr. L'Angelier, Mrs Jenkins, 11 Franklin Place, Great Western Road, Glasgow.

9th February, Monday Night.

Emile, I have just had your note. Emile, for the love you once had for me do nothing 'til I see you. For God's sake, do not bring your once loved Mimi to an open shame.

Emile, I have deceived you. I have deceived my mother. God knows she did not boast of anything I had said of you, for she, poor woman, thought I had broken off with you last winter. I deceived you by telling you she still knew of our engagement. She did not. This I now confess, and as for wishing for any engagement with another, I do not fancy she ever thought of it.

Emile, write to no one, to Papa or any other. Oh, do not 'til I see you on Wednesday night be at the Hamilton's at twelve, and I shall open my shutter, and when you come to the Area Gate, I shall see you.

It would break my mother's heart. Oh, Emile, be not harsh to me. I am the most guilty, miserable wretch on the face of the earth. Emile, do not drive me to death. When I ceased to love you, believe me, it was not to love another. I am free from all engagement at present.

Emile, for God's sake, do not send my letters to Papa. It will be an open rupture. I will leave the house. I will die. Emile, do nothing 'til I see you. One word to-morrow night at my window to tell me or I shall go mad. Emile, you did love me. I did fondly, truly love you, too.

Oh, dear Emile, be not so harsh to me. Will you not? But I cannot ask forgiveness, I am too guilty for that. I have deceived. Love for you at the time made me say Mama knew of our engagement. To-morrow one word and on Wednesday we meet. I would not again ask you to love me, for I know you could not. But oh, Emile, do not make me go mad.

I will tell you that only myself and Christina. H. knew of my engagement to you. Mama did not know since last winter. Pray for me for a guilty wretch, but do nothing. Oh, Emile, do nothing. Ten o'clock to-morrow night one line, for the love of God.

*

Tuesday morning.
I am ill. God knows what I have suffered. My punishment is more than I can bear. Do nothing till I see you. For the love of heaven, do nothing. I am mad, I am ill.

*

Mr. E. L'Angelier, Mrs. Jenkins, 11 Franklin Place, Great Western Road, Glasgow.

[Posted between 8.45 a.m. and 12.20 p.m., at Osborne Buildings Receiving Office, Glasgow, 14th February, 1857; deliverable between half-past 1 and 3 p.m. same day.]
Saturday.

My dear Emile, I have got my finger cut, and cannot write, so, dear, I wish you would excuse me. I was glad to see you looking so well yesterday. I hope to see you very soon.

Write me for next Thursday, and then I shall tell you when I can see you. I want the first time we meet, that you will bring me all my cool letters back, the last four I have written, and I will give you others in their place. Bring them all to me.

Excuse me more; just now it hurts me to write, so with kindest and dearest love, ever believe (me),
Yours with love & affection, M.

32 EXACTING REVENGE
GLASGOW, 9th FEBRUARY 1857

Emile sat at the kitchen table with his good friend and colleague, Thomas Fleming Kennedy. Kennedy, a lot older than Emile, was someone in whom he often confided. The pot belly stove, around which they sat, was pumping out heat, while at the same time, boiling water in the enamel kettle for their mugs of tea.

"How are you feeling these days, Emile? Have you recovered from that bad bout of yours last month?"

"My health has been poorly since being laid up for a week last month, and then just as I recovered, I was ill again last week. I was so ill I fell down on my bedroom floor before being able to crawl into bed. I did not even have the strength to call out to Mrs. Jenkins, my landlady. I've never been so ill in my life. To be sure, I thought I was dying."

Thomas removed the kettle, washed out the teapot with some of the hot water, placed a few teaspoons of loose tea in the bottom, and half-filled it up with the boiled water. Leaving it to draw he turned back to their conversation and brought up a more intimate topic.

"Emile, besides your poor health, I see something has been bothering you of late. Would you care to share that burden?"

"I wasn't aware it was obvious, Tom."

Tom Kennedy chuckled and said, "Emile, you wear your heart on your sleeve. Are you having more problems with your betrothed?"

"As you know my relationships never run smooth, but this one has reached an intolerable state of affairs. After months of promising to marry me, and to introduce me to her family, I've since heard rumours of late she is seeing William Minnoch, a very wealthy family friend, and it sounds as if the relationship is becoming quite serious. Of course she's denying it, but now she wants me to return her letters."

His eyes filled with tears as he relayed to his friend further details of his fragile courtship with Madeleine that he saw slipping away from him.

"She intimated in her last letter that she no longer loves me, and that there's coolness on both our sides. For me there's never been a coolness. I love her as much now as I did then."

"Do you think it's a rumour or an excuse? Do you have grounds for concern?"

"She trifles with my feelings, Thomas. One minute she tells me she loves me and wants to marry me, and the next she tells me she wants to end it all and demands her letters back. I'm not sure what to think. But I can tell you now I'll not return her letters. They are my leverage against her. She's mine and mine alone.

"If she wants to break up the relationship I'll expose her. I'll show the letters of where she describes our intimacy to both her father and her new love interest, William Minnoch. By the time I'm finished, Minnoch will want nothing to do with her. I'm not sure how her father will react, as I've never met the man. Not for want of trying, mind you. However, I'm hoping he'll save her from the shame that would follow if word got out, and have no choice but to allow us to marry, and save the family from a scandal they would want to avoid.

"I can assure you, if I showed you the letters there would be no misunderstanding of the full nature of our relationship. As such we are already man and wife under Scottish law. I'll never allow her to marry another man, as long as I live. Never!"

Thomas was stunned at the vehemence attached to what was being said.

"My God, man, talk some sense! You're talking about seduction and blackmail! Surely you wouldn't do that, Emile? You wouldn't expose the woman you love out of malice just to force her hand to be your wife? It would never work. She would be cast out from her family, disinherited, and left destitute. You hold this woman's reputation in your hands. Think of her, Emile. What you are proposing is dishonourable to the extreme."

"She leaves me no choice."

"Don't you think your behaviour is unbecoming as a gentleman?"

Emile thought about it for a moment, and then replied, "No doubt there'll be much talk about the way I have conducted myself, both during our time together and now, but I want to marry her, Thomas. She'll belong to none other, except me. It is the only way I can see the family agreeing to the arrangement."

"Emile, think of the type of marriage you'll have if you force her into marrying you. A marriage forced can bring no happiness. If she wants to end the relationship, let her go. And do the gentlemanly thing, even though you still love her, return her letters. Don't open her up to scandal and shame. You have to shoulder the main blame here. She's young and impressionable. You seduced her. You should've known better. Think of her, Emile. Don't ruin her because she has spurned you. She has a lot more to lose than you do. Do the right thing. Return the letters."

"Thomas, we've been friends for almost five years now, and being much older than myself, I've always valued your advice. And I can see why you would advise me against this, but this time I cannot agree with you. I've been mistreated by women numerous times and it's time they started to pay. I'll never return the letters. She will become my wife. I'm infatuated with her. She's my life, my universe. I fear though, one day she will also be the death of me."

33 PRUSSIC ACID
GLASGOW, APPROXIMATELY
10 FEBRUARY 1857

William Murray joined the Smith household as a houseboy back in November of the previous year. He was young and lazy, with a preference to standing around on street corners late at night talking to friends, rather than rising early and doing work for which he was employed. Living with the servants downstairs, Madeleine was more aware of his behaviour than the rest of her family. She made it her duty to keep a watchful eye on him, and occasionally, she used him to run errands for her.

On this particular morning, he was not shirking his responsibilities. He was diligently blackening the family's boots when he heard Miss Madeleine call out to him from her room nearby.

"William! Where are you?"

"Coming, miss. I'm in the kitchen, miss."

Replacing the lid to the Warren's blackening paste so it wouldn't dry out, he left the boots and walked the short distance to her bedroom further down the passageway. Because of her close proximity to the servants, calling out was preferable than ringing the bell.

"I need you to go to the apothecary for me this morning, William. Leave whatever you're doing. I want you to go now."

"Yes, miss. What do you need?"

"I want you to fetch me some prussic acid."

She handed him a note. He wasn't the best reader in the world, but he reached for the scrap of paper and held it at the edges in his grubby hands, still smeared with boot polish. He mouthed the words, 'a small phial of prussic acid'.

"Any apothecary will do. Off you go, and don't you dawdle on the way back, because if you do I'll box your ears on your return."

"No, miss. Yes, miss."

She shouted after him as he was disappearing down the passage, "And you be careful with that prussic acid. It's poisonous!"

He jammed his cap onto his head, and clutching the coins she had given him for the purchase, he left in search of the acid. The rest of the servants, who had heard the conversation, remained unperturbed, and returned to their morning duties.

Young William dashed off to 154 Sauchiehall Street to Dr. George Yeaman's surgery, the nearest shop from the house, which was also on the corner of Cambridge Street.

George Yeaman, a recently qualified M.D. from the class of '54, earned a reputation as a good practitioner. People knew him for his firm character, a clear intellect and one who was kind-hearted and faithful to his patients, and the public he served.

On entering his establishment William had to wait. He entertained himself by spinning the coin on the top of the counter and counting the revolutions, trying to beat his last record.

Dr. Yeaman reached out and flattened the coin.

"What can I do for you this morning, laddie?"

"I'd like a small phial of prussic acid, please."

"Is this for you?" enquired the doctor.

"No, sir, it is for Miss Madeleine. I work for Mr. James Smith on Blythswood Square."

"Ah, right. Well, you tell young Madeleine she'll have to come and ask me herself. I cannot give this over to you, it's a rank poison."

William did not dawdle on his way home. The threat of a box to the ears had not been forgotten. His face was flush with exertion by the time he arrived home.

"You didn't buy it then?"

"No, miss. I walked to Dr. Yeaman's surgery on Sauchiehall Street, but he says you'll have to come in and purchase it yourself. He says it's because it's a rank poison, miss."

"Never mind, then. I only wanted it for my hands. It wasn't important."

34 KEEPING A DIARY
GLASGOW, 11 - 17 FEBRUARY 1857

Emile had never kept a diary. However, all that changed after his evening spent with his good friend, Thomas Fleming Kennedy. On the following Monday morning he walked up Great Western Road in search of a stationery shop. There he purchased his first diary.

It was not expensive. It was not even distinguished. More like a notebook, he grudgingly admitted. However, it would suit the purpose.

The diary remained unused for two days until Wednesday, when he held a pencil, sharpened the point, and wrote:

"Wed. 11th Feb: Dined at Mr. J. Mitchell's
Saw M. @ 12 p.m. in C.H. Room."

Thereafter he made a couple of more entries. Some entries, discovered much later, did not happen on the dates that were entered. However, nevertheless, the diary entries were still written.

"Thurs. 12th Feb: Spent the even. @ Pat Kennedy's
Major Stuart and wife
Dr. Jameson & family"

"Friday, 13th Feb: Saw Mr. Philpott
Saw Mimi
Dinned at 144 Renfrew St"

"Sat. 14th Feb: A letter from M–"

"Sun. 15th Feb: St. Judas"

"Mon. 16th Feb: Wrote M–
Saw Philpotts"

"Tues. 17th Feb: Dined at 144 Renfrew St."

35 FALLING ILL
GLASGOW, 19 FEBRUARY 1857

Madeleine sat in the circle stall with William Minnoch and his two sisters. The four of them were at the opera hall that evening waiting for the curtain to go up. The three women giggled and gossiped from behind their fans, talking about people they knew. They fixed their pairs of pearl inlaid binoculars on the subjects under scrutiny, commenting on who was wearing what, and who was with whom for the evening.

Behind the scenes, most actors who were dressed were practising their lines. Others were waiting for the final touches to their makeup. Stagehands were bringing on the sets and final pieces of furniture to complete the effect. The director was fretting. He wrung his hands and wondered if the first show this evening would be better than the dress rehearsal the night before.

The opera this evening was *Lucrezia Borgia,* and the critical Glasgow audience, often hard to please, were looking forward to this performance. Madeleine thumbed through the program, and libretto with the music score that she could play at her leisure when she had the chance. It had an excellent cast, and with the opera receiving rave reviews in London, she was sure they were not going to be disappointed with tonight's performance.

The lights dimmed, voices were hushed, and the ruched velvet curtains with the gold detail rose. Those who did not have good seats shuffled forward for a better view. Excitement and expectation rippled across the hall. The orchestra struck the first chords, and the actors swarmed the stage. Act One had begun.

*

Emile's ill health continued. He could not put his finger on it. Other than the usual bile upsets and bouts of cholera, there were odd things happening to his body never experienced before. A lesion on his tongue brought him discomfort each time he ate or drank. After that, unsightly boils appeared overnight on the back of his neck.

However, nothing would prepare him for the illness that followed. After receiving the pass key from Mrs. Jenkins, Emile fastened the buttons to his coat, reached for his new hat and cane, before closing the door behind him. However, hours later, he couldn't remember much of the night's events. The following morning he felt as if he were at death's door. His mind was like thick treacle he was struggling to swim through, not even recognising the sound of knocking at his door.

"Come in," he finally managed.

His landlady peered at her lodger who lay on his back, and was immediately shocked at his pallor. His complexion, usually clear and fresh, was now yellow and dull, dark rings encircled eyes that looked sunken and hollow.

"I was wondering if you were alright as you didn't come down for breakfast this morning. Are you?"

"No, Mrs. Jenkins. I've been very unwell. Look what I've vomited." He pointed to the chamber pot sitting on the floor within easy reach in case it was needed in a hurry.

Annie Jenkins glanced at the pot and could see the contents were thick and greenish in colour.

"It looks like bile, Mr. L'Angelier. You need to stop eating those herrings and vegetables you're so fond of. I think you eat far too many vegetables. They're not good for you."

"Do you think so, Mrs. Jenkins? When I lived in France I suffered no ill-effects from a similar diet."

"Well, you're clearly not well now, are you? Why didn't you call on me?"

"I fell ill while I was on the road coming home. It seized me so sudden-like. I was seized by the most violent pains in my bowels and stomach. When I managed to return, I was so bad I collapsed on the floor trying to get undressed. I swear I thought I was going to die right there on the carpet and no human eye would see me. I was too weak even to ring the bell."

"My goodness! It sounds more serious than the last episodes. How do you feel now? Can I get you anything?"

"I'm feeling a bit better, thank you, Mrs. Jenkins. If I could trouble you for some tea, I'd be grateful. I don't feel strong enough to go out today. No breakfast, please, Mrs. Jenkins, just tea. I'm ever so thirsty."

"What you need is a doctor, Mr. L'Angelier. Do you want me to fetch one for you?"

"No, not at the moment, but if I feel a little better later on, I'll call on Dr. Steven."

After his tea, Emile fell into a restless slumber until about nine o'clock when, once again, Mrs. Jenkins tapped on his door.

"I've come to see how you're feeling. Are you any better?"

"Yes, thank you. I'm feeling a little better now, and I think I'll go out after all. I need to see to things at work. Just as well it is only two streets off. You've been very kind, thank you."

Emile left between ten and eleven o'clock and talked briefly with his fellow lodger, Amadée Thuau, before going to his place of work. However, the duties of his job were too much for him in his weakened state, and by three o'clock he had returned.

"Still no better, sir?" asked Annie Jenkins anxiously.

"I'm certainly better than last night, but definitely not better than the night before that. I still can't quench this thirst, no matter what I drink. If I may, can I have another cup of tea?"

"Of course. Go on up, and I'll bring you some."

"Thank you, Mrs. Jenkins. I also did as you bid and visited Dr. Steven. He has given me some medicine. Says he thinks I have picked up a touch of cholera."

"Cholera!" exclaimed Annie, looking most perturbed. "Not from this house, I can tell you."

"No, no, please don't upset yourself. Dr. Steven says it's doing the rounds in some places, so I could've picked it up from anywhere."

"Well, the illness has made a great change to you. You look yellow, and you've dark rings under your eyes. Take to your bed, sir, and I suggest you stay there until you're absolutely well."

"I think I will, Mrs. Jenkins. I'm so cold. All day I've been thirsty and cold."

*

Despite being so ill, Emile managed to update his new diary.

"Thurs. 18th Feb: Saw Mimi a few moments.
Was very ill during the night."

*

Glasgow, Mr. E. L'Angelier, 11 Franklin Place, Mrs. Jenkins, Great Western Road.

Wednesday.

Dearest, Sweet Emile,

I am so sorry to hear you are ill. I hope to God you will soon be better. Take care of yourself, do not go to the office this week, just stay at home 'til Monday. Sweet love, it will please me to hear you are well. I have not felt very well these last two days, sick & headache. Everyone is complaining; it must be something in the air.

I cannot see you Friday, as M/ is not away, but I think Sunday P/ will be away & I might see you, I think, but I shall let you know. I shall not be at home on Saturday, but I shall try, sweet love, and write you, even if it should be a word.

You did look bad Sunday night and Monday morning. I think you got sick with walking home so late and the long want of food, so the next time we meet I shall make you eat a loaf of bread before you go out.

I am longing to meet again, sweet love. We shall be so happy. I have a bad pen, so excuse this scroll, and B/ is near me. I cannot write at night now.

My head aches so, and I am looking so bad that I cannot sit up as I used to do, but I am taking some stuff to bring back the colour.

I shall see you soon again. Put up with short notes for a little time. When I feel stronger you shall have long ones. Adieu, my love, my pet, my sweet, Emile. A fond dear tender love and sweet embrace.

Ever with love,
Yours, Mimi

36 MORE HEALTH PROBLEMS
GLASGOW, 21 FEBRUARY 1857

George Murdoch, of the druggist Murdoch Brothers on Sauchiehall Street, was busy in the backroom of his apothecary one morning, when the bell above the door rang to announce a new customer. Madeleine had walked a mere three or four minutes from her house to the shop she now entered.

His young assistant Dickie was at the counter. Dickie looked up to see an unaccompanied, well-dressed woman in front of him.

"Good morning, madam. How may I assist you?"

"Good morning. I'd like to buy sixpence worth of arsenic please."

"Arsenic? One moment please."

James Dickie searched the back room looking for his employer. George Murdoch was counting out tablets and placing them in brown glass bottles. He waited until he had finished counting before speaking.

"Mr. Murdoch, I have a customer wanting to buy arsenic."

"Good you called me."

Murdoch approached the young lady. He knew her as one of his regular customers. "Oh, it's you, Miss Smith. Good morning."

She inclined her head in recognition.

"Is it arsenic you're after, Miss Smith?"

"Yes, it is, Mr. Murdoch. I'd like sixpence worth please."

"For what purpose do you require the arsenic?"

"For the garden and country house."

"Ah, the country house. Fine place your family has up on the Gareloch. Have a rat problem, do you?"

"Yes, yes, exactly."

"James Dickie will measure out the arsenic, but I'll need you to fill in the poison's register before you go."

He reached under the counter, opened up the book, and started writing in the details.

"*February 21 – Miss Smith, 7 Blythswood Square, 6d. worth of arsenic for garden and country-house. – M. H. Smith _____.*"

Madeleine signed her name in the space provided, and George Murdoch placed his own signature under hers as a witness.

Dickie arrived with the arsenic, which he double bagged, and handed over to Madeleine.

"How would you like to pay for that, Miss Smith?"

"Oh, could you please charge it to my father's account, if that's suitable?"

"I shall do that for you, Miss Smith. I see someone from your household has already been in today and ordered soda water. I'll add it to the same entry. Is that all?"

"Yes thank you. Good day to you."

*

Several days passed before George Murdoch saw Madeleine Smith once again. She did not want to purchase anything, but rather to ask a question.

"Mr. Murdoch, regarding the arsenic I bought from you the other day. I thought arsenic was white. However, on opening the packet I noticed it rather grey."

"Yes, that's right. Arsenic is white, but we mix ours with soot, to prevent accidental deaths. It's also laid down by the Act. Thus the colour. However, it doesn't affect its efficacy."

"Oh well, that would explain it then."

*

Emile's Diary Entries:

"Sat. 21st Feb.: Don't feel well
Went to the Kennedy's"

"Sun 22nd Feb: Saw Mimi in Drawing Room
Promises me French Bible
Taken very ill."

37 VIOLENTLY ILL AGAIN
GLASGOW, 23 FEBRUARY 1857

At four o'clock in the morning, Annie Jenkins's sleep was again interrupted by a ringing bell. She lit the candle to see which of her lodgers was calling. Before she even knocked on Emile's door she could hear him retching. It was the same kind of vomit as before, green in colour with a thick porridge-like consistency. This time, there was not as much of it in volume, but the colour was the same.

She stood and patted his back as he finished emptying the last of his stomach's contents into the china chamber pot. Passing him a cloth to wipe his mouth, she left to empty the pot out, and brought it back in case he needed it again.

He flopped back on the bed, eyes closed, sweating, and looking weak.

"Same as before?" she asked.

He managed a weak nod.

"Shall I call the doctor?"

His eyes remained closed. He shook his head.

"I'd like another blanket please. I'm very cold."

She fetched an extra blanket for him, and returned with a fresh pitcher of water, and a clean glass.

He managed a weak smile as she fussed about him.

"Thank you. I've such a great thirst."

"Did you go out after you dined here last night, sir? I thought you stayed home all night?"

"I ate supper and went straight to bed. I didn't go out at all."

"Well you rest now and I'll go boil some water for hot water bottles for your feet, and make you a nice cup of tea. Perhaps some slices of lemon with the water?"

Anne Jenkins spent the whole day running from the kitchen to the sickroom. During this time, she brought him blackened toast to eat, and a good many drinks; water, lemon water, tea, lemon tea, more water. He seemed unable to slake his thirst, no matter what she provided.

She was growing alarmed at his recurring illness, more so because of the other lodgers, and children of her own. What if he did have cholera, as the doctor thought he did? Would they all catch it?

She spoke in hushed tones to Thuau without telling him too much. She didn't want to share her thoughts with all her lodgers at this stage. He promised to fetch Dr. Thomson.

When Thomson arrived, he ordered Emile to tell him his symptoms.

"I'm not well, Doctor. I'm nauseous, and I've been vomiting and purging for several hours now. The pains in my stomach were so bad at one stage my legs just wouldn't support me."

"How long have you been feeling poorly?"

"For a couple of days now, but last night it became really bad."

"Open your mouth, please L'Angelier, I'd like to have a look at your tongue."

Emile did as he was instructed. The doctor noted the tongue was furry and patchy in appearance. He felt his pulse and found it running fast. Next, he felt his hot brow, and noticed his skin had taken on a yellowish hue.

"Well, Mr. L'Angelier, I don't think you have cholera. I think it's an oversupply of bile in your system. I also suggest you give up smoking. It's not doing your health any good. Take these powders, one a day, and I'll check on you tomorrow."

Annie Jenkins was most relieved to hear her house was cholera-free, but she was still concerned for her lodger, who remained in bed for more than a week. The doctor came to the house once more before Emile felt well enough to make a journey to the Bridge of Allan.

*

"Mon. 23rd Feb: Received a letter from Mrs. L"

38 INCRIMINATING LOVE LETTERS
GLASGOW, 27 FEBRUARY 1857

It was Friday afternoon and Auguste de Mean had started clearing his desk, as he did most weekdays before leaving the office for the weekend. There was a rap on his door. Looking up, he saw it was Emile L'Angelier.

The last time he had seen him had been at Helensburgh. He was relieved to see his friend looking better, although he refrained from enquiring about his health, in case he heard about it in detail. Instead, he stuck to a much safer topic, the weather.

"Dreadful weather, what? Can't believe how cold this February has been this year. Come and stand by the fire and warm yourself up. Tea? Coffee?"

"Tea please, coffee doesn't agree with me."

"Ah, yes. I forgot. So, to what do I owe this pleasure?"

He rang the bell, ordered a pot of tea, and continued clearing his desk as Emile sat in the chair opposite.

"I've come to ask your advice."

"Go on."

"Well, you know I've been seeing Madeleine Smith for a few years now.

"Yes."

"And I know you told me to go and speak to her father about our courtship, but I told you I couldn't because he forbade it."

"Yes."

"Well, I never could. It's been the most disastrous relationship with no way forward, and no way out."

"There's always a way out of these things, Emile. It's not as if you're married. You could break it off anytime you liked. However, I think your Miss Smith has solved all your problems, for I hear she's engaged to William Minnoch."

Emile's face curdled. The vein on his forehead pulsated, until with great restraint he managed, "That cannot be true! Madeleine assured me there was nothing between them. Who told you this, her father?"

"No, I've heard it from several public sources, but not from anyone in the family."

"Rumours, that's all they are."

"Are you sure, Emile? My sources were not the usual type to listen to frivolous gossip."

Emile sat for a while and said nothing.

"Well, if it comes to this, and it's true, I have documents in my possession sufficient to stop the banns. Her wedding to Minnoch will not take place."

By now Emile had Auguste de Mean's full and undivided attention.

"What possible documents could you have in your possession important enough to stop wedding banns being posted?"

"Love letters, de Mean, her love letters to me. I have kept each one of them, hundreds of them. Letters declaring her undying love for me and details of our sexual intimacy. Whoever reads those letters will be left in no doubt as to the true nature of our liaison."

*

Mr. E. L'Angelier, Mrs. Jenkins, 11 Franklin Place, Great Western Road, Glasgow.
[Posted at Glasgow, 27th February, 1857; deliverable next morning, first delivery.]

Friday.

My Dear, Sweet Emile,
 I cannot see you this week, and I can fix no time to meet you. I do hope you are better. Keep well, and take care of yourself. I saw you at your window. I am better, but have got a bad cold.
 I shall write you, sweet one, in the beginning of the week. I hope we may meet soon. We go, I think, to Stirlingshire about the 10 of March for a fortnight, excuse this short note, Sweet love.
 With much fond tender love and kisses. And ever believe me to be
 Yours, with love,
 Mimi

39 PLEADING FOR COMPASSION
GLASGOW, 2 - 4 MARCH 1857

The thought consuming Madeleine's time these days was not her recent engagement to William Minnoch, or the impending wedding set for 18th June, but how to persuade Emile to return her letters.

She bitterly regretted the love letters. At the time they were a channel through which she had expressed her feelings, unreservedly. Now they were damning evidence of her licentiousness and shameful behaviour.

If they were made public they would destroy her relationship with her family, her happiness with Minnoch and her social standing. She needed them returned. She would have to place herself at Emile's mercy and beg him to not expose her, to plead for clemency and compassion.

She knew he was angry with her. He was hurt by the constant swirling rumours of her connection to Minnoch. He no longer believed her when she told him they were unfounded. She knew it would only be a matter of time before someone would confirm her engagement. Would he be so cruel to carry out his threat?

At first she wondered if she could enter his rooms while he was at work and retrieve them. However, she realised she didn't know where they were kept. Perhaps they were not at his lodgings. Perhaps they were at his place of work instead.

Mr. E. L'Angelier, Mrs. Jenkins, 11 Franklin Place, Great Western Road, Glasgow.

Tuesday evening, 12 o'clock

Emile,

I have this night received your note. Oh it is kind of you to write me. Emile, no one can know the intense agony of mind I have suffered last night and today.

Emile, my father's wrath would kill me, you little know his temper. Emile, for the love you once had for me, do not denounce me to my Papa. Emile, if he should read my letters to you – he will put me from him, he will hate me as a guilty wretch. I loved you, and wrote to you in my first ardent love – it was with my deepest love I loved you. It was for your love I adored you. I put on paper what I should not. I was free because I loved you with my heart.

If he, or any other, saw those fond letters to you, what would not be said of me? On my bended knee I write you and ask you as you hope for mercy on Judgment Day, do not inform on me – do not make me a public shame.

Emile, my life has been one bitter disappointment. You and you only can make the rest of my life peaceful. My own conscience will be a punishment that I shall carry to my grave.

I have deceived the best of men. You may forgive me, but God never will. For God's love forgive me – and betray me not – for the love you once had for me, do not bring down my father's wrath on me. It will kill my mother (who is not well). It will forever cause me bitter unhappiness. I am humble before you and crave your mercy. You can give me forgiveness – and you, oh you can only make me happy for the rest of my life. I would not ask you to love me – or ever make me your wife. I am too guilty for that.

I have deceived and told you too many falsehoods for you ever to respect me. But oh, will you not keep my secret from the world? For Christ's sake, do not denounce me. I shall be undone. I shall be ruined. Who would trust me? Shame would be my lot. Despise me, hate me – but make me not the public scandal. Forget me forever. Blot out all remembrance of me. I have borne you ill. I did love you, and it was my soul's ambition to be your wife. I asked you to tell me my faults, and you did so, and it made me cool towards you gradually.

When you have found fault with me I have cooled – it was not love for another, for there is no one I love. My love has all been given to you. My heart is empty, cold. I am unloved. I am despised. I told you I had ceased to love you – it was true. I did not love as I did – but oh, till within the time of our coming to Town, I loved you fondly. I longed to be your wife. I had fixed February. I longed for it. The time I could not leave my father's house I grew discontent, and then I ceased to love you.

Oh, Emile, this is indeed the true statement. Now you can know my state of mind. Emile, I have suffered much for you. I lost much of my father's confidence since that September. And my mother has never been the same to me. No mother – she who gave me life, spare me from shame. Never, never while I live can I be happy. No. No. I shall always have the thought that I deceived you. I am guilty it will be a punishment I shall bear till the day of my death. I am humbled thus to crave your pardon. But I care not. While I have breath I shall ever think of you as my best friend if you will only keep this between ourselves. I blush to ask you. Yet Emile, will you not grant me this last favour to never reveal what is passed? Oh, for God's sake, for the love of heaven hear me. I grow mad. I have been ill with worry all day. I have had what has given me a false spirit. I had to resort to what I should not have taken but my brain is on fire. I feel as if death would indeed be sweet. Denounce me not.

Emile. Emile, think of our once happy days. Pardon me if you can, pray for me as the most wretched guilty miserable creature on the earth. I could stand anything but my father's hot displeasure. Emile, you will cause me death. If he is to get your letters I cannot see him anymore. And my poor mother. I will never more kiss her – it would be a shame to them all. Emile, will you not spare me this? Hate me, despise me, but do not expose me. I cannot write more. I am too ill tonight.

M.

*

Mr. E. L'Angelier, Mrs. Jenkins, Franklin Place, Great Western Road, Glasgow.

[Posted, Osborne Buildings Receiving Office, Glasgow, 3rd March, 1857; posted between 8.45 a.m. and 12.20 p.m.; deliverable between half-past 1 and 3 p.m. same day.]

My dearest Emile,

I hope by this time you are quite well, and able to be out. I saw you at your window, but I could not tell how you looked. Well, I hope. I am very well.

On Friday, we go to Stirling for a fortnight. I am so sorry, my dearest pet, I cannot see you before we go. I cannot. Will you, sweet one, write me for Thursday, eight o'clock, and I shall get it before I go which will be a comfort to me as I shall not hear from you till I come home again. I will write you, but, sweet pet, it may only be once a week as I have so many friends in that quarter.

I shall see you very soon, when I get home again and we shall be very happy, won't we, sweet one? As much so as the last time, my pet. I hope you feel well. I have no news to give you. I am very well and I think the next time we meet you will think I look better than I did the last time.

You won't have a letter from me this Saturday, as I shall be off but I shall write beginning of the week. Write me for Thursday, sweet love, and with kind love, ever believe me to be yours, with love and affection,
Mimi

*

Mr. E. L'Angelier, Mrs. Jenkins, 11 Franklin Place, Great Western Road, Glasgow.

[Posted at Glasgow, 4th March, 1857; deliverable between half-past 1 and 3 same day.]

Dearest Emile,

I have just time to give you a line. I could not come to the window as B/, and M/ were there, but I saw you. If you would take my advice, you would go to the south of England for ten days; it would do you much good. In fact, sweet pet, it would make you feel quite well. Do try and do this. You will please me by getting strong and well again.

I hope you won't go to B. of Allan, as P/ and M/ would say it was I brought you there, and it would make me to feel very unhappy. Stirling you need not go to as it is a nasty dirty little Town. Go to Isle of Wight.

I am exceedingly sorry, love, I cannot see you ere I go it is impossible, but the first thing I do on my return will be to see you, sweet love.

I must stop as it is post time. So adieu, with love, and kisses, and much love. I am, with love and affection, ever yours
Mimi

40 A LETTER FROM EMILE
GLASGOW, 5 MARCH 1857

Glasgow, March 5th, 1857

My dear, sweet pet Mimi,

I feel indeed very vexed that the answer I read, yesterday to mine of Tuesday to you should prevent me from sending you the kind letter I had ready for you.

You must not blame me, dear, for this, but really your cold, indifferent, and reserved notes, so short, without a particle of love in them (especially after pledging your word you were to write me kindly for those letters you asked me to destroy), and the manner you evaded answering the questions I put to you in my last, with the reports I hear, fully convince me, Mimi, that there is foundation in your marriage with another; besides, the way you put off our union 'til September without a just reason is very suspicious.

I do not think, Mimi dear, that Mrs. Anderson would say your mother told her things she had not, and really I could never believe Mr. Houldsworth would be guilty of telling a falsehood for mere talking. No, Mimi, there is a foundation for all this.

You often go to Mr. M/s house, and common sense would lead any one to believe that if you were not on the footing reports say you are you would avoid going near any of his friends. I know he goes with you, or at least meets you in Stirlingshire.

Mimi, dear, place yourself in my position and tell me am I wrong in believing what I hear. I was happy the last time we met yes, very happy. I was forgetting all the past, but now it is again beginning. Mimi, I insist in having an explicit answer to the questions you evaded in my last.

If you evade answering them this time, I must try some other means of coming to the truth. If not answered in a satisfactory manner, you must not expect I shall again write you personally or meet you when you return home.

I do not wish you to answer this at random. I shall wait a day or so if you require it. I know you cannot write me from Stirlingshire, as the time you have to write me a letter is occupied in doing so to others. There was a time you would have found plenty of time.

Answer me this, Mimi. Who gave you the trinket you showed me? Is it true it was Mr. Minnoch? And is it true that you are, directly or indirectly, engaged to Mr. Minnoch or to any one else but me? These questions I must know.

The doctor says I must go to B. of A. I cannot travel five hundred miles to the I. of W. and five hundred back. What is your object in wishing me so very much to go south? I may not go to B. of A. till Wednesday; if I can avoid going I shall do so for your sake. I shall wait to hear from you.

I hope, dear, nothing will happen to check the happiness we were again enjoying. May God bless you, pet, and with many fond and tender embraces believe me with kind love,

Your ever affectionate husband,

Emile L'Angelier

*

"Thurs. 5th March: A letter from Brown
Saw Mimi. Gave her a note and received one.
Saw 'Midsummer's Dream' "

41 MARY JANE BUCHANAN
GLASGOW, 6 MARCH 1857

The two girls collapsed with laughter as they emerged from the house on Blythswood Square. For a moment both were stuck in the doorway not big enough to accommodate their large, but very fashionable, crinoline dresses. After much merriment and jostling, they spilled out onto the landing, and stood underneath the portico taming the steel cages that had ridden up in the fracas.

Mary Jane Buchanan made sure her chignon was undisturbed, and retied the silk ribbons to her straw bonnet that had become unravelled. They descended the stairs gingerly, having no idea where to place their feet next, due to the enormous circumferences of their dresses. Once at the bottom, they opened up their stylish silk parasols, more for affect than to protect their skins from the weak March sun.

"It's good of you to come, Mary. I'm sorry I was late in returning, but had an unexpected errand to run. I would've hated to have missed you."

"Oh, I couldn't have gone back to Dumbarton without seeing you. I've been ever so looking forward to this day! I so miss those days of being with you at Mrs. Gorton's. We used to have so much fun! Didn't we?" Mary rushed off headlong into the next sentence without waiting for a reply.

"Tell me, Madeleine! Is it true? I hear you're engaged to be married?"

The girls waited for a horse and cab to pass before they could cross Bath Lane.

"I am. Oh, he's a wonderful man, Mary. You'd like him. I know you would. He's older than me by fifteen years, but he's established and so handsome."

"What's his name?"

"William. William Minnoch."

"Madeleine Minnoch..." She tried out the name several times before turning to Madeleine and saying, "It suits you Minnie!"

She started calling Madeleine 'Minnie' not long after they met at the London finishing school for young ladies. Both girls had arrived from Scotland with thick Scottish brogues. Countless elocution lessons eventually softened these by teaching them to open their vowels. Since meeting, the girls had formed a strong bond.

"I shall buy you a set of towels from Browne & Browne with personalized monograms of MM on each of them! So, when will you be wed then? Will it be soon?"

"William would like us to wed in June."

"I think June is a perfect time for a wedding. The flowers are out, the weather is warmer, and the April showers will be long past."

"Mary, do you remember when we were at Mrs. Gorton's and we made the pact that whoever marries first, the other would be the bridesmaid? I was wondering if you'd do me the honour."

Mary Jane shrieked with joy, finding it difficult to contain her excitement. Natural instincts of wanting to hug her friend were prevented by the large steel spring cages beneath the layers of fabric that placed several yards between them. She reached out and squeezed her hand instead.

"Honoured? I'd be more than honoured, Minnie! When's the exact date?"

"It's planned for 18th June."

For the next couple of blocks the girls discussed the proposed wedding in detail, but as they walked along Sauchiehall Street the coloured carboys sitting in the window of Mr. Currie's Apothecary shop caught Madeleine's attention and she slowed her pace.

"Oh! Stop a moment, Mary, would you? I want to go into the apothecary. Are you in a terrible hurry to return to Woodside Terrace, or will you come in with me?"

"No, I'm in no hurry. I'll come in with you. I need to buy a few things myself."

As Madeleine opened the door, a tiny brass bell heralded their entrance. Crossing the wide wooden floor planks, they stood in front of a gleaming mahogany counter. Against the wall were rows of handmade pills nestling snug inside glass. They stood alongside piles of roughly cut soaps, and tins of ointments, and salves.

The air was thick with the rich smells of herbal ingredients coming from the dispensary at the back for patent medicines to cure a plethora of ailments, real or imagined.

Madeleine, a regular customer, enjoyed trying the new perfumes, and examining the brightly hued bottles of lotions and potions, set out on purpose-built shelving that lined the walls. Ruddy cobalt liquids suggested syrups, while the greens were almost always poison. Small wooden drawers nested underneath were filled with paper envelopes of aromatic dried herbs, and mysterious powders. She turned, and her eyes were automatically drawn to the secluded corner where she knew inside the ornate jar writhed medicinal leeches waiting for their next feed.

As she returned to the counter a young boy pushed his way to the front. He was covered in grime, clothed in rags, with toes peeping out of gaping holes at the top of his boots; his head just reaching the top of the counter. He banged his money on the curved glass top to gain their attention.

"Sir! Sir! Five pounds of daft for Mr. Johnson, please, sir."

The daft was fetched and he struggled away with his purchase, back to his master's confectionery business a short distance away.

The elderly chemist, black hair now a salt and pepper grey, with a beard to match, was clattering away with a pestle and mortar making oil of earthworm. Strings of worms, swimming in olive oil and red wine, were being crushed and mashed as he continued the vigorous action. After the mixture was boiled a salve for wounds and bruises would be the end result.

The rimless glasses perched on the end of Mr. Currie's nose seemed superfluous as he stopped grinding and peered at Madeleine and Mary over the top of them. He knew the one lady, but not the other.

George Caruthers Haliburton, his pock-faced apprentice, hovered close by, eager to serve. Thirty years younger, with hair still black, parted at the side and slicked down with pomade, he stepped forward.

"Ladies, how may I be of assistance this morning?"

"I'd like to buy a tin of Zam-Buk herbal balm and some arsenic. How do you sell the arsenic?" asked Madeleine, giving him a disarming smile.

Haliburton was rather surprised at the request. Mr. Currie, who had gone back to working the mortar, now looked up sharply and fixed his eyes on his young customer with interest.

"It comes in powdered form, ma'am. May I enquire what you want it for?"

"We have a rat problem in the cellars, and I wish to be rid of them."

"Madam, may I suggest you use phosphorus paste instead? It's far safer and less dangerous than having arsenic lying about the cellar. We're not fond of selling it for that purpose. The phosphorus will answer very well."

"Oh, phosphorus doesn't work. We've tried it before. I hear arsenic is more effective."

Mr. Currie cleared his throat. He removed his glasses, folded them, and placed them next to the soupy maroon gloop before addressing his customer.

"Madam, if you purchase the arsenic, I'll have to ask you to sign your name in the registry book for the sale of poisons."

Madeleine smiled and said, "Oh, I'll sign anything you like."

"Exactly how much are you wanting then?" asked Mr. Currie.

"Will sixpence worth be a large quantity?"

"An ounce will cost you a sixpence. That is a large quantity to kill a great many rats."

"I'll have an ounce then. Thank you."

Madeleine found a shilling in her reticule drawstring purse and paid the pharmacist for the three items. She watched him disappear into a backroom and emerge several minutes later with the arsenic that was made off-site by Dr. Penny. Again she was told that this was not pure arsenic but mixed with indigo, again to prevent accidental ingestion.

He measured the powder out on a set of fine brass scales, removing and adding the tiny weights to measure the exact amount. Once satisfied, he shook the contents onto a square of white paper, collected each of the four corners and turned the bottom half around and around until the package was sealed.

He brought over the registry book and handed it to young George Haliburton, before going back to his earthworms.

George wrote down the particulars as directed. "6th March, 1857 Miss Smith, 7 Blythswood Square, 1 ounce arsenic, kill rats." He turned the book around and Mary watched Madeleine sign her name in a round bold hand next to the entry; "M. H. Smith." The pen scratched noisily across the paper as she did so.

"Will that do?" she inquired, as she replaced the ink pen back into the well.

"That will be all, Miss Smith, unless you need anything else?"

"No, not today, thank you."

The young ladies bid the men good day, and stepping out into the afternoon sun, resumed their journey towards the house of Mr. Dickson, where Mary was staying.

"Oh do be careful with the arsenic, Minnie. I would hate anything to happen to you," said Mary, rather concerned with her friend's purchase.

"Mary, you're a silly goose! I'll be fine! I'll give it to the gardener and he can sprinkle it around the cellar when we're all away this weekend in Bridge of Allan. And besides, don't you remember the reading at Mrs. Gorton's in Clapton, given by Miss Augusta Guibilei, the pupil-teacher? The one where the Styrian peasants were taking it to give them breath to climb steep hills and their having a peculiar plumpness and rosiness of complexion?"

"No, I don't. I'm sure I should have, how peculiar!"

She laughed away her friend's concern and the subject of the arsenic was quickly forgotten, when the conversation circled back to the eminent wedding. They were soon deep in discussion as to whether it would be better to have primrose yellow or periwinkle blue for a bridesmaid's dress.

*

"Friday 6th March: Mimi goes to B.of A."

42 MAKING ACCUSATIONS
GLASGOW, 9 MARCH 1857

Emile and Mary Perry sat in her drawing room in comfortable silence. She studied him closely, and could see he was much changed in appearance. He looked older than his thirty-three years; haggard would best describe him, with his skin hanging loose around his jowls. Mary knew him to be vain and meticulous about his appearance, but of late this had seemed neglected. His hair lay several inches past his collar, and his moustache and beard wild and unkempt. Preoccupation for his health had overtaken vanity.

"Are you not well, Emile?" she asked with concern.

He turned and his eyes looked glassy and unfocused. He shook his head.

"Well, I never expected to see you again, Mary. I've been so ill. I collapsed onto the floor in my room, unable to even reach the bell to call Mrs. Jenkins."

"Oh, my goodness, Emile! Have you seen a doctor?"

"I did. Well, you know I had planned to see Madeleine on the nineteenth of last month. I think I remember telling you."

He looked for affirmation and she nodded, looking at him over her china tea cup as she drank small sips from the rim.

"Well I did, and while there I had a cup of chocolate, and before long, I left to come home. However, during the journey, I suffered a terrible attack, as if a vice were clamping down on my intestines. I was in such a bad way, Mary. I don't wish it upon my worst enemy. However, it wasn't the last time I was so ill. I had another bout, two weeks later."

Mary Perry looked at him in alarm. He continued.

"However, a week later, after having some cocoa Madeleine prepared for me, I was just as sick as the time before. I can't think why I'm so unwell after receiving coffee and chocolate from her."

"But what did the doctor say?"

"At first they thought it might be a touch of cholera. However, then they said my liver is playing up with an over-supply of bile to the system. I don't agree, I think it is something else."

While Miss Perry tut-tutted, Emile sipped his tea before he continued.

"I really love that girl, Mary. I want her to be my wife, but as you know the situation is complicated. It's a perfect fascination, my attachment to that girl. If she were to poison me, I certainly would forgive her."

China clashed against china as Mary Perry dropped her cup back onto the saucer.

"Emile!" she admonished. "You ought not to allow such thoughts to pass through your mind. What motive would she have for giving you anything to hurt you?"

He looked at Mary Perry for a few seconds, before taking a few more slurps of his tea. Finally he spoke.

"I don't know. Perhaps she might not be sorry to be rid of me."

*

"Mon. 9th March: Tea @ 144 Renfrew Street"

43 A COOLING-OFF
BRIDGE OF ALLAN, 10 - 13 MARCH 1857

Madeleine and her family travelled to Bridge of Allan for a short four day vacation. She hated the place. It was cold and miserable, and the people matched the weather. The town itself lay three miles north of Stirling and two miles south of Dunblane. It might be a fashionable summer retreat later on in the year, but in its current state she found it not in the least attractive, and yearned to go back to Town.

She wrote several letters while she was there, to help pass the time. However, letters to Emile continued to be written in a way where she hoped she was withdrawing from the toxic relationship without raising suspicion.

Mr. E. L'Angelier, Mrs. Jenkins, 11 Franklin Place, Great Western Road, Glasgow.

[Posted at Bridge of Allan, 10th March, 1857 ; reached Glasgow about 5.30 p.m. ; deliverable between 6 and 8 same evening.]

My own best loved pet. I hope you are well. I am very well, but it is such a cold place. Far colder than in Town. I have never been warm since I came here. There are very few people that we know staying in the Village.

Have you ever been here, my own dear, little pet? I hope, sweet one, it may make you feel well and strong again, and that you will not again be ill all the summer. You must try and keep well for my sake, will you; my own dear little Emile?

You love me; do you not? Yes, Emile, I know you do.

We shall be home Monday or Tuesday. I shall write you, sweet love, when we shall have an interview. I long to see you, to kiss and embrace you, my own, only sweet love.

I know your kindness will forgive me if I do not write you a longer letter, but we are just going to the train to meet friends from the north, so I shall conclude with much, much love tender embraces and fond kisses.

Sweet love, Adieu !

Ever with love, yours, Mimi

44 STILL POINTING FINGERS
PORTOBELLO, 16 MARCH 1857

It had been a year since Emile last saw Mary Perry's sister, Jane. Jane Towers and her husband, James, lived in Portobello. He called on them one Monday afternoon, after starting out from Glasgow, and arriving by coach just before mid-day. The journey had taken several hours. Alighting at Brighton Place, he walked the short distance to their house, rapped on the door with his cane, and was met with a warm welcome.

"Emile, it's wonderful to see you! When you said you were going to call, I said to James it'd been a while since we saw you last. Come in."

Emile said, as he sat down, "Yes, indeed, far too long. It must be about a year now. Are you still enjoying Portobello? I was admiring the view along the Firth."

"I've been telling Jane for some time we should move to Glasgow. That's where all the jobs are, not here in Portobello."

Jane excused herself to see to the tea and finish off the jam scones with some double whipped cream. It gave her the perfect chance to avoid answering. She missed her sister, but she did not miss Glasgow.

As she returned she heard her husband ask, "So how are you doing, Emile? Still working at Huggins?"

"Yes, still there. They've been so good to me of late, due to my ill-health. You may have heard. I've been off for several days due to a reoccurring illness."

"I'm sorry to hear that, Emile. I wasn't aware you'd been poorly. Are you better now?" asked James.

"Yes, I think I may be."

"Excellent!" interjected Jane. "Now, how is my sister? Tell me all the news, and don't leave anything out."

Emile chatted for about twenty minutes, telling them about Mary and their shared church interests and events. How she partook in last month's fête and general chit-chat pertaining to their lives in Glasgow. However, before long he circled back to his ailing health.

"I was hoping to help her with the fête, but I let her down badly, through no fault of my own. I was afflicted with a mysterious illness so bad I thought my time had come."

"When you said you were sick, Emile, I wasn't aware you were that ill. What's been the matter?"

By now, Jane was genuinely concerned.

"I've been struck down with a violent bilious attack, twice now, each time after I've taken hot chocolate and cocoa."

"Do you not usually drink these, Emile?" enquired Jane.

"No, not usually, I don't drink coffee as a rule as it doesn't agree with me. But on these occasions I was so ill I collapsed in my bedroom and the pain so bad I was unable to put myself to bed. However, I managed to crawl to the door and ring through to my landlady, Mrs. Jenkins. It's quite strange I'm always sick after consuming these drinks. I fear I'm being poisoned."

"Poisoned!" exclaimed James. "Are you sure? Do you think you're being poisoned by something, or someone?"

Emile bit into his strawberry jam scone unable to speak for a while. When he was, he said, "Well then, enough about my health, when are you moving to Glasgow?"

*

The same evening, William Minnoch received his first letter from Madeleine.

William Minnoch Esq., 124 St. Vincent Street, Glasgow

[Posted at Stirling, 16th March, 1857; reached Glasgow 5.30 same afternoon; deliverable between 6 and 8 same night.]

My dearest William,

It is but fair, after your kindness to me, that I should write you a note. The day I part from friends I always feel sad. But to part from one I love, as I do you, makes me feel truly sad and dull. My only consolation is that we meet soon.

To-morrow we shall be home. I do so wish you were here to-day. We might take a long walk. Our walk to Dunblane I shall ever remember with pleasure. That walk fixed a day on which we are to begin a new life, a life which I hope may be of happiness and long duration to both of us. My aim through life shall be to please you and study you.

Dear William, I must conclude, as Mama is ready to go to Stirling. I do not go with the same pleasure as I did the last time. I hope you got to Town safe, and found your sisters well. Accept my warmest kindest love and ever believe me to be, yours with affection,

Madeleine

45 SHOPPING FOR ARSENIC AGAIN
GLASGOW, 18 MARCH 1857

Madeleine was again at Curries Apothecary, this time, in the company of her sister Elizabeth. They stood waiting to be served for the room bustled with a good many people for a Wednesday afternoon. George Haliburton rushed back and forth to placate and help the half-dozen or so customers ahead of her.

While she waited, she followed Elizabeth over to inspect some jars displayed on a table nearby.

She picked up a container called *Crème Céleste*, a cold cream for ladies' complexions. She turned it around and read the ingredients: white wax, spermaceti, sweet almond oil, and rosewater. It promised moisturising properties, to hide blemishes, and to provide a light smooth complexion. She made a note to herself. When she came back, she would buy a jar. She still had the jar in her hand when she heard someone ask, "Can I help you, Miss Smith?"

They both turned around, and Madeleine smiled, placed the jar back on the table, and moved towards the counter.

"Mr. Halliburton. I've come to buy some more arsenic. Another sixpence worth, please."

"More arsenic, Miss Smith? Whatever are you doing with it?"

"We've a real rat problem in our cellar. Purchasing the last lot seemed most effective. Eight or nine large rats were lying around afterwards, quite dead. As a result of its efficacy, I'd like to purchase some more. Just to make sure those are the last of them."

"One moment, Miss Smith, I'll need to speak to Mr. Currie."

He disappeared and found Mr. Currie in the back room.

"Mr. Currie, I have a customer wanting to purchase some arsenic."

"Well, I don't sell arsenic to just anyone, George, I only sell it to people I know, and parties of respectability, at that. Otherwise, they could do heaven knows what with the stuff."

"Mr. Currie, I do understand, but you see, sir, we've already sold some arsenic to the young lady, on another occasion. It's Miss Madeleine Smith, the architect's daughter who's enquiring."

"James Smith?"

"Yes, sir."

"Well why didn't you say so before, laddie?'

"How much did you say she wanted?"

"Sixpence worth, for rats, sir."

"Very well, prepare the register. I'll be over in a minute."

46 THE LAST DAYS
BRIDGE OF ALLAN, 20 - 21 MARCH 1857

*M*iss Perry, 144 Renfrew Street, Glasgow.
[Posted at Bridge of Allan, 20th March 1857; reached Glasgow 10.45 p.m. same night; deliverable first delivery next morning.]

Bridge of Allan, 20th March.

Dear Mary,

I should have written to you before, but I am so lazy writing when away from my ordinary ways. I feel much better, and I hope to be home the middle of next week.

This is a very stupid place, very dull. I know no one; and besides, it is so very much colder than Edinburgh. I saw your friends at Portobello, and will tell you about them when I see you.

I should have come to see someone last night, but the letter came too late, so we are both disappointed. Trusting you are quite well, and with kind regards to yourself and sister

Believe me, yours sincerely,
P. Emile L'Angelier

I shall be here 'til Wednesday.

*

W. A. Stevenson, Esq., 10 Bothwell Street, Glasgow.
Bridge of Allan, Friday.

Dear William,

I am happy to say I feel much better, though I fear I slept in a damp bed, for my timbers are all sore and scarcely able to bear me, but a day or two will put all to rights.

What a dull place this is. I went to Stirling to-day, but it was so cold and damp that I soon hurried home again.

Are you very busy? Am I wanted? If so, I am ready to come at any time just drop me a line at P.O. You were talking of taking a few days to yourself, so I shall come up whenever you like.

If any letters come, please send them to me here. I intend to be home not later than Thursday morning.

Yours sincerely,
P. Emile L'Angelier

47 EMILE'S FINAL HOURS
GLASGOW, 23 - 24 MARCH 1857

Emile arrived back at his lodgings after being away for over a week. He had travelled from Bridge of Allan to Glasgow, spending the last two hours in the excellent company of Mr. Thomas Ross, an auctioneer from Glasgow. They had walked from Coatbridge and found the walk arduous, but pleasant, and they parted ways at the top of Abercrombie Street and Gallowgate.

Annie Jenkins looked up from her needlework as she heard the key turn in the latch, a few minutes after seven-thirty in the evening. Emile popped his head into the front room, saw his landlady, and doffed his hat.

"Nice to see you again, sir, I wasn't expecting you back so soon."

"No, except I received a letter while I was away, that brought me back sooner than expected."

"Ah, yes. I gave it to Mr. Thuau whom I presumed would forward it on to you. I'm glad you got it."

"Not half as glad as I am Mrs. Jenkins. When exactly did it arrive?"

"Yesterday afternoon, I believe."

He didn't respond, which prompted Mrs. Jenkins to ask, "Did you have a pleasant week away?"

"I did indeed, Mrs. Jenkins."

"And how are you feeling now? You look a great deal better now than before you left."

"Oh, yes! I'm a great deal better. I'm always well these days, I'm pleased to say. In fact, I've walked fifteen miles today."

"Well, that's a relief!"

She returned to her needlework. An hour later he crossed the doorway once again.

"Do you think I can have the pass key, Mrs. Jenkins? I shall be stepping out for a few hours this evening and may be late in returning. Also, I would be grateful if you could call me first thing tomorrow morning as I would like to be away with the first train."

He never said where he was going that night, or any previous nights before that, and as she handed over the key she did not ask. It was not her place.

*

Emile walked from his lodgings at Franklin Place to Charing Cross. He saw an acquaintance in passing; James Galloway. Galloway knew L'Angelier by sight only as Emile lived next door to one of his relatives, and therefore he saw him often. They acknowledged the other with a tip of the hat as they walked on Sauchiehall Street. Emile headed east and James Galloway could not help but notice the man seemed in no hurry to be wherever he had to be. He himself needed to pick up the pace if he was to be on time for his own appointment. He delved into his waistcoat pocket and stood under the gaslight to read the time, making it a little after nine o'clock.

At about nine twenty p.m. Emile called at lodgings on Terrace Street, which ran between Bothwell Street and St. Vincent Street. They were the lodgings of a clerk, Mr. Edward Lyon McAlester. Emile knocked on the door with the top of his cane, as was his habit, and stood back from the door.

Mary Tweedle, servant to the owner of the lodgings, peered out.

"Can I help you, sir?"

"I've come to call on Mr. McAlester. Is he in?"

"I'm afraid not, sir. Was he expecting you?"

"No, I thought he may be here on the off chance."

Emile hovered, but an invitation did not come.

"Who shall I say called, sir?"

"Emile L'Angelier."

"Very well, sir. Good night to you."

Emile lit a cigar before continuing his journey. Church bells struck the half hour after nine. He was a five-minute walk away from Blythswood Square.

*

Police Constable Thomas Kavan was also out that night, walking his usual beat. Temperatures had plummeted and he pulled up the collar of his uniform to protect his exposed neck from the biting cold. He had finished an uneventful shift, for the cold weather had kept most sensible people off the streets. He did not bump into anyone he knew in his line of duty that evening, not even the young man who sometimes shared his cigars with him at Blythswood Square.

*

At two o'clock the following morning, the doorbell's violent ringing shattered sleep. Repeated long, urgent pulls not only rudely awoke Mrs. Jenkins, but also a stray dog that howled and barked, adding to the din. Annie smoothed her nightgown over her knees, straightened her nightcap, and shuffled over to the window. She swore as she stubbed her toe on the chest at the foot of the bed, darkness cloaking the obstacle. Despite using both hands on the casement, it stuck fast for the frame had swelled in the damp weather. Finally, after several attempts, it grudgingly gave way and she managed to push it halfway up before it stuck, yet again. She ducked her head into the opening and looked down.

Shadows cast from the gaslight lamp made it impossible to make identification. All she could see was a figure leaning with his head on her door, one arm outstretched onto the wall closest to the bell, the other clawing at his stomach.

"Who is it?" she shouted above the cacophony of both dog and doorbell as the bell continued to ring. As the figure looked up, the face, caught in the pale gaslight, reflected skin waxen-white and covered in a soft sheen.

"THE LANDLADY WAS ROUSED BY A VIOLENT RINGING OF THE BELL." (p. 149).

"It is I, Mrs. Jenkins. Emile. Can you open the door, please?"

It was unnecessary to ask why he had not opened the door himself. By the time Anne Jenkins lit a candle, threw a cloak over her nightgown, and made the short journey down the stairs, Emile L'Angelier was dry heaving. He stood on the threshold with both hands crossed over his stomach, bent double with pain. He looked up as she opened the door, sweat beads clung to his face and upper lip.

"I'm very bad," he said unnecessarily. "I'm about to have one of those vomiting spells." He looked ghastly.

"Let's get you upstairs then as soon as possible. Lean on me if you like."

They reached his room when he started to retch. Hurriedly setting down the candlestick, she snatched up the basin used for the same purpose weeks before and thrust it into his hands. No sooner had she done so, than he filled it with the same thick green, gruel-like vomit.

He mopped his face and wiped his mouth with a cotton handkerchief as he handed her back the washbowl with its ghastly contents.

"I thought I'd never reach home," he said weakly and fell back onto the bed. He stared at her vacantly and then lay down; unaware he was still wearing his boots.

"I was so tired on the road, coming home."

He turned his face to her and asked, "Do you think I could trouble you for some water to quench my raging thirst"?"

She reached for the ewer of water on his desk and poured him a long drink. He tried to sit up, failed, and tried again. With one elbow on the bed, propping him up, he extended a shaky hand, clutched the glass, and drank the water like a marooned man.

"Thank you, Mrs. Jenkins, you're very kind. May I bother you for another, and a cup of tea please?"

She filled the tumbler again, and he drank just as thirstily as before.

As Anne Jenkins lifted up her gown on the way down to the kitchen, her thoughts crowded with worry. Where did he go and what did he eat to have this reaction once more? Strange, she thought, him being ill when in Glasgow, but well when he spent the week away in Bridge of Allan. What was it about Glasgow that upset him so?

By the time she returned with the tea, she found Emile partially undressed and vomiting again, but this time worse than before. The vomit was consistent in colour and substance, but with each heave, he clawed at his stomach and cried out in excruciating pain.

Anne Jenkins felt compelled to ask. "Sir, what have you been taking that disagrees so greatly with your stomach?"

"I cannot say, Mrs. Jenkins. I don't understand it myself. I was never better during those few days at the coast. However, now I'm poorly. So poorly. I've the chills and cold to the bone. Do you think I could have some hot water for my feet and stomach, if you wouldn't mind?"

Anne returned with several hot water bottles. Once he was in bed, she added four pairs of blankets, and two mats to cover him but still he complained of the cold, and his teeth started to set off on a chatter.

She stayed with him, dozing nearby in the solitary armchair as her patient slept on his side, knees drawn up and crying out as the next wave of pain, lasting several long seconds, seized his bowels. At about four o'clock in the morning he started to heave once more and she brought a clean basin for him to fill, yet again.

Emptying his stomach was not his only problem. His bowels started to weaken and she helped him to the water closet to empty those as well.

"Mr. L'Angelier, I need to call the doctor. Let me see if I can fetch Dr. Thomson for you. You cannot go on like this. You're very bad."

He lay back on the bed exhausted, eyes closed, sweating profusely, his breathing heavy and laboured. His lids were heavy, and when he managed to open them, they were slits, nothing more. He said, "If it's not too much of a bother for you Mrs. Jenkins. Perhaps I do need the doctor. My intestines are no better. It's as if a red hot ball of fire is travelling through them. I could do with some relief. I'm in agony."

"It's no bother at all. I think I'll call on Dr. Steven, if you don't mind, as he's closer. Now, you have a little sleep and I'll fetch him for you. I'm sure you'll feel better in no time at all."

She tried to keep her voice light but she was watching him sink fast with extreme concern. With her cloak still covering her nightgown, she buttoned up her boots, before unlatching the door. As she slipped into the dark cobbled street in the small hours of the morning, making her way to Stafford Place, the sound of her boots echoed and bounced off the granite walls of the narrow lanes. Her thoughts were not on her personal safety, nor how the boots may attract attention to those lurking in dark alleyways. Instead, they were on the lodger who was at death's door, wondering if a doctor could save him at all.

James Steven shuffled towards the door. He cracked it slightly and peered out, looking disheveled and gaunt.

"Can you come to eleven Franklin Place, Doctor? One of my lodgers is very poorly."

"I too am ill, ma'am, otherwise I would come, if I could. Give me a few hours and if he's still bad, come back and fetch me. In the meantime, give him twenty five drops of laudanum and a mustard plaster."

By seven o'clock Emile had not improved. She returned to the physician's house to convince him it was now a matter of urgency.

Steven arrived, and examining his patient turned to Mrs. Jenkins, saying, "Mrs. Jenkins, I need that mustard. I take it you have some?"

"Yes Doctor, I do. Do you want me to make the mustard plaster?"

"Indeed, I do, Mrs. Jenkins. How do you make yours? Do you use egg white?"

"No, Doctor. I use equal parts of black mustard powder and flour, with a little warm water to make a paste."

"That'll do. Good woman! Bring it up when you're ready. But before you go..." He lifted the cover from the washbowl on the nightstand. "Ah, this is what I was looking for."

He peered at the vomit and then asked her several questions.

"Has he been consistent in what he's been vomiting up? Does it all look like this? The same colour?"

"Yes, Doctor, every time."

"Hmm..."

Once the mustard plaster was ready, Dr. Steven placed it on Emile's stomach.

"Thank you, Mrs. Jenkins. I'll wait with the patient twenty or thirty minutes, if you don't mind, to see if he rallies. We don't want to leave the plaster on too long and allow him to blister. I'm also going to administer a little morphine."

"Tea, Doctor?"

"Lemon if you have any, no milk."

Mrs. Jenkins made her way to the kitchen to boil more water, and to see to her children's breakfast.

When she returned, Emile was awake. He turned to her and said, "Oh, Mrs. Jenkins. This is the worst attack I've ever had. Far worse than the others."

"I think so, sir," she replied.

Emile tapped his forehead and said to the doctor, "I feel something here."

"Now, now, Mr. L'Angelier, what you have is not perceptible. It's inward. I've given you morphine for the pain. Try to rest," ordered the doctor.

Anne Jenkins let the doctor out but before he left she asked, "Doctor, what's the matter with Mr. L'Angelier?"

The doctor paused before replying, and then looked at her intently.

"Is he often tippling?"

"Tippling, Doctor? No, sir, quite the opposite, he never drinks. Not to my knowledge. I've never seen him drunk in all the time he's been living here. But I do find it strange; for this is the second time he's been out and came in badly."

"Where does he go?"

"I don't know, Doctor. He never says."

"Well, good day to you, Mrs. Jenkins." He doffed his hat before adding, "I'll be back between ten and eleven to check on him."

Anne Jenkins saw her daughter off to school and then checked her patient. L'Angelier looked no better. His face sweating profusely, despite the chilly weather, blended in with the slightly yellowed cotton bed linen.

"What did the doctor say?" he wanted to know.

"The doctor says you'll get over it."

"I'm far worse than the doctor thinks, if that's what he's saying."

She avoided replying by crossing the room and drawing the curtains.

"I'd like to see Miss Perry. She lives at one forty-four Renfrew Street. Do you think you could call on her and ask her to come?"

"I don't want to leave you, but I'll send for her."

"Thank you, Mrs. Jenkins. You've been so kind to me. Now, if you could please close the curtains I think, if I could have five minutes sleep, I'd be better."

Annie Jenkins kept popping into the room to check on him. She called out his name on one of her trips up, but he did not stir, and she left him to sleep in peace.

As promised, the doctor returned.

"How's your patient, Mrs. Jenkins?" enquired the doctor, already removing his hat and coat before waiting for the reply.

"He's only newly fallen asleep, Doctor. It would be a pity to wake him."

"Nevertheless, I'd like to see him."

The doctor placed his bag on the side-table and, his eyes still not adjusted to the darkness, asked Annie if she would be so kind as to draw back the curtains.

A pale light shone through the small panes and the physician turned to look at L'Angelier lying on his right side, with his back towards the light, knees drawn up slightly to his chest with one arm outside the covers tightly clenched, the other remaining tucked inside.

Dr. Steven stood at the side of the bed, felt the man's pulse, and frowned. He then lifted Emile's head off the pillow. It fell back and lolled to one side, eyes open but unseeing.

"Is there something wrong, Doctor?"

With little bedside manner the doctor retorted, "The man's dead. I need to consult his regular doctor before I write a death certificate. What did you say his name was?"

"Doctor Thomson."

"Doctor Thomson? Right."

With that, he closed his bag, replaced his hat and coat, and left the room, leaving Annie Jenkins to deal with the shock on her own.

The House in which L'Angelier died, Franklin Place, Glasgow

The room he occupied is on the first floor, immediately over the doorway.

48 MAKING ARRANGEMENTS
GLASGOW, 24 MARCH 1857

Ann Jenkins's mind was awhirl. She could not believe Emile was dead. One week he was fine, and dead the next. She did not quite know what to do, or who to fetch. Her husband worked away and was seldom at home, and so she stood in the death room for a while, all in a quandary.

She wondered where Miss Perry was. She had sent for her, but she had not yet arrived. She paced the space between the foot of the bed and the window, all the while wringing her hands as she tried to think.

As she walked up and down, she dabbed at her eyes with the bottom of her apron. She wept tears for the polite man who was her lodger, but no more. He had been a good lodger, never giving her trouble, always paying his rent on time. She would miss him, including the money. She felt guilty wondering so soon how long it would be before they could rent the room out again.

The strident voice of her young son interrupted her thoughts.

"Miss Perry's coming, Ma. Soon, she said."

He wiped his snotty nose across his right sleeve, eyes darting about before noticing Emile's unfocused eyes. It slowly dawned on him the man was dead. He crossed himself and scurried down the stairs.

"Jimmy Jenkins! You come back here!"

He looked a little sheepish as he climbed his way back to the landing. Annie peered over the balcony with her hands on her hips and chided him,

"Don't you disappear on me, boy! Go and find Mr. Clark and bring him here. He should be in his room. Then you need to go and fetch Mr. Chrystal, the grocer, on North Street. Tell him, it's urgent and he has to come straightaway."

"Yes, Ma."

Annie waited for the men to arrive. Mr. Clark, a fellow lodger, was the first to appear. Due to his close proximity, he had heard and wondered about the commotion, but initially had decided to stay where he was. As soon as he heard why Annie Jenkins had summoned him, he refused to enter Emile's room. Instead, he recoiled, patted down his trouser pockets until he was able to dig out his handkerchief, and held it up to his nose.

"What did you say he died of, Mrs. Jenkins? Not contagious, I hope. You know I couldn't stay here a minute longer if he has died of some dreadful disease."

Before she could allay his fears, Mr. Chrystal arrived. He had locked up his shop as soon as he was summoned, his rotund figure, face, and pate sweating from the exertion of his quickened pace. His face was grave as he listened to what had transpired.

"Right, don't you worry about a thing, Mrs. Jenkins. I'll go over to the cotton place and speak to Emile's employer. Once I've done that, I'll fetch Mr. Scott. He's the foreman to Menzies, the undertaker. He'll come over and lay out the body. Now, you go and make yourself a nice pot of tea."

The luxury of a cup of tea was soon forgotten as the house filled with people connected to Emile through life or death, except Mr. Clark, who melted away to his room.

Annie Jenkins descended the stairs when she heard rapid knocking. The door creaked in protest as she opened it.

"Yes?"

"You called for me. I'm Miss Perry."

"Oh! Come in, Miss Perry. I'm Annie Jenkins. Come in. This is a dreadful state of affairs."

She ushered Mary Perry in before extending a hand.

"I am sorry to tell you this, Miss Perry, but you're too late."

"Too late? Too late for what?"

"Emile died this morning."

"No! That cannot be! Oh, no! Surely not!"

She let out a wail from deep within, collapsed into a nearby chair, and sobbed.

Mrs. Jenkins hovered and waited for the tears to dissipate before she asked, "Are you his intended?"

"No," she managed, in between sobs. "I'm a close friend. He was a dear man, a sweet man. I cannot believe it. I saw him just the other day and he was fine, better than I've seen him in ages. Oh, my goodness. This is such a shock."

"I know. I know what you mean. I can hardly believe it myself." She paused, before asking, "Would you like to see him?"

Mary Perry hesitated for a fraction of a second, before she replied quietly, "Yes, I...I think I would."

As they entered the room, the undertaker's foreman was already laying out the body, so Annie Jenkins guided Mary Perry into another room, and they spoke in hushed voices waiting for the undertaker to finish.

"I can't believe he's gone. Mrs. Jenkins, is it? I can't believe it. What a dreadful, dreadful tragedy. And one so young! Just thirty-three years old. We were born five years apart, almost to the day ..."

She trailed off, deep in thought and then cried a great deal more before saying, "His poor mother. She'll be very sorry to hear the news."

"Indeed. No doubt the lady he intended to marry will feel the same."

Mary looked up sharply.

"It would be best not to say too much about that for the time being."

Mary Perry dabbed at her eyes, blew her nose and then sobbed some more.

After a while, they entered the bedroom to look at Emile, eyes closed, mouth hanging slightly open. Mary Perry moved over to the bed and gazed at her former friend while breaking out in a fresh round of sobs. She kissed him several times on the forehead, unaware others had now arrived.

William Stevenson waited for the right time to make his entry. Having had no reply as he knocked and stood on the street, he had let himself in. As the two women looked up, he doffed his hat, and made his introductions.

"Sorry to arrive unannounced, ladies, I did knock. The name is William Stevenson. I'm Emile's manager at the cotton factory. Mr. Chrystal asked me to come by."

He turned and the women saw several other faces hovering behind him. "I've brought with me Dr. Hugh Thomson, Dr. James Steven, and Mr. Amadée Thuau, who works at the French consul, as you know."

Annie Jenkins nodded her head to those she knew and thanked those she did not, for coming.

Dr. Thomson crossed the room and looked at the man he had not seen in nearly a month. The body lay on a stretcher placed on top of the table, now washed and dressed in grave clothes. The skin had assumed a jaundiced tinge. He examined the body externally, and lifting the shirt, explored the area of the liver. He knocked over the area, each time the action emitted a dull sound. He moved to the heart region, but where the liver sounded 'full', the heart area appeared normal.

Neither Thomson, nor Steven, could account for the death with any degree of certainty.

"Doctors, can you tell me if the death of Mr. L'Angelier is suspicious in any way?"

Both doctors hesitated before Thomson said, "I'm sure my learned colleague, Dr. Steven will agree with me when I say, to my knowledge, there is nothing suspicious about his death, nothing at all. However, we can only ascertain this knowledge fully by examining the body further."

Steven nodded in agreement.

"How soon can you do the examination then?" pressed Stevenson.

"Do you have some concerns?"

"We do."

"Well then, we'll need to discuss these somewhere more private. Steven, are you free tomorrow for an examination of the body?"

"I can avail myself, yes."

"Right, well that's settled then. Mrs. Jenkins, is there anything we can do for you while we're here?"

"I'd like someone to take charge of Mr. L'Angelier's belongings. They need to be gathered up and locked up somewhere before we can pass them on to his next of kin."

Stevenson offered to take charge and bent down to pick up the clothes off the floor that Emile had discarded the night before. He examined the pockets, turning them inside out, and placed the contents on a small table. There lay a bit of tobacco, three finger-rings, five shillings, seven pence, and a bunch of keys. There was nothing of value, or of interest, until he moved to the vest pockets. Here he found an envelope within which was a letter. The paper was crisp white, with handwriting familiar to a few in the room.

After he read the note William Stevenson said, "Well this explains all!"

They passed it around to sounds of murmurs, and shakes of heads, before Annie Jenkins read it herself, first looking at the envelope in which it had arrived.

"This is the letter that came for him on Saturday," she confirmed.

Mr. E. L'Angelier, Mrs. Jenkins, 11 Franklin Place, Great Western Road, Glasgow.
Posted at Glasgow, General Office or pillar-box, 21st March, 1857, between 9 a.m. and half-past 12 p.m. if pillar-box, and if General Office between 11.45 a.m. and 1 p.m., and deliverable between 1.30 and 3 same afternoon.

Well, my beloved, you did not come to me. Oh, beloved, are you ill? Come to me, sweet one. I waited and waited for you, but you came not. I shall wait again tomorrow night, same hour and arrangement. Do come, sweet love of my dear love of a sweetheart. Come, beloved, and clasp me to your heart. Come and we shall be happy. A kiss, fond love. Adieu with tender embraces, ever believe me to be your own, ever dear fond,
  Mimi

49 SCRAMBLING TO SAVE A REPUTATION
GLASGOW, 24 MARCH 1857, MORNING

Auguste de Mean sat perched on the edge of his seat in the grand drawing room with James and Janet Smith. The only other occupant in the room was Madeleine. The atmosphere was heavy. James Smith's face was unreadable. He had arrived home unaware of anything, other than being told his wife needed him instantly.

Janet Smith looked as if she had done a great deal of weeping, for her lashes were wet, her face red and blotchy. From time to time she dabbed at her puffy eyes etched in red, and clutched the cambric handkerchief in a frail hand, at the ready.

James Smith glowered at Madeleine who sat a little way off from them. Her back was straight, her head held high, and in no way did she look intimidated or perturbed by the events of the last few hours.

"Mr. Smith, I understand Mr. Thuau and Miss Perry informed the house earlier of the demise of Mr. L'Angelier."

"L'Angelier? Why does that name sound familiar?"

"He was courting your eldest daughter, Miss Madeleine, sir."

"Yes, yes. He was trying to, but we put a stop to that. Some years back now. The man is dead? What does that have to do with us now?"

De Mean cleared his throat.

"There is an issue of some delicacy I need to bring up. Forgive me, sir, but due to the nature of the frequent correspondence between your daughter, Miss Madeleine, and the late Emile L'Angelier, there is great urgency to exonerate her and make pressing application to retrieve these letters."

"Letters?" He frowned. This time he spoke directly to Madeleine.

"Did you continue to write to this Frenchman after I forbade you, Madeleine?" The tone was not a decibel over normal conversation, but there was no confusion at the level of his anger.

"Yes, Papa." The tone was meek. She dropped her gaze.

"For how long, Madeleine? How long have you being meeting and writing to this man? How long?" He asked the last question in a slightly raised voice, rage and indignation simmering.

"For more than two years, Papa." Madeleine could not look at her father.

Both women jumped as her father leaped out of his chair, spun around and smote his hand onto the table next to him. "Christ! Two years?"

Her father never swore. Janet Smith mopped at fresh tears, and blew her nose in the ensuing silence. Madeleine bit her fingernails, but said nothing more.

James Smith paced the room unable to think straight, unable to stand still, such was his turmoil.

"Sir, if I may interject. Forgive me, because I know this is a difficult time for all of us, but you need to know it's the content of these missives that's exceedingly damning, to Miss Madeleine in particular. She was...." He hesitated. He fumbled for the right words, not wanting to enflame an already explosive situation.

"I assume, she expected at the time, that L'Angelier would destroy each letter. Unfortunately, he did not. He kept every one of them. He threatened several times to show these to you and to her intended, Mr. Minnoch, over the last few months. The contents were such that...that they would have stopped her marriage to Minnoch. As a result, it is imperative we retrieve them as soon as possible."

The silence was palpable. Janet Smith looked stunned. A good few seconds passed for De Mean's words to sink in, but even James needed clarification. What he heard seemed unfathomable. He looked at Madeleine aghast, hoping for her to deny everything. Instead, when she met his gaze, she dropped it just as quickly. She stared back at her folded hands on her lap, saying nothing.

"What's in these letters to have made this man comment so, De Mean?"

"I honestly don't know, sir. I've not read them, but I can only guess, after what I was told. What I do know, is that Emile was confident this would be the outcome when we spoke about this some weeks before his passing. He said there would be no misunderstanding, once read, as to the true nature of their relationship, and marriage to another would be out of the question."

Janet Smith's tears turned to hysterical sobs, and not willing to listen to anymore left the room. James Smith slumped into the closest chair. Madeleine's cheeks burned as she continued to stare at her lap, biting her bottom lip.

"Madeleine, for Christ's sake, what have you done? Tell me none of this is true!"

De Mean continued.

"It's because of the content, sir, I urge you to secure these letters. If these letters were to fall into the hands of strangers, once read, they would cause untold damage to your family and to Miss Madeleine's reputation. It would be prudent to find and destroy them."

James Smith mumbled something inaudible, and nodded his head.

De Mean turned his attention to Madeleine. "Miss Madeleine, I need to ask you something. Did you write to L'Angelier while he was away at Bridge of Allan?"

"I wasn't aware he was at Bridge of Allan. I wrote to him on Friday, to his lodgings in Franklin Place, asking to see me the following day, Saturday."

Did you see Emile on Sunday night?"

"I did not." Her voice was clear and steady. She looked De Mean in the eye and her gaze did not waiver. "I've not seen him for some three weeks. I've told you. I wrote him to come Saturday last, but he did not."

"Some people are already speculating about his death. Some saying his death was suicide. However, Miss Madeleine, if what you say is true, I don't think it likely he would have committed suicide without knowing what it was you'd asked him to come to Glasgow for."

"I'm not sure what he died of, or how he died, Mr. De Mean. I heard the news but a few hours ago."

"Miss Madeleine, there is one particular letter existing, and it's certain it is this letter of yours sent on to L'Angelier that brought him back to Glasgow. In the circumstances, I urge you to tell the truth. It's sure that someone, anyone – a servant, a policeman, even a stranger passing your house - will confirm they saw L'Angelier at or near your home on Sunday night. By concealing the truth, Miss Madeleine, and denying he was here, when he was, would cause strong suspicion as to motive and why he died."

Madeleine spoke with conviction and sincerity. She left her seat and stood opposite De Mean.

"I swear to you, Mr. De Mean, I've not seen L'Angelier, not Sunday, nor three weeks prior."

"With regards to this letter to L'Angelier, where you invited him to see you, why would you continue your covert correspondence with a former sweetheart, now you're engaged to be married to another?"

"I only did it to encourage the return of my letters."

"Is it true you signed your name as L'Angelier at the end of your notes to him?"

"Yes, sir."

De Mean made to leave before he felt compelled to ask one more question.

"Before I take my leave, Miss Madeleine, please place me in a position to contradict the statements being made about your relations with L'Angelier."

She hesitated for a second, dropped her head and said, "I am sorry, sir, for I cannot. They are true."

James Smith had heard enough. He stood up abruptly, yanked open the door and cleaved his way through scattering servants while Auguste De Mean and Madeleine remained standing in uncomfortable silence.

50 GRAVE SUSPICIONS
GLASGOW 24 MARCH 1857, AFTERNOON

Hugh Thomson, one of Emile's doctors, entered the office of Mr. William Huggins. Seated was a man whose name he had forgotten as soon as they were introduced. William Huggins had summoned him to the office to discuss the case of their employee of four and a half years, Pierre Emile L'Angelier.

"Dreadful business this death of L'Angelier this morning, what do you make of it, Thomson?"

"To be honest, sir it's all rather odd. The symptoms are such it could have been a number of things; excessive bile, cholera... There is nothing conclusive pointing to one particular illness."

"Could he have been poisoned?"

"I've heard that you have suspicions but they have little grounding. I suppose the symptoms are such that they might have been produced by an irritant poison, yes. However, it would be very unlikely."

"Well, how do we make sure?"

"It's customary, under conditions of suspicion such as this, for a coroner's inquest to be held. I'll ask Dr. Steven to accompany me, if you like. We'll send you the report once we have our findings."

*

Huggins & Co. suddenly seemed to be a place of great interest to the outside world, for no sooner had William Huggins seen off Dr. Thomson, than someone else was knocking on his door.

This time it was a gentleman who introduced himself as Mr. Auguste De Mean, attached to the French consul.

"I apologise for my unannounced visit, but this is a matter of importance. I'm a friend of the Smith family, Madeleine Smith was unofficially betrothed to L'Angelier. Apparently, there were a number of love letters exchanged between the pair, and the family asks if they could have these back, due to the content that could harm the young lady's reputation. Would you have some of these on the property? Perhaps in L'Angelier's desk?"

"With all due respect, sir, the answer is no, you may not have access to these. The letters were collected and sealed this morning. There is a distinct possibility they could be used in a future inquest."

"Inquest?"

"Yes, sir. You see, we don't believe our late employee died of natural causes. We believe there was foul play. We have asked for an autopsy and a full investigation into the cause of his death."

51 RUNNING AWAY
GLASGOW, 26 MARCH 1857

As dawn broke, Madeleine crept out of bed, stood on the tips of her toes and fetched the portmanteau from the top of the wardrobe. She unclipped the clasp and started packing it with a few clothes and essentials. She could not bear to be in the house a moment longer. Ever since De Mean's visit, her parents had been relentless in extracting from her minute details of her time spent with Emile.

With great reluctance, she had told them the sordid story, from the time she met him, until the last time she saw him, three weeks prior to his death. However, once they learned the truth, they immediately wished they had not.

Her deception and depravity left them in shock and total disbelief. How could a child of theirs resort to such immorality? They were not able to hide their abhorrence. She sat in the dark, musty study with her mama and papa and found the room oppressive. Her chest heaved in anticipation of what was to come.

"I can't tell you what a disappointment you have turned out to be, Madeleine. What did we ever do to deserve a daughter like you?"

"I'm sorry, Papa."

"Sorry? Sorry? Not half as sorry as I am! Your behaviour has been reprehensible. Why? Why would you indulge in such baseness? You were brought up better than that! Think of the scandal that is sure to follow. Did you think of that while you were cavorting around like a lusty kitchen maid with this man we kept telling you, you couldn't see?"

"I always said having Madeleine down with the household staff was a bad idea, James."

Her mother's comment was ignored.

"Well, it's too late for that now, isn't it? What a selfish, stupid, rebellious, wicked girl you are. Your immoral actions will taint this family forever, affecting every single member! You've even trampled on your sisters' prospects of securing a respectable marriage. Do you realize that?"

"I wasn't thinking, Papa."

"That much is obvious. You've brought mortification and humiliation to your mother and me. We'll never be able to hold our heads high in polite society ever again. You've damned the lot of us, in the blink of an eye. Everything I worked for, gone in a moment of shameless debauchery and wilful disobedience. As for Minnoch, do you think he'll still want you after he hears of your shenanigans? Well, do you? Look at me, Madeleine, when I am talking to you."

"Yes, Papa. No, Papa."

"You are no longer a daughter of mine. I hardly know the strumpet you have become."

They raged, fumed, and harangued relentlessly until the girl who seldom cried, finally broke down.

Then the admonishments stopped. No one spoke to her, not even her siblings. They gave her the cold shoulder instead, more painful than the tirade of questions and rebukes. Her mama retreated to her bed and had not surfaced since. Her father retreated to his study, taking his meals there on the first day. On the second, he remained in bed.

After two days of this treatment, she made up her mind to leave. Today, she had learned, was Emile's funeral. She wanted to find solace somewhere more peaceful. No one had thought to ask her how she was feeling after Emile's death. Going to Rowaleyn was the obvious choice. A caretaker lived on the property, and the house was always open. If she made haste before the family awakened, she would be long gone before anyone was aware of her disappearance.

Clutching her bag, making sure she had left nothing behind, she moved up the stairs, praying their creaking would not give her away. She dared not leave through the kitchen courtyard for the wrought iron gate always squeaked on its rusty hinges. Not wanting to draw attention to herself, for the servants were already up lighting the range and preparing for the new day, she left via the front door.

The streets were still dark when she stepped out, and Madeleine's heart pounded as her buttoned boots echoed on the cobbles. She drew her cape closer and hurried on, glancing nervously behind her. She held her breath as she came to every dark recess or deep doorway, fearing her path would cross the many garrotters Glasgow had spawned over the years. She clutched her bag and quickened her pace.

*

It was William Minnoch who raised the alarm that Madeleine was missing. The previous evening he had taken her out to a pre-arranged dinner party held at Mr. Middleton's. Madeleine had seemed a bit peaky to him, not her vivacious self at all, and it prompted him to call on her, to see if she was in better health. In addition, he wanted to enquire after the health of Mr. Smith who, like his wife, had taken to his bed with an illness. He hoped an awful virus was not the cause of their affliction.

On arrival, after enquiring about Miss Madeleine, the house was in chaos; Miss Madeleine was missing. On further inspection, it appeared she had removed some clothes, for her portmanteau was gone. The family sent James, her brother, to the drawing room to tell Minnoch the news.

"Gone? She never mentioned any of this last night. Was this something planned?"

James had been forbidden to tell Minnoch anything. Instead, he said, "Madeleine's been rather upset over the last few days. It appears an old sweetheart died recently, and it's affected her rather badly."

Minnoch frowned. He had not been aware of any recent deaths of people within his circle of friends, or beyond.

"We think she's run away as she packed a bag."

"Run away? Why ever would she do that? Do you know where she might have gone?"

"We are guessing, Rowaleyn. It would be the first place I'd look."

"Well, James, we need to bring her back. I'll go out onto the street and hail a cab. Be outside as soon as possible and we'll be on our way."

James and William flagged down the first cab they could and travelled as far as Queens Street Station. From there they caught a train to Greenock. No one stopped to admire the beautiful scenery, the embracing hills of Argyllshire and Dunbartonshire, or the elegant customs house on the quay. Instead, as soon as they alighted they sought out the ticket office to catch the steamer already pumping black palls of smoke into the air, signaling its imminent departure.

They embarked the quarterdeck steamer, *Roseneath*, bound for Helensburgh with a final destination to Row, minutes before it pulled away from the shoreline. By now, it was two o'clock and they had all been travelling for several hours.

"I think we should find ourselves a seat and have something to eat. By the looks of it the passage could be a little rough," said Minnoch.

Jack was not a good sailor, more importantly they had not eaten a morsel since leaving Glasgow. He readily agreed.

They moved to the first class saloon when suddenly Jack shouted out, "Madeleine!"

Madeleine had not seen them approach, and looked just as surprised to see them.

"Madeleine, where've you been? The family has been worried sick about you. *I've* been worried sick about you."

William Minnoch could not mask his displeasure.

She was about to answer when he pulled her aside and said, "Don't answer now. There are too many people about. Let's not draw attention to ourselves."

It was not until they disembarked that Minnoch asked her again, "Why did you leave the house? Leaving your friends and family so distressed, without so much as a word?"

"I needed some time to think on my own. I cannot tell you the reason now, William. Please just accept that I needed to leave for a while." .

"I don't know what has happened to you, Madeleine, nor will I pass judgment. I hope you will trust me enough to tell me, in due course. I'll not embarrass you by prying into your personal affairs. However, we've been sent to bring you back to Glasgow, and that part is not open to discussion."

For the duration of the return trip, no one spoke to Madeleine directly. It was as if she were invisible.

*

Stevenson arranged for Pierre Emile L'Angelier's funeral and burial to take place at Glasgow's Ramshorn Parish Church.

That afternoon, a small circle of friends, and his immediate family, attended the funeral. The majority of the mourners were made up of Emile's colleagues. His distraught mother, Victoire Melanie de ste Croix, and his sister Emilie Anastasie were inconsolable. Over the years Melanie, as she was better known, had buried her husband, Pierre Francois; her youngest daughter, Zephrine Emilie; and her youngest son, Jean Achille. Now she was burying her remaining, and eldest son, Pierre Emile.

As Huggins sat in church, listening to the quiet sobs of the women, he looked more closely at the small gathering of mourners dressed in black suits and bombazine. He couldn't help but notice there was one person he was not able to identify - Emile's fiancée of whom he always spoke.

Once they left the church and gathered outside, he confirmed his suspicions. She was not among the mourners. He found this most peculiar. Who was she, where was she, and why had she not come?

52 THE POST-MORTEM REPORT
GLASGOW, 28 MARCH

The report on the post-mortem was finally finished. Thomson and Steven read it carefully, before placing their signatures at the bottom of the last page.

At the request of Messers. W. B. Huggins & Co. of this city, we, the undersigned, made a post-mortem examination of the body of the late Mr. L'Angelier at the house of Mrs. Jenkins, 11 Great Western Road, on the 24th March current, at noon, when the appearances were as follows:

The body, dressed in grave clothes and coffined, viewed externally, presented nothing remarkable, except a tawny hue of the surface. The incision made on opening the belly and chest revealed a considerable deposit of sub-cutaneous fat.

The heart appeared large for the individual, but not so large as, in our opinion, to amount to disease. Its surface presented, externally, some opaque patches, much as are frequently seen on this organ without giving rise to any symptoms. Its right cavities were filled with dark fluid blood.

The lungs, the liver, and the spleen appeared quite healthy. The gall bladder was moderately full of bile and contained no calculi.

The stomach and intestines, externally, presented nothing abnormal. The stomach, being tied at both extremities, was removed from the body. Its contents, consisting of about half a pint of dark fluid resembling coffee, were poured into a clean bottle, and the organ itself was laid along its great curvature.

The mucous membrane, except for a slight extent at the lower curvature, was then seen to be deeply injected with blood, presenting an appearance of dark-red mottling, and its substance was remarked to be soft, being easily torn by scratching with a fingernail. The other organs of the abdomen were not examined.

The appearance of the mucous membrane, taken in connection with the history as related to us by witnesses, being such as, in our opinion, justified a suspicion of death having resulted from poison. We considered it proper to preserve the stomach and its contents in a sealed bottle for further examination by chemical analysis, should such be determined on.

We, however, do not imply that, in our opinion, death may not have resulted from natural causes, as for example, severe internal congestion, the effect of exposure to cold after much bodily fatigue, which we understand the deceased to have undergone.

Before closing this report, which we make at the request of the procurator-fiscal for the country of Lanark, we beg to state that, having had no legal authority for making the post-mortem, examination above detailed, we restricted our examination to the organs in which we thought we were likely to find something to account for the death.

Given under our hands at Glasgow, the 28th day of March, 1857, on soul an conscience.

(Signed) Hugh Thomson M.D.
(Signed) James Steven M.D.

53 WARRANTS
GLASGOW, 30 MARCH 1857

John Murray, a sheriff-officer from Glasgow, applied for four warrants in the L'Angelier case, all of which were granted. The first warrant was to secure Madeleine's letters. It came to the authorities' attention, that the family of L'Angelier's rumoured fiancée had sent an agent to retrieve these. They clearly, were of some importance.

He visited the office of Huggins & Co., accompanied by Mr. Bernard McLauchlin. It was there he saw William Stevenson and Thomas Kennedy. The sheriff secured the letters between the two lovers, bundled them up carefully, sealed them in the presence of all concerned, and sent them to the Procurator Fiscal's office for examination.

His next stop was L'Angelier's lodgings at 11 Franklin Place on Great Western Road. Here his assistant, Mr. Bernard McLauchlin and William Stevenson, from Huggins & Co., accompanied him. Annie Jenkins allowed them into Emile's room, left untouched since his demise the week before. While they were there, they made a thorough search. They found more letters in a portmanteau as well as more lying inside the drawers of Emile's desk. These too were sealed and sent to the authorities.

All medication found in his room was also itemized and removed. There appeared to be a good number of potions L'Angelier used for treating a variety of illnesses, despite telling people he did not like to take medicine. They examined the bottles and phials, making note of the labels on each.

1. *A bottle containing a brown liquid; turkey rhubarb labeled, 'a tablespoonful to be taken thrice daily'.*
2. *A bottle of sugar and ammonia.*
3. *A bottle of camphorated oil*
4. *A bottle containing a colourless liquid; a very weak solution of aconite.*
5. *One phial marked 'laudanum'.*
6. *A bottle containing a white or other powder marked, 'for cholera'.*
7. *Four packets containing powders; sulphate of quinine.*
8. *A bottle of olive oil.*
9. *A bottle containing a brown liquid and sediment; chalk, cinnamon and an astringent like catechu.*
10. *A bottle of eau de Cologne.*

The third warrant allowed them to exhume the body of L'Angelier for further testing. The fourth warrant allowed them to search the premises of Number 7 Blythswood Square.

54 CLOSING IN
GLASGOW, 31 MARCH 1857

Four gravediggers helped remove the coffin from the family vault, placed there mere days earlier. In the process, one of them stumbled, and the coffin hit the surface with a thud.

"Let's try and keep him in there a little longer, shall we, gentlemen?" admonished Thomson as he watched the scene unfolding from the side. Hugh Thomson was not alone. Alongside him stood the sheriff, and the doctors; Dr. James Steven, Dr. Robert Telfer Corbett, and Dr. Frederick Penny.

The procurator fiscal asked Dr. Penny, a respected chemist and professor of Chemistry at the Andersonian University, Glasgow to examine the contents of the stomach. The same stomach Thomas and Steven had sealed in a washed and rinsed out pickling jar, used for safekeeping, during the preliminary post-mortem.

They handed over the stomach to Dr. Penny on 27 March, trussed up and lying snug in the jar manufactured for a more pleasurable purpose. What he found over several days of study caused alarm, and he insisted they exhume the body for further tests.

When they prised open the coffin, considering the time since death, nine days prior, the body of L'Angelier was surprisingly well preserved. They now aimed to remove other organs and do further assessments.

*

William Minnoch called on Mrs. Smith in the morning, to see how she was. She had been in bed for a week, and people were concerned. He stood in the hallway ready to depart when the front door flew open and Madeleine and her sister appeared at the door.

"Madeleine, Miss Elizabeth." They bowed to each other before he said, "Madeleine, may I have a few moments please?" Elizabeth continued to hover.

"Alone."

Madeleine shot a look to her sister before replying, "Yes of course, William, come into the drawing room. Would you like some tea?"

"No thank you, I have another appointment in town, but I'd like to discuss something of importance with you."

Behind closed doors, William turned to Madeleine and said, "Madeleine, you promised me at Rowaleyn you would tell me why you ran away. You still have not spoken of the reason. I've heard some startling rumours this past week, and would like to hear about this from you."

"I had a row with Mama and Papa. I wrote to the Frenchman for him to return my letters. However, he died last week, and I needed time to think."

"You never spoke of him before."

"There was never a need."

"There are rumours going around that he was poisoned."

The blood drained from Madeleine's face and she sat down hard onto her seat. For several seconds her eyes were unfocused and she swallowed several times. Thoughts swirled around in her head. All she could think of was how she had purchased all that arsenic, and how it must look to others.

She swallowed hard again before saying in an unsteady voice, "William, you will no doubt hear more rumours in the future, and I'm afraid my situation looks quite black. You see, I was in the habit of buying arsenic to soften my skin. A mere coincidence, I assure you, but I understand how it must appear."

Horror swept over William Minnoch's face.

"You bought arsenic? A man is dead. Your old sweetheart, thought to be poisoned during the time you were trying to retrieve your love letters. Madeleine, tell me this is not true?"

"Alas, William it's all true, but as God is my witness, I had nothing to do with his death."

William looked at her, and wished he could believe her. The evidence was damning indeed for the woman he had wanted to marry. He felt a mixture of confusion, horror, even revulsion.

"Madeleine, I think it best if we do not see each other for a while. I hope you understand my decision."

*

The afternoon started like any other, but did not end so, when there was a knock on the Smiths' door. Much excitement followed, when the men gave in their cards to one of the servants. They were kept waiting for a good three minutes before being ushered into the drawing room. There they found the person of their interest; she was working a piece of hardanger for a set of pillowcases, and she did not leave her seat as they entered.

"Gentlemen, I'm told you wish to see me."

"May we?" John Murray, the sheriff-officer indicated a chair.

"Forgive my rudeness. Please, be seated."

"Are you Madeleine Hamilton Smith?"

"I am she."

"Did you know Pierre Emile L'Angelier, native of this country?"

"I did."

"Were you the intended of the late L'Angelier?"

"We had an understanding."

"How long did you know the deceased?"

"About two years."

"You wrote to him on occasion?"

"Frequently."

"Were you aware there was a possibility he was poisoned?"

"I have heard."

"Do you deny you purchased arsenic in the past?"

"I cannot."

"Did you, in any way, have something to do with the death of Pierre Emile L'Angelier?"

"I did not."

"Miss Smith, I have a warrant to search your room. I must ask you to stay here with Officer McLauchlin until the search has been conducted. We may remove items that we may not return. Do you understand all I've told you?"

"I do."

"Is there anything you wish to ask me or tell me, before we start?"

"No, sir, I've nothing to hide."

The sheriff marveled at her composure and calmness in answering his questions. He had never seen someone so in control of their emotions.

The officers spent several hours in Madeleine Smith's bedroom. They left nothing unturned. During the search, they found some items of interest. There was a phial containing a yellowish liquid, a tin of cocoa, and a photo of Emile in a small, unlocked trunk in a wall recess, showing a connection between herself and the deceased. They also discovered a couple of Emile's letters.

From there they searched the kitchen, but found nothing of interest.

They returned to the drawing room to find the young lady still engrossed with her needlework, and engaging in small talk with officer McLauchlin.

"Miss Smith, is your father at home?"

"Yes, I believe he's in the study."

"I suggest you ask him to join us."

James Smith looked drained as he entered the room and showed little interest of names attached to introductions. He remained standing as the officer addressed his daughter, who resumed her seat.

"Madeleine Smith, please set down your needlework and stand."

"Am I a suspect, officer?"

"Yes, Miss Smith, I'm afraid you are. I hereby arrest you on suspicion of the wilful murder of one Pierre Emile L'Angelier."

55 RESULTS OF THE SECOND POST-MORTEM
GLASGOW, 3 APRIL 1857

The medical men were meticulous in their second examination of the body, as they were in the first, and were now ready to present their findings.

Glasgow, 3rd April, 1857

By virtue of a warrant from the Sheriff of Lanarkshire, we, the undersigned, proceeded to the post-mortem examination of the body of Pierre Emile L'Angelier, within the vault of the Ramshorn Church, on the 31st March ult., in presence of two friends of the deceased.

The body Thomson removed from the coffin, two of our number, Drs. Thomson and Steven, who examined the body on the 24th ult., remarked that the features had lost their former pinched appearance, and that the general surface of the skin, instead of the tawny or dingy hue observed by them on that occasion, had become rather florid.

Drs. Thomson and Steven likewise remarked that, with the exception of the upper surface of the liver, which had assumed a purplish colour, all the internal parts were little changed in appearance; and we all agreed that the evidences of putrefaction were much less marked than they usually are at such a date the ninth day after death and the fifth after burial.

The duodenum, along with the upper part of the small intestine, after both ends of the gut had been secured by ligatures, was removed and placed in a clean jar. A portion of the large intestine, consisting of part of the descending colon and sigmoid flexure, along with a portion of the rectum, after using the like precaution of placing ligatures on both ends of the bowel, was removed and placed in the same jar with the duodenum and portion of small intestine. A portion of the liver, being about a sixth part of that organ, was cut off and placed in another clean jar.

We then proceeded to open the head in the usual manner, and observed nothing calling for remark beyond a greater degree of vascularity of the membranes of the brain than ordinary. A portion of the brain was removed and placed in a fourth clean vessel.

We then adjourned to Dr. Penny's rooms in the Andersonian Institution, taking with us the vessels containing the parts of the viscera before mentioned.

The duodenum and portion of small intestine were found to measure together 36 inches in length. Their contents, poured into a clean glass measure, were found to amount to four fluid ounces, and consisted of a turbid, sanguinolent fluid, having suspended in it much flocculent matter, which settled towards the bottom, whilst a few mucous-like masses floated on the surface.

The mucous membrane of this part of the bowels was then examined. Its colour was decidedly redder than natural, and this redness was more marked over several patches, portions of which, when carefully examined, were found to be eroded.

Several small whitish and somewhat gritty particles were removed from its surface, and, being placed on a clean piece of glass, were delivered to Dr. Penny.

A few small ulcers, about the sixteenth of an inch in diameter, and having elevated edges, were observed on it at the upper part of the duodenum.

On account of the failing light, it was determined to adjourn till a quarter-past eleven o'clock forenoon of the following day. All the jars, with their contents, and the glass measure, *with its contents, being left in the custody of Dr. Penny. Having again met at the time appointed, and having received the various vessels, with their contents, at Dr. Penny's hands, in the condition in which we had given them to him, we proceeded to T* to complete our examination.*

The portion of the largest intestine, along with the portion of the rectum, measuring twenty-six inches in length, on being laid open, was found empty. Its mucous membrane, coated with an abundant, pale, slimy mucus, presented nothing abnormal, except in that part lining the rectum, on which were observed two vascular patches, about the size of a shilling.

On decanting the contents of the glass measure, we observed a number of crystals adhering to its interior, and at the bottom a notable quantity of whitish sedimentary matter.

Having now completed our examination of the various parts, we finally handed them all over to Dr. Penny. The above we attest on soul and conscience.

Signed by:
Dr. Thomson
Dr. Steven
Dr. Corbett.

Examination resumed: *The appearance of the mucous membrane of the duodenum denoted the action of an irritant poison. The patches of vascularity in the rectum might be also considered the effects of an irritant poison. But they were not very characteristic of that. There were ulcers there. We could not form any opinion as to their duration.*

All these substances removed from the body were left in charge of Dr. Penny. The ulcers might have resulted from an irritant poison, but I am not aware that they are characteristic of that. They might have been produced by any cause which would have produced inflammation.

56 RESULTS OF DR. PENNY'S FINDINGS
GLASGOW, 6 APRIL 1857

*I*n compliance with the request of William Hart, Esq., one of the Procurators-Fiscal for the Lower Ward of Lanarkshire, I have carefully analysed and chemically examined the said stomach and its contents, with a view to ascertain whether they contained any poisonous substance.

This liquid measured eight and a half ounces. On being allowed to repose it deposited a white powder, which was found on examination to possess the external characters and all the chemical properties peculiar to arsenious acid; that is, the common white arsenic of the shops.

It consisted of hard, gritty, transparent, colourless, crystalline particles; it was soluble in boiling water, and readily dissolved in a solution of caustic potash; it was unchanged by sulphide of ammonium, and volatilised when heated on platina foil. Heated in a tube it gave a sparkling white sublimate which, under the microscope, was found to consist of octohedral crystals.

A small portion of the powder was also subjected to what is commonly known as 'Marsh's process,' and metallic arsenic was thus obtained, with all its peculiar physical and chemical properties.

These results show unequivocally that the said white powder was arsenious acid; that is, the preparation of arsenic which is usually sold in commerce, and administered or taken as a poison under the name of arsenic or oxide of arsenic.

I then examined the stomach itself. It was cut into small pieces, and boiled for some time in water containing hydrochloric acid, and the solution, after being filtered, was subjected to the same processes as those applied to the contents of the stomach.

The results in every case were precisely similar, and the presence of a considerable quantity of arsenic was unequivocally detected.

I made, in the last place, a careful determination of the quantity of arsenic contained in the said stomach and its contents. A stream of sulphuretted hydrogen gas was transmitted through a known quantity of the prepared fluids from the said matters, until the whole of the arsenic was precipitated in the form of tri-sulphide of arsenic. This sulphide, after being carefully purified, was collected, dried, and weighed. Its weight corresponded to a quantity of arsenious acid (common white arsenic), in the entire stomach and its contents, equal to eighty-two grains and seven-tenths of a grain, or to very nearly one-fifth of an ounce.

The accuracy of this result was confirmed by converting the sulphide of arsenic into arseniate of ammonia and magnesia, and weighing the product. The quantity here, is exclusive of the white powder first examined.

The purity of the various materials and re-agents employed in this investigation was most scrupulously ascertained.

Having carefully considered the results of this investigation, I am clearly of opinion that they are conclusive in showing -

Firstly, that the matters subjected to examination and analysis contained arsenic; and,

Secondly, that the quantity of arsenic found was considerably more than sufficient to destroy life.

All this is true on soul and conscience.

(Signed) Frederick Penny, Professor of Chemistry. Glasgow, April 6, 1857

57 MOVING THE PRISONER
GLASGOW TO EDINBURGH, 24 JUNE 1857

The noise of keys turning in iron locks jolted Madeleine from a restless sleep. Through the blackness, human shadows created by the swinging light from Bullseye lamps, came down the corridor towards her cell. She had been forewarned about the move from Glasgow to Edinburgh's Calton Prison. It was another step closer to her murder trial which would take place within weeks.

People spoke in half-whispers and low voices. It was an hour before rising time, but the volume was not for the consideration of the prisoners. It was to keep the news of moving Madeleine as quietly as possible. Emotions were running high, and not everyone believed the young Miss Smith was innocent.

Matron entered and allowed her to pack her few belongings into the small carpet bag she had arrived with. In it she placed her spare prison dress, her dress for court, her writing equipment and reading matter she had been allowed. The Glasgow prison governor Mr. Stirling, arrived some minutes later, and together with Matron, the party of three made their way to Glasgow Railway Station in a pre-ordered carriage to catch the early train.

The pair of horses pawed at the ground, iron hitting flint as the three travellers waited inside for the train to arrive. The privacy of the carriage sheltered her from the station's public waiting room, affording protection from scrutiny. The conversation inside the vehicle was stilted, the occupants unsure of what to say under the circumstances.

For more than ten minutes they engaged in small talk, before alighting and making their way to the first class train carriage. With a heavy veil pulled over her face, and flanked on either side by the stout middle-aged couple, no one recognised the young lady fast gathering infamy in journals and newspapers throughout Scotland, and beyond.

During this leg of the trip, they journeyed in silence so as not to draw attention. Instead, Madeleine glanced out the window at the passing landscape and wondered if this would be the last time she would see the heather-clad hills and lochs she had had twenty summers to appreciate. She had taken it all for granted. Now her future hung in the balance. The outcome could go either way. It was a frightening thought for the twenty-one year old who should be worrying about which dress to wear to the next ball, not which dress she should wear to a hanging.

They alighted at Haymarket Station with the cab already waiting for them, and again she was flanked by her companions as they made the short distance to the south side of Regent Street, to Calton Prison.

They stood outside the prison walls waiting for the guard to open the yawning doors. Calton Prison had a terrible reputation. It was known for being one of the most brutal places to be incarcerated. Madeleine had heard the stories; how the majority of women inmates were prostitutes and common thieves. She had given an involuntary shudder on first sighting the crenelated walls. The building looked more like Edinburgh Castle than a prison, but the soot covered stonework, black and grimy, hinted at the squalor within.

The governor had seen the alarm on Madeleine's face.

"It looks grim, Miss Smith, and it is. However, your father has arranged for you to have a cell of your own, as you did in Glasgow. You'll still be able to write your letters, and have access to your reading material."

"Thank you, Mr. Stirling. That will be a comfort to me. I dared not hope this would be the case. Thank you for your kindness, to both of you, during the journey. It's something I'll not forget."

"Having known you over the last few months, and I'm sure I speak for Matron here too, we wish you a successful trial and a good outcome. We wish you all the very best."

With tears in her eyes, Madeleine shook Mr. Stirling's hand, and that of Matron, who broke protocol and hugged her to her ample bosom. Matron dabbed at her eyes with a hanky clutched in her plump hand as they watched their ward turn and wave goodbye, as she was swallowed up by the doors to the women's section on the other side.

As Madeleine entered her small cell and heard the key turn in the lock, metal grinding against metal, she wondered what awaited her. It was another step further towards the determination of her fate.

58 BARING HER SOUL
EDINBURGH, JUNE 1857

Calton Prison's cells were cold, silent, damp, and poorly ventilated; a far cry from her baronial-styled summer home in Row, or the stately home on Blythswood Square.

The barred window to her room faced south overlooking the crowded buildings of the Old Town, rising gradually along the sloping ridge of the lower part of Holyrood to Castle Rock. Over this grim assemblage of rooftops, chimney stacks belched plumes of smoke remaining in perpetual suspension on the cold air, earning it the well-coined name, 'Auld Reekie'.

Madeleine's meals were almost unpalatable. She was given thick oat porridge and sour milk for breakfast. At midday it was soup and a piece of dry bread. For supper another bowl of thick porridge and sour milk was served. Seven days a week, the food didn't change. Even the soup didn't seem to vary.

Before breakfast, like the rest of the inmates, Madeleine was expected to rise when the bell rang at six o'clock, and to wash every day using the enamel jug of cold water provided. She was allowed to change her prison uniform once a week, and her bedding was cleaned once a month. Madeleine was given access to her books, and granted permission to write letters to friends and family, who were concerned for her health and welfare, as she waited for her trial date. She considered herself lucky not to have to share a cell with other female inmates far less privileged.

From time to time, she was allowed visitors. Her father had come several times, but his stays had always been brief. He had visited only on the insistence of his wife, who had threatened to make the trips herself, if he would not. This morning it was the prison chaplain who visited. He was there to offer spiritual comfort.

"I'm not here to judge you, my dear," said the chaplain, sitting precariously on a small chair that could have been a milking stool in another life. "Only God can do that. However, if you are guilty, you need to confess to Him so he may cleanse you of your sins."

"I did not commit murder, minister. I am innocent. There is nothing I am guilty of, other than being rebellious and failing to be a dutiful daughter. I should have listened to Mama and Papa, but I did not. I ignored their advice for I thought I knew better. They forbade me to see Emile, whom I loved a great deal. I wish I had listened. I'm too ashamed to tell you anymore. For that too, I'm guilty."

"We are all sinners in the sight of God, my child."

Madeleine studied his face before deciding whether she should unburden herself to this man. For so long she had told no one of the inner turmoil that had weighted her down. She looked into his eyes, and saw them as kind, not accusatory.

"Please understand, I love my papa and mama, but Papa is very strict. When I was much younger my parents did not allow me to socialize often with my friends. I was kept apart from the world and what was going on. We weren't even allowed to read the newspaper.

"Papa always said *The Times* was full of crime and business that would contaminate and taint our souls. So instead of reading current events to Papa, I read only books he pre-approved. I would read these to him, and Dr. Beattie, who can no longer read for himself.

"When I was sent to boarding school, I was unprepared for the world. I learned of shocking things the other girls talked about quite openly, but to which I was never exposed."

She stopped but the minister remained passive, merely nodding encouragingly.

Finally he said, "My dear, knowledge is the source of resistance, and the only foundation of conquest."

"I guess that's true, minister. I really had no knowledge of life in general, and when Emile came along I did not truly understand the course of my actions. I'm guilty of rebelliousness, for it was a period in my life where I wanted to be free of my mama and papa. But look where it has brought me."

Her face crumpled as if she would cry, but she managed to restrain herself.

He bent over and patted her knee.

"There, there, child, don't upset yourself. None of us is perfect."

"I did a wicked and sinful thing, minister. I allowed myself to be seduced by the man who is now dead. Am I not married in the eyes of the law and God?"

"Ah. Yes indeed. Did you not try and speak to your father about your love for this young man, before it reached that stage?"

"I did, several times. However, he was very angry, and ordered me to stop thinking of poverty, and to think rather of riches. When I told him I cared not for riches he became exceedingly irate, and forbade me to see Emile again. If only I'd listened. Now Emile's dead, and they think I killed him."

"I can see you've been struggling with a lot on your own, my child. Let us pray for your forgiveness, and ask God to give you strength for whatever may lie ahead."

Calton Prison where Madeleine was kept for three months before her trial began

59 THE TRIAL OF THE CENTURY
EDINBURGH, 30 JUNE 1857

The 30th June, 1857 finally arrived, and Madeleine Smith was on trial for her life. For three months, she had sat in her cell governed by bells and routine, both yearning for, and dreading this day.

The accused, and her official fiancé, William Minnoch, were well-known socialites in both Glasgow and Edinburgh circles. As a result, immediately after her indictment, and when the date of the trial had been posted, applications flooded in for seats at Court. Judges, advocates, legal agents, officers of Court, the police - everyone from the highest to the lowest official, who possessed any authority, or connection to the case, was besieged by eager applicants.

The death of a working class man like L'Angelier may not have even made the tabloids, a paragraph at best, were it not for the fact a young socialite was now accused of his death.

Before the newspaper ink was dry, and the pages cold, the public at large was titillated by the daily revelations, drip-fed to them by the journalists of the day. The question on everyone's lips was, had she killed the man who had threatened her social respectability? Had she poisoned him for fear of him exposing her intimate love letters, shared between them? What exactly was in these letters to push her to kill him, in the first place?

That Tuesday, the morning of the trial, was wet and dismal, but it did not deter the crowds that jostled, shoulder to shoulder, outside the Justiciary Court on Parliament Square trying to secure a better view of the prisoner rumoured to be arriving shortly. People had gathered in the square long before daybreak to ensure they did not miss this grand event.

Many more ran behind the cab as they transferred Madeleine from the prison to Court. They banged on the windows, threw rotten vegetables and fruit at her, and there were shouts of, "Hang the Witch! Hang the Witch!" as she tried to remain out of view, shrinking back into the seat, as far as she could.

At eight o'clock, officials flung open the doors and the portion assigned to the public was immediately packed. Not a seat was spare. The scene was set like a play unfolding. However, murder was no light relief entertainment. Voices were hushed. The room hummed with whispers and titters. On every face was stamped curiosity and expectation. The pomp and circumstance of the event, caused by the entrance of the large gathering of Faculty of Advocates, looked suitably academic and serious in their court attire as they filed in and took their seats.

There was also a long array of Edinburgh reporters. In the gallery, on the right, sat the judges. In the gallery on the left, and the greater part of the slope in the lower area, sat the public, whose entry was by ticket only.

The authorities had only allowed twelve women into the courtroom, and it would appear they were there for the duration, as most of them had brought their needlework so they could stitch and listen at the same time.

Voices halted when the three judges entered the room. Everyone stood as the learned men claimed their places on the dais.

The silence was even more deafening when next, the trap door opened and the accused came up from the cell to enter the dock. Numerous pairs of eyes followed as she moved from the side entrance to take her place. They were astonished to see how calm and poised she was, given the circumstances. Her demeanor said some, showed she was innocent, and had nothing to fear. Others said it proved her guilt, and was in perfect keeping with her whole character of subterfuge and cunning.

She walked to the dock with the matron of the Edinburgh prison on her left and two constables flanking her on either side. Some noted how diminutive she was, no more than five feet, two inches. She looked a lot younger than her twenty-one years, and although there was some evidence of strain, she looked quite calm. She cast a hurried glance around the court room in search of some known faces, and then settled herself onto her seat to wait for her trial to begin.

The scrutiny was not over. People noted what the young Miss Smith was wearing. Journalists scribbled furiously, graphite flying across paper, penknives at the ready to keep those points sharp.

Madeleine chose to wear a rich, chocolate brown, silk dress with a mantle of black lace, and a fashionable white scoop bonnet trimmed with white ribbons and blue flowers. When she arrived, a black lace veil had covered her face, and her hands were enclosed in pale lavender, kid gloves. In one hand, she carried a cambric handkerchief, in the other a silver-mounted bottle of smelling salts.

The veil remained drawn over her face, away from judging, prying eyes. However, when she assumed her place she removed it and people immediately leaned forward for a closer look. They strained, looking between and over bobbing heads. Her dark brown hair, neatly braided, matched her eyes, some said. Others said they were lighter than that, perhaps a hazel brown. Others, closer to the defendant, swore they were grey.

An inventory of typewritten and handwritten documents and articles pertinent to the case, were stacked high on the table. More than two hundred of Madeleine's most intimate love letters, considered crucial evidence for the prosecution, were in bundles, tied up with twine, and placed in the order they were to be read to the public.

By now, it was just after ten o'clock. The Lord Justice-Clerk and Lords Handyside and Ivory were on the bench. The counsel for the Crown was the Lord Advocate Solicitor-General, and D. McKenzie, Esquire, Advocate-Depute.

For the defense, there appeared the renowned Dean of Faculty Mr. John Inglis, Mr. George Young, and Mr. Alexander Moncrieff, whose agents were Messrs. Ranken, Walker and Johnston from Edinburgh; Mr. Daniel Forbes of Messers. Moncrieff, Paterson, Forbes and Barr, Glasgow, and Mr. John Wilkie, of Messers. Wilkie and Faulds from Glasgow. Her father had spared no money in hiring one of the best legal teams he could afford. If he could not prevent a scandal, at least he could try to prevent a hanging.

Silence ensued as they read the indictment. Madeleine was accused of wickedly and feloniously administering cocoa or food laced with arsenic, with an intent to murder Pierre Emile L'Angelier on the 19th or 20th days of February, (Thursday or Friday), 22nd or 23rd February (Sunday or Monday), and again on the 22nd or 23rd March (Sunday or Monday) all taking place in the house in Blythswood Square.

"Madeleine Hamilton Smith, how do you plead?"

"Not guilty." The tone was clear and firm.

Madeleine had made a statement to the authorities now read out in court.

"My name is Madeleine Smith. I am a native of Glasgow; twenty-one years of age; and I reside with my father, James Smith, architect, at 7 Blythswood Square, Glasgow."

"For about the last two years I have been acquainted with P. Emile L'Angelier, who was in the employment of W. B. Huggins; & Co., in Bothwell Street, and who lodged at 11 Franklin Place. He recently paid his addresses to me, and I have met with him on a variety of occasions. I learned about his death on the afternoon of Monday, the 23rd March current, from mama, to whom it had been mentioned by a lady named Miss Perry, a friend of M. L'Angelier."

"I had not seen M. L'Angelier for about three weeks before his death, and the last time I saw him was on a night about half-past ten o'clock."

A hum of disagreement from the camp who believed her guilty echoed around the chamber. The official looked up briefly, before resuming.

"On that occasion, he tapped at my bedroom window, which is on the ground floor, and fronts Mains Street. I talked to him from the window, which is stanchioned outside, and I did not go out to him, nor did he come in to me. This occasion, which, as already said, was about three weeks before his death, was the last time I saw him".

Titters and fierce whispers simmered under the voice of the court official as he plodded on.

"He was in the habit of writing notes to me, and I was in the habit of replying to him by notes. The last note I wrote to him was on the Friday before his death, viz., Friday, the 20th March current. I now see and identify that note, and the relative envelope, and they are each marked No. 1. In consequence of that note, I expected him to visit me on Saturday night, the 21st current, at my bedroom window, in the same way as formerly mentioned, but he did not come, and sent no notice."

"Liar!" shouted one spectator. Several more followed his lead, until there was a chorus of accusations.

"Order! Order!" demanded one of the judges as he struck the gavel several times. "We will not tolerate this type of behaviour in this courthouse. You have been warned. Any more outbursts and I will have you removed."

"There was no tapping at my window on said Saturday night, or on the following night, being Sunday. I went to bed on Sunday night about eleven o'clock, and remained in bed 'til the usual time of getting up next morning, being eight or nine o'clock."

"In the course of my meetings with L'Angelier, he and I had arranged to get married, and we had, at one time, proposed September last as the time the marriage was to take place, and,

subsequently, the present month of March was spoken of. It was proposed that we should reside in furnished lodgings; but we had not made any definite arrangement as to time or otherwise."

Madeleine shifted her gaze to William Minnoch who stared straight ahead, ignoring her and those in the gallery who knew him, all waiting for a reaction that did not come.

"He was very unwell for some time, and had gone to the Bridge of Allan for his health; and he complained of sickness, but I have no idea what was the cause of it. I remember giving him some cocoa from my window one night some time ago, but I cannot specify the time particularly. He took the cup in his hand, and barely tasted the contents; and I gave him no bread to it. I was taking some cocoa myself at the time, and had prepared it myself. It was between ten and eleven p.m. when I gave it to him."

"I am now shown a note or letter, and envelope, which are marked respectively number two, and I recognise them as a note and envelope which I wrote to M. L'Angelier, and sent to the post. As I had attributed his sickness to want of food, I proposed, as stated in the note, to give him a loaf of bread, but I said that merely in a joke, and, in point of fact, I never gave him any bread."

"I have bought arsenic on various occasions. The last I bought was a sixpence worth, which I bought in Currie, the apothecary's, in Sauchiehall Street, and, prior to that, I bought other two quantities of arsenic, for which I paid sixpence each - one of these in Currie's, and the other in Murdoch, the apothecary's, shop in Sauchiehall Street. I used it all as a cosmetic, and applied it to my face, neck, and arms, diluted with water. The arsenic I got in Currie's shop I got there on Wednesday, the 18th March, and I used it all on one occasion, having put it all in the basin where I was to wash myself."

"I had been advised to the use of the arsenic in the way I have mentioned by a young lady, the daughter of an actress, and I had also seen the use of it recommended in the newspapers. The young lady's name was Guibilei, and I had met her at school at Clapton, near London. I did not wish any of my father's family to be aware that I was using the arsenic, and, therefore, never mentioned it to any of them; and I don't suppose they or any of the servants ever noticed any of it in the basin."

Some of the ladies momentarily suspended their needlework and nodded at each other in agreement.

"When I bought the arsenic in Murdoch's I am not sure whether I was asked or not what it was for, but I think I said it was for a gardener to kill rats or destroy vermin about flowers, and I only said this because I did not wish them to know that I was going to use it as a cosmetic. I don't remember whether I was asked as to the use I was going to make of the arsenic on the other two occasions, but I likely made the same statement about it as I had done in Murdoch's; and on all the three occasions, as required in the shops, I signed my name to a book in which the sales were entered. On one occasion I was accompanied by Mary, a daughter of Dr. Buchanan, of Dumbarton."

"For several years past Mr. Minnoch, of the firm of William Houldsworth & Co., has been coming a good deal about my father's house, and about a month ago Mr. Minnoch made a proposal of marriage to me, and I gave him my hand in token of acceptance, but no time for the marriage has yet been fixed, and my object in writing the note No. 1, before mentioned, was to have a meeting with M. L'Angelier to tell him that I was engaged to Mr. Minnoch. I am now shown two notes and an envelope bearing the Glasgow postmark of 23rd January, which are

respectively marked No. 3, and I recognise these as in my handwriting, and they were written and sent by me to M. L'Angelier."

The focus was on Minnoch again. This time he had his head down and was scratching at an imaginary flaw in his pinstriped trousers.

"On the occasion that I gave M. L'Angelier the cocoa, as formerly mentioned, it must have been known to the servants and members of my father's family, as the package containing the cocoa was lying on the mantelpiece in my room, but no one of the family used it except myself, as they did not seem to like it. The water which I used, I got hot from the servants. On the night of the 18th, when I used the arsenic last, I was going to a dinner party at Mr. Minnoch's house."

"I never administered, or caused to be administered, to M. L'Angelier arsenic, or anything injurious. And this I declare to be truth.

(Signed) Madeleine Smith"

Each day of the trial, Madeleine Hamilton Smith stood in the dock totally composed, listening intently to the arguments on both sides. Only once, when the Court read the letter she had been dreading, to those in the courtroom of when she had lost her virginity, did she lean forward and throw her hands up to her face to hide her mortification. *Who could blame her?*

When William Minnoch took the stand, her face remained unchanged. She was calm and serene as he spoke of how she had run away, and how he had gone with her brother to bring her back. However, during his testimony he could not even look in the direction of the dock, where sat the source of his humiliation in good Glasgow society.

Poor Minnoch! He who had made honorable proposals of marriage, which she had accepted, with a marriage date fixed, and through his fiancée's folly and sin, now stood in the unenviable position of being betrothed to a woman who was already the wife of another.

The trial lasted for nine lengthy days before a verdict was made. The prosecution argued a strong case. They reasoned that the accused had murdered her lover, because William Minnoch was a wealthy merchant, earning £4000 a year. She had poisoned Emile because he was threatening to expose their love affair to her father and fiancé with their letters he refused to return. She had tried buying prussic acid at first, no one had ever heard of this being used for one's hands as she professed, and the arsenic she purchased on several occasions thereafter, coincided with the times L'Angelier fell ill.

The defense, however, argued there was no motive for the murder. After all, killing L'Angelier did not result in her securing her letters. By his death, the letters became subjected to public consumption. Emile was sick many times before. On the first date the prosecution accused her of administering Emile the poison, she had not even purchased her first lot of arsenic by then.

The times she had bought arsenic, it was twice in the company of others. The first instance was with a friend, the second, with her sister. The poison had been purchased openly, even charging the initial purchases to her father's account. That the first lot of arsenic was enough to kill fifty men. Why go on to buy more, if the intent was to kill in the first place?

The deceased was a man who saw the prisoner as an opportunity to improve his social position. He had seduced her deliberately to prevent marriage to another, this wicked deed securing his future. The defense said the deceased was excitable, and often expressed suicidal thoughts, and that several times he had tried to commit suicide. When he came back from Bridge of Allan something snapped, causing him to take the poison himself.

They concluded the prisoner told the truth. That she had not seen L'Angelier for three weeks prior to his death, and there was no proof she saw him on the night he fell ill.

Next to speak, was the Lord Justice Clerk who summed up the case, reiterating pertinent evidence for both sides of the argument. He urged the jury to proceed on suspicions, or even strong suspicion, but there was to be strong conviction in their mind; and if there was any reasonable doubt it was their duty to give the prisoner the benefit. But, if they came to that clear conclusion of her guilt, they were not to allow any suggestion made for the defense to deter them from doing their duty.

THE LORD-ADVOCATE, COUNSEL FOR THE CROWN.

The jury retired to their room to decide her fate. They were working class men - farmers, merchants, shoemakers, a clerk, a cabinetmaker, and a teacher. Would they be prejudiced against the defendant? The deceased was one of them. Would they be impartial and look at the evidence before them?

The appearance of the court was impossible to describe. The learned judge moved some spectators to tears by his impressive address. For the many baying for a hanging at the start of the trial, by the end, they were no longer sure if hanging was appropriate.

For once Madeleine's calm exterior was beginning to crack. She had listened to the evidence for and against her, looking anxious, at times leaning back with her head down, deeply affected.

While the jury deliberated, the court retired for refreshments, and Madeleine remained in the dock, under guard, as she did each time Court had taken recess. During this time, people paid a guinea or two, to have a look at the infamous Madeleine Smith. Today, on the final day, several women were admitted through a side door, and were allowed to approach the prisoner. They stood and gazed at her for so long, and so rudely, a hum of disapproval from the other spectators in the courtroom forced them to make a retreat.

A small bell rang out, signaling the jury had made their decision. Voices and breaths held. Tension filled the air. Madeleine's vision focused totally on the foreman as he rose to read the verdict. Her mouth was dry, her hands sweating under the lavender gloves. She moved to the edge of her seat and leaned in to hear what they had decided to do with her life.

DEAN OF FACULTY, COUNSEL FOR THE PRISONER.

"Gentlemen, have you agreed to your verdict?" asked the Clerk of the Court.

"We have," answered the Foreman.

"How say you, gentlemen; do you find the prisoner guilty or not guilty?"

The Foreman hesitated slightly. The silence was tangible.

"We find the prisoner not proven on the first account, and not proven on the second and third."

On the verdict of not proven on the third charge, Madeleine's head fell slightly forward, her face broke into a bright, but somewhat agitated smile, and her hand was warmly grasped by her agent, Mr. Ranken, on the one side, and the gaol matron on the other.

There was a loud and long continued burst of applause following the announcement, but was immediately suppressed with, "Order! Order!"

The not proven verdict was cruel. Some members of the jury believed she had murdered Emile, they just did not have enough evidence to prove it. Before the public could bombard Madeleine, they whisked her away, down through the trap door for the last time.

Outside the court house, Parliament Square heaved with people wanting a glimpse of the prisoner whose trial had been dubbed the *Trial of the Century*. Removing her unmolested would need a clever ruse.

A young girl of Madeleine's age and height had bothered court officials for days to see the prisoner. Each time they had refused. Despite the constant refusals, the young woman resumed her spot, still hoping to see the Madeleine Smith who had become the subject of notoriety.

When an official collared her immediately after the trial, and asked if she would still like to meet Miss Smith in person, she was elated. However, there was one small detail to be agreed. She had to pretend to be Miss Smith by wearing one of her dresses, and to use the waiting cab, flanked by two police officers. She readily accepted the conditions.

Madeleine met and dressed the young lady herself, while outside, rumours spread that the prisoner was coming out. They were told they needed to clear a space, to allow her through. Sure enough, a cab drew up. A young girl came out, dressed like Madeleine Smith and, with a little difficulty, climbed into the carriage, along with the usual police. It drove off, at breakneck speed followed by the rabble, and in no time at all Parliament Square was quite empty.

Miss Smith was taken down to one of the witness rooms where she changed her dress, wore a cloak of a different colour to that which she had worn to court, a different straw bonnet with darker ribbons and a green veil. She remained there until five minutes past four, when she was brought upstairs, taken through the several passages of the Exchequer, and quietly walked away, accompanied by her elder brother and an unnamed young gentleman.

The trio walked as far as St. Giles Church where her cab was waiting and they entered without any fuss. They drove to Slateford where she met the five o'clock Caledonian train from Edinburgh, proceeded to Greenock, and then caught the steamer to her father's house at Row. On arrival, it distressed her to find her mother confined to bed, and in very poor health. Her incarceration had affected everyone.

That evening, and for weeks to come, a considerable crowd gathered at the Blythswood Square house wondering if she, who had invested it with such romantic publicity, was again its occupant. Policemen were sent to warn off those who attempted too curiously to pry into keyholes and window chinks, or those whose morbid curiosity led them to chip off bits of the house and carry them away as mementoes.

Within the family, she tried to mend broken fences, but she had no idea how difficult that would be, nor at what price her freedom had come.

She soon learned that a dark cloud of suspicion would always envelope her. That she would never escape a lifetime of stigma, wagging tongues, vicious rumours, and a perpetual interest in her life, no matter where she lived, what she did, or where she went. That despite the verdict, she would always be known as Madeleine Smith, the young woman who poisoned her lover.

The verdict that had saved her from the gallows condemned her to a miserable future, forever coloured by the actions of her past.

60 WHAT HAPPENED TO MADELEINE HAMILTON SMITH?

The enigmatic Ms Smith was formally abandoned by her betrothed-to-be, William Minnoch, shortly after the scandal developed. Although he was initially supportive of Madeleine, whether pressured by his own family or the revelation through the letters read out in court that revealed his bride-to-be was no longer the virgin he thought she was, he eventually broke off the engagement.

Madeleine soon found it impossible to live in Scotland. The long finger of suspicion followed, and she became the fodder of scandalous gossip and ribald humour at Scottish and English dinner parties, and even further afield. Madeleine's own defense lawyer was once asked at a dinner party, "Well, then! Do tell! Did she do it?"

To which he had replied, "I would rather have danced, than supped with her."

Raucous laughter erupted, scant thought to the young girl's tattered reputation, and a guilt that had not been proved.

During the rest of July and August, Madeleine remained secluded away with her family. Even there she was barraged with hundreds of letters asking for her autograph, and as many as ten letters from potential suitors arrived offering her marriage.

False reports started to appear. In the *Morning Advertiser* there appeared the following; "Miss Smith will positively take an action for breach of promise of marriage against Mr. Minnoch, should that gentleman now decline her hand."

In *The Ulsterman*, Belfast, July 17, 1857 there appeared another false report:

"Throughout the whole of Saturday afternoon, every third person who met every other third person revealed in the intelligence that Miss Smith had taken a passage to New York, in the royal mail steamship, Asia.

"Every particular in connection with the flight was known. Immediately the verdict was given a telegraphic communication was forwarded, as the story ran, to the office of Messers. MacIver, in Water Street, Liverpool conveying instruction to secure two first cabin berths, one for a lady and the other for a gentleman under assumed names.

"On Friday, Miss Smith left Edinburgh for the Adelphi Hotel, until the last moment for proceeding on board arrived, when a cab was called, and she was driven to the landing stage. She wore a hat with a huge over-hanging brim, with the capacious tip of which she concealed her face by keeping vigilant guard with the elastic.

"She was accompanied, it was said, by a gentleman about thirty-five years of age, whom rumour, to give the proper colouring to the sketch, represented as Mr. Minnoch.

"The news of her coming had preceded her arrival, and when the unfortunate lady stepped on board, eye-glasses were ruthlessly directed against her, and was keenly scrutinized by her fellow lady passengers, who quickly discovered unquestionable signs of extreme criminality in her features..."

In September of that year, a newspaper needed to refute a rumour circling that Christina Haggart, Madeleine's trusted house servant, confessed on her deathbed that poison was indeed administered to L'Angelier on the night preceding his death. The response by the *Illustrated News*, Saturday, 26 September, 1857 was: *It is a fabrication.* Christina Haggart was alive and well.

Finally, her family decided it would be best, for all concerned, if she left the family home. They simply could not accept what had become of her. James Smith organized the move, sending her to live with the Rev. George Mason and his family, an Anglican minister in Devonport. He ran a refuge for fallen women, and she lived there from the summer of 1857 until 1861 when she married George Wardle. George Mason introduced Wardle, who had lodgings close by, to Madeleine.

She married George Wardle on 4th July, 1861. He was a year older than her, a drawing teacher, and a pre-Raphaelite painter. He was also a bit of a fop who was known to frequent the streets wearing an outlandish Spanish coat and a broad-brimmed hat. He too, was not the kind of man whom the Smith family would have welcomed into their home before the scandal, for he was not considered of their class, making a mere £80 a year.

George Wardle's finances improved slightly when he worked for William Morris, the English textile designer. However, he was still giving painting lessons until 1868, in order to augment his meagre annual wage.

Madeleine had two children with George Wardle. Mary, her daughter, whom she nicknamed "Kitten", was born in 1863 and her son, Thomas, was born a year later. In her spare time, Madeleine continued to play the piano, sing, and paint with watercolours. She was well read and particularly fond of art. What inspired this interest was Vasaris' *Lives of the Painters*.

Madeleine tried desperately to reinvent herself. She no longer called herself Minnie, Mini, Mimi, or even Madeleine. Instead she adopted the name Lena, the name her sister Bessie had called her from time to time.

Lena Wardle, for a while, was involved in the Fabian Society in London, and worked as a hostess, ironically making the coffee for those attending the meetings.

In 1883, June 6 William Harper Minnoch, who later became a very successful businessman and the leader of the Glasgow Chamber of Commerce, died at a house in Craven Street, London. He was living at 6 Woodside Crescent, Glasgow at the time. He left behind a widow and several children.

After twenty-eight years of marriage, for some unknown reason, George left Madeleine and lived in Naples, Italy. Some spread the rumour she was growing tired of her husband. Having been given "the look" he had decided to beat a hasty retreat to Italy in order to avoid meeting the same fate as Pierre Emile L'Angelier. However, there was no basis to this rumour, and the reason for his move to Italy was purely speculative.

There is possibly a far more practical reason – gossipmongers who just would not go away. In 1890, her salacious love letters to L'Angelier were once again the centre of scrutiny when a clerk to the Justiciary was tried for theft of these very letters that ended up being sold to a local bookstore. The intimate correspondence, once again became evidence, and many were read publicly, all over again.

It was probably the last straw for George, who for twenty-eight years had endured being part of the never-ending cycle of gossip. Once her husband left she relied on the financial support of her husband's relatives with whom she lived in Staffordshire.

Madeleine was not prepared to sit around and feel sorry for herself. She decided to make the move to New York City to join her son, who had been living there for some time. She arrived in America on the *Arizona*, on 11th September, 1893, claiming to be thirty-six on the passenger list, when in reality she was fifty-eight. Moving to America was a subject of discussion for some time, and therefore, it seemed a natural progression, after the fact.

In America, she met husband number two, William Sheehy. William Sheehy was a much younger man, and when her first husband died in a Plymouth nursing home in 1910, she was finally able to marry Sheehy, whom it is said, she lived with for many years prior to their wedding.

This marriage lasted until his death in 1926. During her lifetime, despite avoiding Scotland by going to London, and then on to New York, scandal followed. Trying to cloak herself in anonymity by calling herself Lena Wardle before her second marriage, did not escape detection. Even Hollywood film directors wanted her to star in their films as herself, to tell her story. She always refused.

Madeleine died on 12 April 1928 at the age of ninety-three, still maintaining she was only in her sixties. She was buried in the Mount Hope Cemetery at the corner of Saw Hill River Road and Jackson Avenue in Hastings-on-Hudson, Westchester, New York under the name of Lena Sheehy. It is a simple headstone sitting low off the ground, with little pomp and ceremony. It reads: *"Lena Sheehy, died April 12, 1928."*

Lena Wardle's children did not outlive her long. Tom died in 1931, Kitten in 1935. Kitten's son Stephen died childless, in 1967. Tom's descendants, John and Violet, had children who still live in the USA, in the eastern states of Maine and Connecticut.

Madeleine Smith - now Lena Wardle - pictured in America around 1920. Picture: TSPL

Picture courtesy of the Mitchell Library, Glasgow

See Author's Final Word and an Analysis of the Case.

FINAL WORD
"IF SHE DIDN'T KILL HIM, PERHAPS SHE SHOULD HAVE!"

These are not my words, but a quote from a journalist of the day. Emotions ran high, and there were strong arguments for and against this case. Because of this, when it came to trial they could not secure a unanimous decision. Out of the twelve jurors, ten thought she was not guilty, and two thought she was. No amount of persuading would change their vote. In the end, a not proven verdict was the only other option.

L'Angelier was a narcissistic cad. He was dishonorable, vain, boastful, a fabricator of the truth, a namedropper, a seducer of women, a blackmailer, and a social climber. However, none of these traits meant he deserved to die in the manner he did. What is up for discussion is who killed Pierre Emile L'Angelier, and why?

A crime has three things: motive, means, and opportunity.

Madeleine had motive. She was about to be exposed by Emile through her love letters that would have ostracized her from her family and polite society, and ruined the opportunity of a good marriage with Minnoch who was worth £4000 a year, a handsome sum, even in those days. In today's economy, that equates to roughly £316,000 ($405,200) per year. Emile was living on 10 shillings a week. With 20 shillings to a pound, Emile earned £28 a year.

Madeleine had the means. She bought arsenic, lots of arsenic, readily and openly. The arsenic found in Emile's body – nearly 83 grains of arsenic, is about one fifth of an ounce (5.67 grams), or just over a teaspoon. It was enough arsenic to kill fifty men, let alone one.

She had the opportunity. He came to her house regularly, and she could have slipped the arsenic into his cocoa and coffee.

However, the motive may look sound on the surface, but if she were guilty in killing Emile why did she make no attempt to retrieve her letters? Those all-important letters she so desperately needed to prevent the rest of the world from knowing about her immoral behaviour.

It was De Mean, a mutual friend, who acted as a gentleman after suspecting the nature of the correspondence. He was the one scrambling to find these in order to save her reputation, and not even at her bidding. By killing Emile, the letters were immediately placed in the public eye, being key material evidence. What was the point in killing the man for letters she could not obtain?

Madeleine was no fool. Her first thoughts must have immediately gone to the love letters on hearing of his death. Yet, she did nothing. Had the murder been pre-meditated and planned, retrieving these would have been the next logical step. If this was a pre-meditated killing, she would have known he would be violently ill. She would have stuck to his bedside until she had the opportunity to rifle through his possessions to find them.

Let us now look at Emile. He had motive. He wanted revenge. She was the third woman to have dumped him at the eleventh hour. He had told friends this would never happen again. When rumours started circulating of Madeleine's engagement to Minnoch, he set out to frame her, out of sheer malice and spite.

The motive was perhaps to cast suspicions that his illness was due to a poison administered by Madeleine. He wanted to destroy her and any chance of her happiness with another. If he could not have her, no one else could.

He had the means. He was a known arsenic eater. He showed people arsenic in his possession, and spoke about it to several people as a way in which he controlled his asthma, back pain and other ailments, even though his name was not found in any poison's register.

He had the opportunity. Each time he made contact with Madeleine, on or near the date, he could have dosed himself up with more arsenic than usual and then spread the rumours to all who would listen, that Madeleine was poisoning him. Coupled with this, he now starts keeping records of his meetings in his new diary to help further spread the seeds of doubt.

L'Angelier could not obtain an introduction to James Smith on an ordinary level, so he set about seducing the young, naïve Madeleine. Being 10 years her senior, he knew exactly what his actions would be for her, thereafter. The seduction that he orchestrated and then refused to take the blame for, questioning her virginity, and blaming her for being so weak was done with sinister calculation. By taking her virginity, he knew, even if she did not, they were now married under Scottish law; legally or illegally, she belonged to him. He often reminded her of this adding further pressure to tell her father that they needed to marry. Being now his wife, neither could belong to another.

Why did he not go to these two men with these letters with which he was blackmailing Madeleine? His end goal was to secure a good marriage out of the deal, along with acceptance into the family. Exposing the letters would have resulted in a possible disinheritance. That was not part of the plan.

With all the times that he had access to James Smith's house, both day and night, why did he not spirit Madeleine away and elope? For the same reasons he mentioned when lacing up Madeleine's corset in his lodgings that day. He did not plan to marry someone who was penniless. In eloping, he again risked the chance of her been disinherited, after the fact. He wanted her status and her money. Without either, there would be no wedding.

One possibility for Emile wanting to frame Madeleine for his illness was that due to his insane jealous of Minnoch, and her rumoured engagement, it was tipping him over the edge. That, coupled with being tired of hearing he was not of her class, and would never be accepted as such, his dreamed life of jumping classes was eluding him. This theory is supported when he told several people he believed Madeleine was poisoning him. Having never kept a diary before, he suddenly makes careful notes of when he is sick, and when he visits Madeleine. This is another suspicious element to the case.

When he knew all was lost, blackmail paled into significance when his malicious plan to frame her for poisoning him came to fruition. He would take delight in making sure, if he could not have her, neither could Minnoch, for she would rot in gaol and he was eager to see her there.

We have to now stop and ask some serious questions. If you suspected someone was poisoning you, would you not avoid that person, if you thought your life was in danger? You certainly would never willingly go and accept another coffee or cocoa from someone you suspected was poisoning you, would you? Yet he did!

When looking at the history of their relationship, Emile was excitable, bi-polar, entertained numerous suicidal thoughts, and tried to commit suicide several times, more for the drama rather than being serious about ending his life.

In his own words, he once wrote to his sister, Anastasia, and said, "*I would never commit suicide if I could not be there to contemplate it.*"

The theory of suicide therefore is not convincing. He had the opportunity for social betterment. He convinced himself that Madeleine and he would marry due to his ruination of her. He had a stable job and did not seem depressed or cast down before, or shortly after, on his return from Bridge of Allan.

Did Emile overdose on arsenic intentionally or by accident? I believe he did not mean to kill himself. There are a number of plausible scenarios for how he died.

When he walked back to Glasgow from Coatbridge, a good eight miles from his home, as witnesses in the trial testified, he was still not in the best of health. He wrote to a friend, complaining his 'timbers (legs) are quite sore', a few days before departing for Glasgow. Perhaps he needed something to give him stamina to complete the trip.

Would he have taken arsenic to give him the strength he needed to complete the journey? After all, he knew how well it worked for those horses in Paris, all those years ago.

According to another witness from the trial, Emile bought a bottle of laudanum at a local pharmacy. So clearly, he was suffering from something before he even embarked on his journey. Did the laudanum play a part in an overdose?

Perhaps there was more arsenic left over in the packet than he realised, and he consumed the lot without thinking? After all, he was a known arsenic eater, confident he knew what he was doing, and did not think he might be giving himself more than he needed. This might account for the fact no arsenic was found in his possession, for he had ingested the whole of what he was currently carrying on him.

Alternatively, he may have taken some arsenic at the start to fortify his journey, started to grow tired, forgetting he had already dosed himself, and had a little more. If he was trying to frame Madeleine, would taking a little more have been the logical scenario in order to be languishing by the time he arrived back from his outing?

Or was it the white powder painkiller that he bought from Miss Kirk at a different chemist, on that Sunday afternoon, on his way home that he confused with the arsenic in his possession? Had he swallowed the arsenic, believing it to be the painkiller?

To me, this is the most plausible cause of L'Angelier's death. However, even this cannot be verified as Miss Kirk had no prior knowledge of L'Angelier, he was not a regular customer, she had seen him only once, and identified him by his purse only. We know now, in the 21st century, that eyewitnesses are notoriously unreliable for a variety of reasons. If this was L'Angelier, then we have a strong case, if this was a case of mistaken identity, we are still back to the more likely cause of death; mistaken overdose, one way or another.

So, why did they not find Emile's name in the poison's register? How did he lay his hands on such a dreadful poison that we know he used with regularity?

During the Victorian era arsenic was used for all sorts of things and they were incredibly careless with how they used it, and where they stored it. Arsenic, for example was the main ingredient used in paper fly strips to kill flies. It was also included in a green dye called Sheele's Green, ending up in the fabric of women's dresses, curtains, and even in paint and wallpaper, eliciting complaints for years by people who said these items made them sick. Manufacturers repeatedly ignored their complaints, disbelieving them.

Dyers and merchants brought in arsenic by the ton, storing it in unsecured wooden barrels in their warehouses with wooden lids loosely covering the poison. Anyone could access who worked there. No one would have missed a few spoonsful, or even a cupful!

Huggins & Co. were cotton merchants. Did they too have dye vats and barrels of arsenic lying around? No one ever thought to ask the question. Moreover, Sheriff Taylor found four shops in Glasgow where one could buy arsenic without a poison's register.

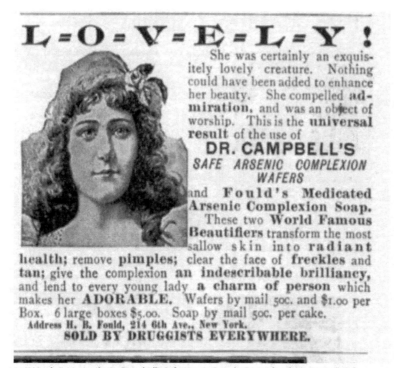

An 1898 advertisement for Dr. Campbell's Safe Arsenic Complexion Wafers. (Photo: lussi/flickr)

Using arsenic as a cosmetic was not as uncommon as the men of the courts thought. Widely advertised, not only in the Blackwoods publications, but in other magazines written for women, arsenic was regularly suggested as a solution for problem complexions.

Madeleine was young, silly, and vain.

Perhaps, she did not want people to know the real reason for her wanting the arsenic, so telling people she used it for rats was far less embarrassing than telling people she was using it for her skin; a practice people would have advised against. Had her parents paid more attention to their accounts after the first purchase, her life may well have had a different outcome!

Articles advocating arsenic were in many publications, well-known beauty recipes included arsenic, and even across the Pond in America, right up to, and after 1898, arsenic soap, and wafers were advertised for eliminating pimples and improving one's complexion.

Madeleine did not need to make three purchases of arsenic when the first lot of arsenic was enough to kill so many, if that was the intention. However, if she used all of the sixpence worth in a basin of water for her skin at one time, this would account for her multiple purchases.

Christina Haggert testified she did not see the evidence of indigo or soot in any basins of water she threw out. If Madeleine was so surreptitious with her use of arsenic as a beauty product, there was nothing stopping her emptying out the contents onto the street from her window, to get rid of the evidence.

If Madeleine was guilty of murder, how do you disguise this amount of arsenic found in Emile's system, equivalent to just over a teaspoon, without detection? Arsenic does not dissolve in water, hot or otherwise.

Dr. Penny stated in his testimony that if he had swallowed a cup of coffee or cocoa doctored with arsenic, the cup would be incapable of holding more than twenty grains in suspension. This would equate to 200 or 300 grains of gritty arsenic mixed with soot.

However, Emile neither tasted the arsenic, if what is proposed as true, nor when lying in similar agony which he had endured before, did the suspicion of poison come to mind. He repeated that it was that 'bile' again. Bear in mind that cocoa in the United Kingdom is thin, unlike France, Belgium and other European countries where it is as thick as porridge. Therefore, administering such a large dose in thin English cocoa would have been an impossible feat, without detection.

This then dispels the theory that Emile had genuine concerns that Madeleine was poisoning him, and reinforces the theory that he was framing her, with no substance for doing so. This would have been the perfect time to raise those concerns. Instead, he was at a complete loss as to why he was experiencing the same illness that kept cropping up. What he was experiencing were the same symptoms of chronic arsenic exposure, sustained over long periods.

When they performed the autopsy, the arsenic found was white. The arsenic Madeleine purchased was coloured with either with indigo, or soot. Unfortunately, none of the doctors responsible for the autopsy thought to examine specifically for soot or indigo deposits in the stomach at the time. Had they done this, we may have had a stronger case to prove, or disprove, her innocence.

The last question is why had he asked to see Mary Perry? Had he wanted to tell her again that Madeleine was poisoning him? If we are maligning him, and he had no such malicious intent, if he thought he was dying, why had he not called for Madeleine? After all, was she not his wife?

Of the first of the three illnesses Emile suffered in the latter months of his life, Madeleine was accused of using poison to cause them. However, her first purchase of arsenic came two full days **after** the first bad bout he had, nor had she hidden these purchases from friends or family.

If you were plotting to poison someone would you not visit a pharmacy out of town, where no one knew you, where you could use a false name?

My fourth cousin, four times removed, was the infamous serial poisoner Daisy de Melker. Yes, one cannot choose one's relatives! However, she purchased poison on several occasions each time at establishments nowhere near where she lived. Each time giving addresses she no longer resided at, and old married names she was no longer known under, using just her initials, never her current name. There were no identity checks in those days. You could call yourself whomever you pleased.

Even the prussic acid, which the male members of the judiciary staunchly upheld was never known to be used for cosmetic purposes, were wrong.

The following is from a website called The Victorian Web.org and says the following,

*"One of the most popular items gaining hold by the 1860s were the cosmetic face washes for removing every kind of freckle, blemish and eruption on the face; though the more they promised the impossible, the more they succumbed to adulteration. They were often based on highly pernicious chemicals such as white arsenic, bichloride of mercury, hydrochloric acid, corrosive sublimate and even **prussic acid** – diluted in distilled water and mixed with rose, lavender or orange water to disguise the chemical smell."*

Emile's illness was not something he developed overnight. He suffered such vomiting and purging bouts over several years before ever meeting Madeleine Smith. Was this the result of chronic arsenic poisoning, sustained over a long period, rather than bouts of cholera, of which the symptoms are the same?

More telling was the arsenic found in the brain at the post-mortem. With chronic arsenic exposure, the poison does not remain in the stomach but is absorbed into the organs, including the brain. No arsenic would be found in the brain after just three doses, no matter how large the dose, as arsenic leaves the system within three days. He also had an enlarged heart, and jaundiced skin, more evidence for this theory. All evidence of those exposed to arsenic over a long period.

So, did Pierre Emile L'Angelier accidently overdose on arsenic which he was known to take, or did Madeleine Smith slip him something in order to stem the potential scandal and to regain her life?

We will never know the truth. That is between Madeleine Smith, Emile L'Angelier and their maker. However, there can be no doubt everyone has their own opinion on this case!

*****

If you would like to **download a free copy of all the original love letters** between the two main characters, then you can do by going to: www.kathrynmcmaster.com/love-letters/

I do hope you enjoyed my Victorian Era murder mystery. After reading it you will, by now, realise it is a fictionalised account based on a true story set in Scotland during the 1850s. Hopefully, you found my novel to be interesting and would recommend it to others who enjoy historical fact fiction.

If you enjoyed this book, **I would really appreciate a review on Amazon and/or Goodreads.**

https://www.amazon.co.uk/dp/B0758DV8CY/

ABOUT THE AUTHOR

This is the second book of Kathryn McMaster, the first being the highly popular "Who Killed Little Johnny Gill?" A fictionalized account of the murder of young John Gill, said to be, by some, the sinister work of Jack the Ripper.

Her interest in true crime came from her father who would only ever read true crime, and at the age when other girls her age were reading Nancy Drew and the Secret Five she was secretly reading Bernard Spilsbury's cases of Dr. Crippen, the Brides in a Bath and the Brighton Trunk Murders among others!

Kathryn lives on a thirty-acre organic farm in Italy growing olives and grapes and enjoys the solitude that allows her to write. She likes getting her hands dirty and runs a productive orchard and kitchen garden, all grown without the use of deadly pesticides.

Although she has several other manuscripts on the go, Kathryn's passion is writing fact fiction based on true crimes.

***

Visit me on my website www.kathrynmcmaster.com and see more images of the Madeleine Smith case, download the full trial, read all the letters that were written between the lovers.

Finally, visit the website www.onestopfiction.com to see new releases, and get access to free and discounted books of all genres.

Printed in Great Britain
by Amazon